THE LONG JOURNEY HOME

MAUDY G. TESTRO-MEIJER

Copyright © 2024 Maudy G. Testro-Meijer.

All rights reserved. No part of this book may be used or reproduced by any means, graphic, electronic, or mechanical, including photocopying, recording, taping or by any information storage retrieval system without the written permission of the author except in the case of brief quotations embodied in critical articles and reviews.

This book is a work of non-fiction. Unless otherwise noted, the author and the publisher make no explicit guarantees as to the accuracy of the information contained in this book and in some cases, names of people and places have been altered to protect their privacy.

WestBow Press books may be ordered through booksellers or by contacting:

WestBow Press
A Division of Thomas Nelson & Zondervan
1663 Liberty Drive
Bloomington, IN 47403
www.westbowpress.com
844-714-3454

Because of the dynamic nature of the Internet, any web addresses or links contained in this book may have changed since publication and may no longer be valid. The views expressed in this work are solely those of the author and do not necessarily reflect the views of the publisher, and the publisher hereby disclaims any responsibility for them.

Any people depicted in stock imagery provided by Getty Images are models, and such images are being used for illustrative purposes only.
Certain stock imagery © Getty Images.

ISBN: 979-8-3850-3045-3 (sc)
ISBN: 979-8-3850-3046-0 (hc)
ISBN: 979-8-3850-3044-6 (e)

Library of Congress Control Number: 2024915727

Print information available on the last page.

WestBow Press rev. date: 08/15/2024

*Dedicated to my late parents, Harry and Christine
Meijer and millions like them
who triumphed over unimaginable adversity, allowing love, hope and
faith to be their destiny at the end of the long journey home.*

Honor thy father and thy mother: that thy days
may be long upon the land which
the Lord thy God giveth thee
Exodus 20:6 KJV

"…………..I know that I'm a prisoner, to all my father held so dear,
I know that I'm a hostage to all his hopes and fears.
I just wish I could have told him in the living years…
………..Say it loud, say it clear,
You can listen as well as you hear!
It's too late when we die,
To admit we don't see eye to eye…"
BA Robertson

PREFACE

"While we look not at the things which are seen, but at the things which are not seen; for the things which are seen are temporal; but the things which are not seen are eternal."

Apostle Paul in II Corinthians 4:18 NASB

The morning began as usual on that blustery, very cloudy January day. Our modest, suburban home, wonderfully nestled at the top of a semi-secluded, residential area called Red Hill, experiences cool, westerly winds every winter. The property surrounding our home is covered by expansions of green lawn and defined by a diverse assortment of many trees which attract crows, mocking birds, dozens of sparrows, and lovely, humming birds. A resident, long-eared owl has made his home in our giant juniper for years. Making their nests in the tallest trees are Cooper hawks who lodge there annually, patiently waiting for their eggs to hatch. Large, red squirrels run up and down the tree trunks and branches, hoping not to become the hawks' meal for that day.

As an avid gardener, I take advantage of the continental climate growing appropriate plants, flora and various palm trees, grateful for the joy gardening provides. Every morning, I drink my coffee appreciating the quiet moments as I feast my eyes on the shade those trees provide, protecting the hedges of delicate jasmine blossoms from the daily Southern California sun. Today is an exception and I hope the clouds above will dispense some desperately needed rain!

The ritual of rising early affords me time to ponder what the Lord has in store for me. Daily I am blessed with the opportunity to meditate on the goodness of God and appreciate my treasured relationship with Him.

Suddenly, my reverie is disturbed by the loud, obnoxious cawing of the crows.

I am not a fan of crows. Many live in our towering, Australian eucalyptus trees as they forage the field behind our house for dead rodents. Not only noisy, the scavenging, black birds dot our property with droppings in our swimming pool and leave unsightly, purple stains on the concrete. Observing the crows outside my kitchen window, I am eagerly waiting for the appropriate time to call my parents and share with them the events of the previous evening. Weeks before, they had arranged to meet me at the California Polytechnic University campus in Pomona where the Gideons were hosting their monthly camp meeting. The Gideons International, established in 1899, is a well-known Christian organization recognized for distributing free copies of the Bible, worldwide. I was the guest speaker for the event and my father had expressed a desire to attend. However, Mom called the day before to cancel their attendance explaining that Dad was not feeling well.

Not wanting to disturb them too early, I wait until 9 AM. Mom answers the phone immediately, sounding out of breath and a bit irate. Perhaps I should have waited a little longer. I apologize but my mother is not concerned about the call. She is speaking rapidly in her native Dutch language, upset that dad would not help her remove the sheets off their bed. My mother explains that earlier, Dad had vomited "iets zwart" 'black stuff' and at the moment, remained seated on the bathroom floor unable to move. Suspecting my father could be seriously ill, I urge Mom to call 911 for emergency services. However, during our conversation she did not agree with me that my father could be in grave, physical distress, grows impatient with me and hangs up the phone! Desperate, I call my brother Jack who assures me he could reason with her. Blessed with a calm and gentle spirit, Jack has an exceptional ability to make a point clear while avoiding any conflict that might arise during an intense situation. Thankfully, Mom takes his advice. In the meantime, my husband Phil, suggests that we drive to my parents' home, but as we walk out of the front door, the phone rings. It is my youngest sister, Mirna. Distraught, between sobs, she explains that the paramedics had arrived too late and pronounced our father deceased.

Mirna, the daughter my parents lovingly characterized as their happy, good-natured child, is struggling to communicate that Dad's body was transported to nearby Queen of the Valley Hospital. Less than six weeks before, Mirna had hosted a delightful party for Dad and her daughter Valoree whose birthdays fell on the same day.

It would be a long time before we would revisit that celebration again. Today, we are overwhelmed with indescribable grief.

As I hung up the phone, my attention returned to a commotion in the field where the raucous squawking of those annoying crows had grown louder. The aggressive scavengers had begun fighting over the carcass of a dead animal. Directing my gaze up, I noticed that the gray, winter sky had grown much darker which coincided with a bleak, dull ache in my heart. The vital, much needed rain never came!

However, for Harry Antoine Diederich Meijer, my beloved father, the morning of Saturday, January 27, 1996 became the dawn of his glorious, long-awaited homecoming.

INTRODUCTION

"I love the Lord because He hears my prayers and answers them. Because He bends down and listens, I will pray as long as I breathe."
Psalm 116:1-2 KJV

As long as I breathe? A lifetime? Yes, prayer for a lifetime as God bends down to listen.

Each of us is given an allotted time to live. For some, one look in the mirror and the reality that decades have passed force us to admit that time marches on swiftly. The realization can be a depressing one, especially if we are struggling in the midst of fiery, life challenges or carry the weight of heavy burdens because of regretful choices made in the past. We are told by numerous writers of poems, authors of books and countless composers of song that it helps to look back at former years, hopefully to see a clearer perspective for the journey ahead. Of course, there are those who disagree and prefer to leave the past behind.

For me memories of days gone by are needful, regardless of whether they were a collection of joyous occasions or pain-filled reminders which bring on debilitating despair. In my personal experience, thoughtful, deep reflections about former mistakes empower me to face each day with hope of doing better.

The journaling of my parents' story is a project I began more than ten years ago as I was dealing with a renewed longing for them. Dismal circumstances in my own life triggered intense emotions which forced me to think about the brevity of life, reviving my long-standing desire to finally write my parents' story. However, conflicting thoughts caused me to hesitate for several reasons and had been my excuse to put off the project for many years.

The challenges included, what parts of the past were worth repeating and questioning if I could remain objective. One reason for hesitating was my greatest conflict of all: could writing about someone else's life bring on possible disputes with individuals whose memories differ? With a suggestion from a friend who had self-published his own work, writing the story as my own memoir, enjoying the freedom with autobiographical license, perhaps this project could be easier!

Was I up to the task? I chose to plunge ahead despite my uncertainty.

So, I began with great enthusiasm, sitting in front of the keyboard, surrounded by pages of historical and geographical research, my desk covered with notes I took while interviewing my siblings, combing through dozens of boxes filled with hundreds of photographs, and examining several binders, journals and diaries my parents had composed over the years. Setting my eyes on their handwritten notes moves me unexpectedly as tears blur my vision. Speculation from friends and family assumed this project would ease my deep feelings of loss but the passion to recount their story had burned inside me for decades and I was missing them more.

Every human-interest story, whether on television, in magazine or newspaper articles has without fail, captured my attention for as long as I can remember. The widely popular, Life Magazine was a publication which emphasized photojournalism, amplifying news stories with large, gripping photo features and photo essays, radically changing the way people viewed the world. As a child, new to the English language, the pictures in Life Magazine kept me engaged in current events, including features of famous or infamous personalities. My father recognized my love of reading, so it was no surprise for my birthday or at Christmastime, he would bring home books which increased my appetite for more. For my tenth birthday, Dad brought home the complete set of Nancy Drew Mysteries. I jumped with joy! The excitement I experienced while reading about the teenaged sleuth replaced my own uninteresting, tedious days and without question, would begin to feed my passion to one day become a writer.

Little did I realize that a real-life documentary was playing out right in front of my very eyes!

Daily, volumes of anecdotal tales were told by my parents about the life they experienced long before I was born. Neither one was timid to share personal experiences, including events rich with meticulous detail and on many occasions, exposed their raw emotion! As youngsters, my siblings and I did not pay much attention to Dad and Mom's ramblings, somehow believing that every home was filled with a normal amount of melodrama. But one day I became aware that my parent's need to vent painted a much larger, more interesting picture. Fascinated by hearing years of their autobiographic narratives, my interest grows and in spite of my young age cause me to brazenly inform them that one day, I would write their story.

Dad and Mom burst out in laughter!

But one, fantastic, glorious morning, I receive a gift!

In January 1961, my father is notified that the local, city newspaper requests to have a meeting with my parents. My eldest brother Johny, who worked as a part-time employee in the circulation department of the La Puente Valley Journal, had shared with their Feature Editor a brief, verbal synopsis of our family's journey. As new immigrants, originally from the Southeast Asian country of Indonesia, we had migrated to a small western nation in Europe called the Netherlands, eventually arriving in America in the winter of 1957.

On the day of the interview, the journalist for the newspaper named Marty Ott enters our home, carrying a large satchel which holds a portable tape recorder. The reporter is accompanied by her photographer whose bag of camera equipment and large tripod dwarfs our small living room. Marty is a kind, middle aged woman genuinely interested in hearing all the relevant details for an exclusive she will publish in the La Puente Valley Journal.

The session includes many questions Marty had written in a spiral notebook. Hours into the meeting, I am disappointed that most of her inquiries are directed towards my parents and my brothers, Johny and Rene. For weeks I had been daydreaming of answers I would give if any questions were asked of me. Alas, Marty never turns her attention to those of us who are younger and after the last photo is taken with the entire Meijer family posed on the living room couch, concluding almost four hours of conversation, Mom happily serves our guests "Dutch-style" macaroni and cheese.

Marty Ott's article and photograph take up five columns and almost the entire front page of the newspaper's feature section. When Johny arrives home with dozens of copies meant to be shared among neighbors, friends and extended family members, I secretly keep one for myself and hide it among my personal items.

It becomes something I treasure and is the inspiration for me to "interview" my parents in the same manner Marty had.

I am thirteen years old!

chapter 1

"By letting go of our own agendas and time-tables we discover that God's plans are mind blowing."

FORMER NBA PLAYER DAVID ROBINSON

Born one year after the onset of World War I on December 9, 1915 in the far Southeast part of the world in a country called the Dutch East Indies, on the island of Java, in the city of Surabaya, Harry Antoine Diederich is the first of five children born to Johann and Mineoh Meijer.

The world's largest archipelago nation, the Dutch East Indies [known today as Indonesia] compromises more than 17,000 islands located in the Indian and Pacific Oceans, covering an area of 735,358 square miles. The three largest, populated islands being Sumatra which is a land mass of almost 183,000 square miles, Java covering an area of 49,536 square miles and Kalimantan, otherwise known as Borneo is 287,000 square miles in size. Only 7,000 of the islands are inhabited, with an estimated 273,000,000 population. Prone to earthquakes, volcanic eruptions and tsunamis, over recorded history these same natural phenomena are responsible for killing thousands. During the tsunami of 2004, caused by an undersea earthquake off the coast of Sumatra, more than 300 Indonesian islands disappeared, drowning an estimated 150,000 Indonesian citizens, and taking 100,000 additional victims all over the Pacific. With an annual rainfall of at least 69 inches, the rich volcanic soil produces vast acres of forests yielding resources which provide teak, sandalwood, bamboo and ebony. Indonesia's abundance in petroleum, spices, palm oil became well-known and vehemently sought after commodities which lured ambitious,

European explorers to the vast continents of Indonesia and her neighboring Southeast Asian countries centuries ago.

Before western civilization became aware of the largest archipelago in the world, ancient peoples occupied the Indonesian islands filling them with artistic, literary, religious and cultural histories, producing a rich Pacific Island history. The earliest inscriptions in the Indonesian archipelago can still be viewed on seven stone pillars from Kutai in East Kalimantan, dated on paleographic grounds as early as 400 B.C. Indigenous sources and Chinese records have enabled scholars to reconstruct much of the history of Indonesia, which include some of the major empires of the ancient world: the Majapahit in East Java, of Hindu-Buddhist roots and the kingdom of Malacca in Malaya, the greatest of the ancient Muslim trading empire. Those ancestors progressively invented and practiced remarkable ocean voyaging and navigation skills in order to reach the expansive distances between the hundreds of islands.

All Pacific Island societies have traditions and stories which relate to their discovery and origins. Ballads tell true stories of regional kings, queens and lords who ruled over vast territories. Bountiful, compelling folklore which describe fierce battles and warrior conflicts are tales told and passed down from one generation to the next, including stories of conquest and defeat, triumph and tragedy. And Indonesia's ancient history is as unique and distinctive as the country itself. The primeval foundation of the archipelagoes is vital to her legacy before Europeans and Asians come on the scene to radically change the island nation culturally, economically, and politically.

Since the beginning of recorded history, earmarked around 100 B.C, the Southeast Asian archipelago had already maintained a major position along the Indian Ocean and South China Sea trading routes promoting economic and societal advances. By the fourteenth and fifteenth century, prospectors were regular surveyors around the hundreds of islands in the Indonesian archipelago.

For two hundred years, seafaring Portuguese and eager explorers from India had begun aggressive explorations around all of the southeast Pacific islands to seek out the endless bounties of agricultural wealth. By the end of the fifteenth century, most of Europe, the Middle East and Northeast Asia have tapped into the abundance of natural resources these islands contain, bringing their influence and imperialism along with their trade practices.

Dutch explorers arriving from the small, European country of the Netherlands take over the islands of Indonesia at the beginning of the 1600's. Dutch ingenuity in business practices and politics overwhelm and outwit the previous Portuguese and Eastern Indian traders monopolizing all of the export commerce from the islands.

With the invasion of foreigners on its unsullied shores, original inhabitants of the Indonesian archipelagoes are dismayed to be taken over by strange languages, and are exposed to alien customs as uninvited interlopers, unwelcome scavengers, survey the verdurous country. Astonished by the lush topography of the islands, clever European explorers, for an exchange of trinkets or flatware, procure the assistance of indigenous volunteers, and traverse over miles of the interior regions of dense, luxuriant terrain and discover thousands of acres of tropical rain forests with flora they have never seen before. Immediately enthralled by hundreds of various types of palm trees, these early explorers walk into acres of distinctive ferns, short, growing close to the ground, in contrast to many species growing taller than most men. Beyond the forests, adventurers arrive upon a panorama of hundreds of miles of lowlands which feature everything from wet marshland to rolling, lime-green hills thick with moss which appears after the monsoon season ends. On the three largest islands, as explorers view the vastness of the terrain before them, massive mountains rise thousands of feet above, sporting magnificent waterfalls creating winding, wildly swirling rivers and waterways. Eventually, the region leads travelers to dry grassland and back to picturesque beaches they landed upon. Surprisingly, it doesn't require an intense search for foreigners to discover numerous varieties of tropical fruit they have never tasted, such as mango, jack fruit, and durian. The archipelagoes are covered by miles of indigenous fruit trees.

Feasting their eyes on the endless beauty of the islands, accentuated by 40,000 breath- taking varieties of flowering plants of which include more than 5,000 species of elegant, opulent orchids, European pioneers are delighted to find that Indonesia is home to the largest of all orchids, the 'tiger orchid' which can reach a height of 25 feet.

Along with magnificent variations of hundreds of types of foliage, dotting the majestic sky above the islands are the splendid sea birds around the coast, the interior birds of ducks, geese and waterfowl including the riverine birds which live along miles of twisting waterways. Filling the air with song are the multi-colored pittas, small passerine birds the size of sparrows and multitudes of noisy parrots whose feathers display a pageantry of vivid, gorgeous colors ranging from azure blue, emerald green, golden yellow, crimson red to royal purple.

With 54,716 miles of coastline, the explorers become enchanted with the splendor of Indonesia's stunningly beautiful beaches and coral reefs. Dutch explorer Abel Tasman characterizes the islands as a "garland of jewels in the backdrop of teal-blue seas."

Java, the island on which Harry Meijer is born, is characterized by a chain of volcanic mountains [130 of them are still active] which forms an east-west spine along the island, with the highlands and other mountainous regions splitting the interior into a series of various regions which are cut off by natural formations of rolling hills. By 1699, those regions are the perfect wet environment for rice cultivation, and Java becomes the first place where Dutch settlers plant coffee seeds smuggled from the Republic of Yemen, grown in the interior places of the island.

All equatorial countries of the Southeast experience hot, humid, wet climate conditions and because of Indonesia's location so close to the equator, the average daily temperature on Java can range from 70 to 92 degrees. With little variation from one season to the next, inhabitants of Indonesia wear traditional dress made of lightweight cotton or linen. It must have seemed comical to the native people as they observe those early settlers, large, white men, in their stuffy, overdressed attire, perspiring profusely under their stiff, starched collars and vestures accompanied by their women-folk, equally clothed in heavy frocks as miles of fabric cover their pale bodies.

What the 16th century, native leaders would not have known, is the sheer force these pallid complexioned, intrusive settlers would employ to enrich their own philanthropic appetites of all the Indonesian islands' agricultural and mineral wealth.

Rice Fields in West Sumatra

chapter 2

"Dominance is one of the most pervasive and important behaviors among wolves in a pack"

AMERICAN BIOLOGIST/ AUTHOR L. DAVID MECH

B eginning in the early 1600's, Indonesia is invaded by hundreds of able seamen of the Netherlands who were seasoned, accomplished navigators culminated by decades of maritime experience. With their own country located on the cold, frigid North Sea, and despite its small size compared to their larger European neighbors, historically the Dutch enjoyed bragging rights as they successfully controlled a large, vast empire from the early 17th to the 20th centuries.

Decades of fighting hostile invaders made the Dutch cunning, brave and strong. Until 1579 the entire region of the "Low Countries of Europe," namely, the Netherlands, Belgium and Luxembourg were intertwined culturally and politically. The territory that became the Netherlands, also, otherwise known as Holland, had struggled long and hard to rid itself of unwanted invaders. In 59 B.C. the Romans under Julius Caesar, conquered a wide region along the Rhine River and its tributaries. Celtic and Germanic tribes, though fiercely independent by nature, bowed to his rule. And the Romans hung on for several hundred years.

Next came the Franks, an aggressive, eastern Germanic tribe who conquered the region in the 7th and 8th centuries but lose their hold to the Vikings who sailed up the Dutch rivers to loot and pillage. Local rulers developed their own fortified towns and made up their own government and laws in order to survive the onslaught of sea-faring pirates and hoodlums.

Meanwhile, many "little lords" across the various regions of the low lands met their match with the Dukes of Burgundy, who gradually took over all of the territory. Duke Philip ruled from 1419 to 1467, greatly limiting the freedom of all local rulers. In October of 1496, Philip married Joanna, the daughter of the king and queen of Spain. By 1555, Philip's son, Charles, bequeaths the "Low Countries" to his grandson Philip II. A staunch Catholic, Philip II wants to rid the territory of all Protestants, especially those active in the Reformation, and goes after the activists with a vengeance by burdening the citizens with increased local taxes.

But the Calvinists and Lutherans are well prepared to fight back. Systematically, destroying art and religious icons of Catholic churches in the Netherlands, the Protestants are also angry with Philip's high taxes on trade and increasing trade restrictions. Decades before, the Dutch had become greatly adept at shipbuilding and were successful merchants selling luxury items such as tapestries, fashionable clothing and paintings along with ordinary, but popular commodities such as herring and beer. The trade restrictions stirred dissent among the merchants, so joining forces with the Protestants in 1568, fight the army of Philip II and begin the Dutch War for Independence which persists a tenacious 80 years, including and interrupted by 30 years of the European War! Finally, through a series of major triumphs and defeats, the Dutch are successful in driving the Spanish out permanently and in 1648, both countries signed the Treaty of Westphalia, recognizing the independence of the Netherlands, Belgium and Luxembourg.

However, decades of conflict does not deter the Dutch government from pursuing its thirst for global navigation, exploration and eventual conquest of unexplored territories. Undaunted by far distances, overcoming horrific challenges at sea and suffering hundreds of sea-faring casualties due to scurvy, ambitious explorers from Holland prove to be pertinacious in acquiring the coveted territories and resources far off lands produced.

Indonesia is just one of her many acquisitions because the Dutch had auspiciously colonized South Africa, parts of eastern United States before the British landed, various Caribbean Islands, Suriname and the territory we know today as Brazil.

Noted in numerous accounts of colonization, aggressive invasions of settlers from various parts of Europe into Indonesian territories is not received well but in 1602, bold and enterprising Dutch merchants successfully overrun the already existing Portuguese and British traders. Portugal had made major strides in the spice trading business in the archipelago one hundred years before, but were sloppy and corrupt in their merchandise operations. More cunning than their competitors, Dutch businessmen set up headquarters in Jakarta with a company naming it the [Dutch East India Company](). Using direct force and craftily schemed alliances with native leaders, merchants and dealers from Holland interfere with and eventually stop the inter-island network of Portuguese and British distributors from engaging in international trade with other countries!

The government of the Netherlands becomes the dominant exporter of Indonesian resources.

However, over decades, opposition from various island warriors begins to grow. As proud island inhabitants, discontent with the pillaging and ransacking of their beloved archipelago, native, Indonesian combatants begin periodic and unpredictable conflicts with the unwelcome invaders which the Dutch government promptly puts down using military force. But fierce, Javanese guerrilla fighters, having experienced hundreds of years of battles with neighboring warriors, refuse to submit, and sporadic conflicts continue over a period of two hundred years, leaving a total of 200,000 dead from both sides. The longest running hostility from 1825-1830 caused widespread famine in parts of Java for the following ten years.

The government of Holland remains persistent, unwilling to give up their hold on the agricultural and mineral wealth of Indonesia. Setting up government, civil law and religious practices common to their order in the Netherlands, indigenous citizens become aware that the "white folk" are committed to stay.

With their intent to remain, one element of Dutch society is primarily concerned with the spiritual condition of the "unsophisticated heathens" and send Dutch missionaries across to introduce the gospel of Christianity.

Soon, hundreds of Protestant and Catholic churches are erected on the island of Java.

Anthropologists differ in their opinions whether or not combining cultures is advantageous for all people involved. The debate continues about the assets versus unfavorable consequences of bringing one culture and forcing it to merge with another. It is an undeniable fact that since the beginning of man, cultures have been colliding as explorers, conquerors and opportunists cared less about the well-being of those they wished to subjugate, and more about the acquisition of human resources and commodities those lands provide.

And the historical facts about the colonization of Indonesia is no exception.

chapter 3

"Always remember, you are absolutely unique. Just like everyone else."

AMERICAN ANTHROPOLOGIST/AUTHOR MARGARET MEAD

At the time Harry Meijer is born in the city of Surabaya on the island of Java, 300 years of colonial rule in the Dutch East Indies had evolved into the accepted social and economic way of life. Dutch citizens have well-established communities in their own, exclusive neighborhoods, successfully industrialized the three largest islands and enjoy the political control of the archipelago nation. The Governor-General is the head of state appointed by the Dutch monarchy and although he rules with an advisory council, the Governor-General is accountable only to the king and queen of the Netherlands.

Three major classes of people compromised society with the European elite as the upper class. Individuals born in Indonesia of only European parents and by birth are given the most social and economic advantages above any other group of citizens. Considered the middle-class are the Eurasian elite who are the mixed offspring of European fathers and indigenous mothers possessing family names of European origin and fortunate enough to receive the same standard of education as their European counterparts which enabled them to hold jobs as teachers, administrators or political office. The largest group of society classified as the indigenous natives of mainly Indonesian ancestry, are primarily employed in servant capacities. Dutch and Malayan are the official languages spoken, with the majority of upper/middle citizens speaking both.

The distinction of class is evident everywhere on the major, populated islands. It is the European elite who enjoy the status and affluence of island life, living in neighborhoods on large, luxurious estates, surrounded by manicured lawns and beautiful floral gardens, separated by and secured with brick walls, noticeably blocking the view from pedestrians. Their palatial homes made of masonry and brick accommodate the style preferred by Europeans, including tall columns in front of the house, framing a sizeable veranda. In stark contrast, removed miles away, native villagers live in crowded communities or villages while the poorest of them call home a thatched roof shanty usually settled in ramshackle squatter settlements called "kampongs".

As industrialization increases on the islands at the turn of the 20th century, it causes the middle-class, predominately made up of Eurasians, to rise significantly. Middle-class communities reveal growing suburbs which in turn improves the much-needed infrastructure in the interior areas of the island on basic necessities like running water, electricity and improved road conditions.

By 1915, the port city of Surabaya, located in East Java has been a major trading center benefitting the larger Indonesian islands for more than two hundred years. It is also an established, important financial, commercial and industrial nerve center for servicing Java, which is the most populated of all the islands. Surabaya, as in all major cities where commerce flourishes, wide, paved roads allow for busy traffic to move safely as a policeman diligently, with precision, directs busy traffic at every intersection including diesel-run trams, automobiles, pedi cabs, bicycles, and pedestrians. The city thrives much like a bustling, congested metropolis in Europe and on every corner, towering, stately buildings, many resembling modern European structures stand as a testament to decades of colonization, and most notably, Dutch soldiers cooperatively stand alongside Indonesian troops guarding large government buildings.

Yet in the midst of the progressive, modern life, centuries of Hindi, Buddhist, eastern Indian, and Muslim influence are evident everywhere. Hundreds of Hindu and Buddhist temples, as well as the mosques of Islam built centuries before westerners arrived, are scattered in major cities, some standing next to Protestant churches or Catholic cathedrals.

Surabaya's economic growth provides employment opportunities for those fortunate enough to have benefitted from an adequate education. In banking, accounting, auditing, and managerial positions are considered prestigious. As a port city, Surabaya also bursts with plenty of jobs for men who are trained to work on the docks, loading and unloading cargo on and off ships, to secure warehouse positions, and those fortunate enough receiving instruction to become successful maintenance or repairmen.

However, the native Indonesian, without the benefit of any education or training becomes the servant for the European and Eurasian elite, validating one major reason the undercurrent of bitterness and resentment characterized the country for three hundred years during Dutch colonial rule. Adding to the tension impacting political and cultural life was the ongoing contention between various ethnic groups of Indonesians made up of the Javanese, Sudanese, and Malayan, Madurese, Acehnese, Dyak and Batak people. These indigenous peoples whose ancestors made up proud, fierce, tribal clans suffer years of repudiation as they consistently dispute and disagree within their own groups about Indonesia's progressive changes, at times causing outbreaks of confrontations mostly concentrated in the poorer sections of the country.

Several million of the population are also of Chinese and Portuguese descent along with smaller numbers of eastern Indian and Arab lineage. All of these ethnicities struggled to hold onto traditional values and principles they believe merit consideration above others, creating neighborhoods exclusively apart from other groups of differing ancestry. Through the years, groups of Indonesians came into conflict with residents of Chinese origin, who historically maintain successful business ventures and enjoyed a higher standard of living. At times, whole neighborhoods of Chinese communities, including Chinese businesses, were systematically wiped out through violence or trumped-up charges leading to false imprisonment and even deaths of many Indonesian citizens of Chinese descent. As the ethnic tensions simmered in Indonesia, the ability to improve the infrastructure is hampered, frustrated and divided by opposing ideals and almost three hundred dialects.

Into this rich, diverse, conflicting society, the child Harry Antoine Diederich makes his entrance. Harry's father, Johann Diederich born of Dutch/Indonesian parents possessing the family name Meijer; a name taken from the original Roman personal name of Magnus (great one) with Dutch, French, German and Swiss roots meaning mayor, overseer or public servant, holds a job as administrator for a Dutch government agency overseeing fiduciary practices in banking. Johann's island wife Mineoh, is a simple girl of Malayan/Chinese origin. Photographs reveal Johann to be taller than the average Indonesian man, with a fair complexion. Mineoh is small in stature, petite, characterized by typically dark features much like her native womenfolk.

Together the Meijers are the parents of five children of whom Harry is the eldest. Johann attends work every week day while Mineoh remains at home caring for the needs of the children and the household. Blessed with European ancestry which gave Johann the privilege of a good education, the Meijer family enjoys their comfortable, middle-class lifestyle with the income Johann makes in his prestigious position. His salary allows for the employment of a baboe, the domestic servant to assist Mineoh in the household duties.

For more than two hundred years, baboes make up a large community of people so well recognized in the Indonesian culture they are grouped in a class of its own. Thousands of domestic servants serve and in some instances, live with the family they tend to in a separate, humble dwelling apart from the main house on the common property, far enough to be separate but near enough to be available at a moment's notice.

Typically, the female baboe works assisting the wife and children of the elite family while baboe's husband's duties involve tasks related to the outdoors, mainly gardening and structural maintenance of the family's house. If baboe has children of her own, her youngsters usually become the playmates for children of the employer. It is not unusual for exclusive, higher economic groups of society to consider their baboe as an extended member of the family.

However, class boundaries still exist. The servant is not privileged enough to weigh in private or personal matters regarding the family in her care. If uncomfortable circumstances occur, baboe understands to keep situations strictly confidential for fear of losing her employment.

At the turn of the 20th century in the archipelago nation of Dutch/Indonesia, in spite of its many diversities, prominent Indonesian culture regarding family values is still dominated by a patriarchal system. Father has the last word and his word is law! Harry's father, Johann Meijer enforced that law in his home, daily communicating the expectations, rules and standard he demands of his wife and children. A strict disciplinarian, Mr. Meijer has earned the reputation in his community as a prideful, impatient task master in the workplace and in his home. For anyone who questions that distinction, all doubt is erased when Johann is questioned by local authorities for throwing his three-year-old son, Harry, through a plate glass window, resulting in extensive, medical treatment for the child's severe injuries.

A typical three-year-old boy is naturally curious, fearless and full of energy. Discovering the world around him is a daily adventure! Conversely, he can be demanding, disobedient or mischievous. Regardless of the circumstances, there was no explanation offered justifying the cruel punishment of the toddler with such brutality. Johann didn't need to explain because officials in charge do not investigate. Young Harry's wounds are bandaged up and the incident is never mentioned again.

Society agrees! Father in the home is king, his word is law and children are expected to be obedient, seen and not heard! If there is abuse in a home, no one mentions it! Family issues are kept private with society designating it a thing of shame to air one's personal business in public. Retaining family honor in the community is each member's responsibility! Determined to maintain the respect he has earned from everyone around him, Johann sustains complete control of his family.

Respect for parents is also earned by raising children who excel in school. Grades in school range from 1 being the lowest mark, with 10 as the highest possible. Each child in the Meijer family understands that Johann does not tolerate marks lower than 7. Harry as the eldest Meijer sibling, is required to tutor the younger children in their school work. His sister Ida, who is passionate about learning, solicits all the help she can from her older brother. Witnessing the benefit Ida receives from his assistance, Harry's younger brothers Jan and Rudy and little sister Ellie, take advantage of Harry's willingness to help. Perhaps Harry is motivated to assist because he receives severe physical punishment from his austere, authoritarian father if his siblings do not perform well in school. Johann's excellent reputation is dependent upon the success his children achieve in keeping their marks high.

Punitive measures are not just the prevailing, acceptable norm in the home as various forms of discipline are used regularly in school as well. Teachers summarily use a switch on a student for any insolence, striking the child on the neck, back or open hand. Corporal punishment keeps students under control. The severity used is left up to the discretion of the assailant.

Regardless of the pressure Harry experiences in the home or at school, his day is always made brighter by the woman he loves most of all!

Harry's affectionate mother, Mineoh is dutiful in her role as a wife and she is supremely devoted to her five children. As her favorite, Mineoh depends on Harry to cushion the physical and emotional blows she receives from Johann. The reserved, island mother is grateful that her eldest son defends her whenever possible, many times receiving the punch meant for Mineoh, Harry will sustain a black eye or bruise from his father's fists. Johann Meijer does not tolerate interference when he is administering his physical power over any member of his family, and his wife is no exception. Harry's regular intervention results in the teenager being sent outdoors to fend for himself until his father's ire is diminished days later. Mineoh sustains her son with food during the day while her husband is away at work. The wife and mother of Johann Meijer's children is grateful for Harry's passion to protect her.

Mineoh's personal story is fraught with maltreatment and abuse.

Born into a wealthy, well established Muslim family whose father proudly serves his community as the most important, influential Sultan in the region, Mineoh is his first-born child. The Sultan is severely disappointed that the infant born is a female. The Islam community mandates the need for men to dominate Muslim society, making male children the priority. A female is viewed merely as the means Allah uses to, one day, dominate the entire world via the wombs of women. Mineoh's father has no interest in his daughter and relegates the care of the child to her mother and two other wives. A Sultan has more important tasks to fulfill.

The role of Sultan in the Muslim region of eastern Surabaya designates him as the superior moral and spiritual authority, not just in his local community, but in the surrounding Muslim neighborhoods as well. He is to enforce all the religious laws in his sphere of influence. Adherents of the Muslim faith must abide by the many decrees of Mohammed which include an important ordinance to control the infiltration of any pagan influence. Mineoh's father enjoys the power of having jurisdiction over many municipalities. Earning the status of a Sultan has also granted Mineoh's father the privilege to marry more than one wife, provided he can financially support equally for each of them.

Mineoh's mother, of mixed ancestry, enjoys the advantage of being the first and eldest of the Sultan's three wives requiring her only child to help with many more children born in her father's household. While the Sultan's wives depend on Mineoh to assist them, they do not hesitate to abuse their authority over her. Mineoh struggles to carry the many burdens and responsibilities of her younger siblings, as days stretch long into the late evening hours.

Educated in the home by the local Muslim tutor teaching her the basic tenets of the Qur'an, Mineoh is dissatisfied but accepts the mandate that young women do not require any further education. Schooling ends for the teenager as her days are filled with preparations for Mineoh to become a dutiful wife in an arranged, Muslim marriage.

However, in her late teens, Mineoh meets and falls in love with a gentleman who works at the local bank, named Mr. Johann Meijer. The Sultan vehemently opposes the plans Johann and Mineoh have to marry! Mr. Meijer is a Protestant, and is told Mineoh cannot marry outside of the Muslim faith! However, the teenager is determined to marry Johann, risking the repercussions of bringing shame upon her father's position and his family. Mineoh is blessed that in the moderate, Islamic culture of Surabaya, excommunication is the most severe consequence.

Years later, Mineoh confesses to Harry the disappointment she experiences not being able to introduce her children to the family she sorely missed. Harry sympathizes and equally treasures his mother, keeping a special place in his heart for the woman who sacrificially placed her husband and children above herself. Sadly, Mineoh's life is tragically cut short at the age of thirty-five with complications from a bacterial infection. The year is 1931 and the penicillin vaccine is not yet available in the Indonesian archipelagoes. Harry is sixteen years old.

Decades later, Mineoh's son is convinced that a simple injection of antibiotics would have saved her life.

Following the death of their mother, the hardships of family life increase on the entire Meijer family, straining the atmosphere at home even more. To reduce his stress, Harry, who enjoys reading, embarks on a self-enlightenment journey through books and magazines about far-off lands which enable him to escape the world of his tyrannical father. Dozens of stories and photographs transport Harry away from his feelings of loss and loneliness. His favorite reading materials includes the historical and political accounts of a country called the United States, describing a lifestyle that would give a young man like Harry more opportunities to live successfully, free from the pressure of the oppression he experiences in his family life and more recently in his community.

Adding to Harry's bereavement in the loss of his mother, is the increasing pressure he experiences in school about social issues centered on the centuries-old disputes about the Dutch occupation of Indonesia.

Debates about colonialism have routinely been part of the domestic conversations in Indonesian homes and academia but until recently, increasing unrest and division about Dutch colonialism in the archipelago nation have been ramping up controversy in local and national Indonesian narratives. Newspaper editorials offer up opposing positions about the possibility of fighting for independence from the Dutch government, making the teenager question all things told to him by teachers in school, his father and adults in authority over him. Harry's concern about their lack of clarity and emotional rhetoric seem to him as unwise, devoid of fact-based discourse. Growing discontent in Johann Meijer's eldest son increases the tension at home as Harry begins confronting his father, accusing Johann's generation of hypocrisy. Harry takes a risk on escalating Johann's outrage as he regularly disrupts their conversations, mocking their duplicity. Like many young people, Harry disagrees with the views of the older generation.

The majority of national debates center on the imprisonment of dissenters against the Dutch government. Some Indonesian nationalists believe that implementing communistic ideologies in business practices would improve conditions for everyone. Johann vehemently disagrees with the communist factions, and is in favor of incarceration for all vocal insurrectionists. Increasingly, accelerating contention for independence is making its way into the public square and Harry believes his personal opinion, contrary to his father's, are relevant in the midst of controversial discussions. The rift between the teenager and his father grows, causing the young man to consider leaving his father's house. For many months the loss of Harry's mother, Mineoh, has made life in the Meijer home unbearable, and Harry decides that he will move out to create some distance between himself and his unreasonable father. Numerous, acrimonious conflicts between father and son about the nationalists' fight for independence and its leaders give the idealistic, young man the rationale he needs to absolve himself of any guilt feelings about leaving his family.

In the most recent episode making headline news is a young, Javanese university student named Raden Soekemi Sosrodihardjo otherwise also known as Sukarno who has gained notoriety as the leader of a group he formed called the Indonesian Independence Movement Party. The PNI's mission statement include a mixture of socialism, nationalism and communistic ideology adding the religious duties to Islam combing all of the influences Sukarno was exposed to in his youth. As the organization increases in popularity with idealistic university students and young professionals, Sukarno becomes more fearless and grows bolder in holding rallies advocating the overthrow of the Dutch government and fighting for Indonesian independence. Sukarno is arrested in 1932 for inciting violence and imprisoned for two years. In the public eye, the arrest elevates him as hero with more frustrated islanders inspired to stand up to the Dutch government and their monarchy.

Johann Meijer and most of his colleagues are jubilant that the troublemaker is put away. But Harry's struggles intensify as society begins to split into two major opinions about fighting for independence from Dutch imperialism. In school, teachers freely express their position about the growing number of citizens who want to rid the country of their colonist oppressors. They advocate protests and hint at promoting violence to achieve their goal. Leaflets begin showing up on students' desks in school, slipped under front doors in residential neighborhoods or hung randomly on tree branches, championing the idea of organizing a major revolt against Dutch sovereignty.

Disgusted with any form of violence, Harry remains pragmatic about his personal choices. During his lifetime, he had witnessed the discontent of fellow countrymen, some which resulted in a skirmish or two, but was immediately put down by local authorities. Harry remains focused, resolute to finish school and makes plans to join the Royal Dutch Air

Force. He is eager to leave his father's controlling authority and believes joining the military will give him an opportunity to grow in the self-confidence he needs to become successful.

It is 1933 and Harry realizes he is powerless to change the political landscape of the Dutch East Indies. Personally, the young man has never been conflicted about his Indonesian/European lineage. He is confident and proud to be part of both cultures. Johann Meijer's eldest son is grateful to have been the recipient of many advantages including the education and training he needed to fulfill his goals. Born and raised in Surabaya where the thriving metropolis helps galvanize the ambitious young man to make plans for his future, Harry has a clear choice about remaining in the city to seek a job in administration or join the military. Either one will bring into his life much sought after adventure and perhaps give him a chance to visit far off lands including a country call the United States! The issue and persistent contentions in his father's house about colonialism will not disrupt Harry's desire to seek the best choice for a good future. The young man is confident that decades of economic progress of his country will override the philosophical arguments in the national debates!

The majority of the public agrees, hoping more moderate voices assuage the agitators.

In the Dutch East Indies, three hundred years of European countries bringing commerce, trading and manufacturing has notably enriched the island nation, and results in economic advantages co-mingling the two major civilizations of west merging with the east. For decades, Portuguese, Dutch, French, German and British entrepreneurships brought into the archipelagoes become successful, well-established companies on the islands. Accompanying the businessmen to the Indonesian archipelagoes are their family members, greatly impacting the Indonesian culture with western influences of social, artistic, and religious practices.

And one major, significant characteristic are the obvious, genetic changes of their children!

Throughout decades of inter-racial marriage, the diverse physical contributions of the Europeans is adjunct to the varied, contrasting qualities of the islanders, as the appearance of their offspring is impacted by the combination of the fair complexion of the Europeans co-mingling with the olive skin of the natives. The result is a change in skin color. A major feature attracting those early explorers to the indigenious female was the island woman's long, black tresses. As youngsters, island girls are taught to care for it by adding coconut oil after washing, adding a luxuriant, striking feature to their physical appearance. The Eurasian daughter inherits the dark, thick mass of hair on her head contrasting with her pale, slightly, olive skin tone. Adding to the comely allure of the Eurasian female are the European facial features of high cheekbones, blending with the islander's full, fleshy lips and exotic shaping of the eyes.

Complementing the DNA of rounded curves of the European female with the contribution of lithe, dainty limbs of the petite, Indonesian girl, many beautiful Eurasian daughters are born, one of whom is Christine Victorine Hall.

chapter

4

"There is nothing permanent except change."
GREEK PHILOSOPHER HERACLITUS OF EPHESUS

Portrayed on a typical post card or tourist brochure of Southeast Asian lands, lovely colored photos depict dozens of men and women in traditional dress, their heads covered with typical wide-brimmed straw hats, as they contentedly gather in sheaves of rice, the main staple of the country. Unbeknownst to most westerners, pictures belie the true story.

In the early years of 20th century Indonesian society, native peasants barely eke out a living because of the extraneous, physical labor required for harvesting rice by hand. Yet in the midst of meager living conditions, native islanders of Indonesia are known for their generosity and hospitality.

First time travelers who visit are delighted with the reception they receive upon arriving on the islands. Visitors who leave typical tourist attractions, make their way inland, and travel beyond the commercial sections of the metropolis, are blessed to discover a charitable kindness of the native people and equally surprised by their poverty. The industrial age of the early 1900's has not yet advanced the living conditions of citizens living on the outskirts of major cities. Managed poorly by the Dutch government, hundreds of surrounding, little villages suffer the lack of infrastructure for decent roads, office buildings, telecommunication lines, proper sewage drains, basic electricity, and delivery of water and natural gas.

Indonesia's villages struggle to have properly maintained streets for pedestrians, bicycles and motorcars in poorer sections of the country.

Over-head, strings of electrical wires span carelessly for miles from one wooden pole to another. In the countryside, the roads are customarily paved with crude blacktop. The wear and tear on those streets of the occasional motor vehicle cause less of a problem than the heavy, deluge of monsoon rains which pelts the country twice of the year. The majority of poor villagers trek on foot from one destination to another.

On the outskirts of the thriving metropolis of the city of Medan, located on the third largest Indonesian island of Sumatra, female residents from the villages walk to their jobs as hotel chambermaids, or domestic servants for suburban, middle-class residents.

With the assistance of a hired midwife, Mrs. Kasmenah Hall gives birth to her first child, Christine Victorine on January 31, 1919. Thankfully the baby is born healthy because the pregnancy had been a difficult one. Kasmenah's young age of fifteen is the main reason the teenager experienced a challenging delivery. The majority of women in the Dutch East Indies give birth at home. Kasmenah is blessed to have a midwife present and the assistance of her faithful baboe. Because of the Hall's middle-class income, Kasmenah enjoys the help of both women.

Kasmenah's husband, Christiaan Ludwig Gustav Hall, is not present when the child is born because he is at work as an auditor in the commerce department for the government in the city of Medan, the perfect job for a man of his temperament. Christiaan Hall has the reputation of being a trustworthy, hardworking individual. Colleagues also describe him as intense and private.

As the son of Eurasian parents, Christiaan and his four younger brothers were blessed to receive the benefits of an education which gave them opportunities to secure well- paying jobs. All the Hall brothers are among many growing the middle-class on the archipelagoes in the beginning of the 1920's.

In as many years, Mr. and Mrs. Christiaan Hall become the parents of three more children after Christine is born, requiring Christiaan to work longer hours. But the young father looks forward to attending his job every day and is happy to be part of a profession which is growing rapidly in the big city.

Christiaan is well aware that he married an ordinary island girl of limited means with no status in the community. His goal is to help his wife understand the opportunities open to him at work and hopes to advance his reputation in the local community too. Every weekend, Christiaan is involved in raising funds for assistance in relief work to help the poorest neighborhoods who suffered from the trade restrictions brought on by the 1914 – 1918 Great War in Europe. He is committed to volunteer in charitable works as a good example for his wife and children.

Kasmenah Hall finds her own level of comfort in the nearby village away from the noise and crowds of the city of Medan. She is happy to walk several blocks down the road to the familiarity of the local, outdoor market, where a large, noisy, colorful area called the pasar, occupies a large open space with the farmers laying out the day's provisions of exotic fruits, root and leafy vegetables, dried, salted or fresh fish, hundreds of various types of herbs and spices, including the choices of well-seasoned poultry, fish and meats. Refrigeration is not widely available, thus, highly seasoning the meat products keep it fresh, even if, for just a few hours. Large areas of the pasar is adequately covered with large, colorful sunshades called payongs.

Immediately upon arrival, Kasmenah recognizes the aroma of oil which flavors the air as someone is frying food for purchase whether sweet or savory with hungry customers buying a morsel or two, munching as they continue their shopping. Around the corner, merchants bring non-eatable items such as yards of beautiful, batik material, the fabric which made the southeast nations popular in the textile industry by dyeing raw material on top of a removable wax design. Kasmenah eyes the delicate ceramic ware made in a nearby, village home but considers the purchase of another aluminum pot instead. In another row of stalls, village homemakers offer tasty home-cooked items hoping to make a rupiah or two. The pasar experience brings joy to Kasmenah Hall as she regularly encounters an amicable friend or neighbor.

All over the market place, patrons can be heard passionately negotiating about the price of an item, because missing feathers on a chicken or ragged edges on the fin of the fish, maybe a bruise on fruit could bring the price down, but not without the emotional ardor of both parties involved. Sometimes, Kasmenah would make nasty remarks about an item with the help of a nearby shopper agreeing, causing the merchant to raise his voice, or slap his forehead, making flamboyant gestures as he argues that his merchandise is the best in the whole pasar! Kasmenah knows that in the end, the customer prevails and she leaves satisfied with the bargains in her basket.

Everywhere in the pasar, mothers joyfully shop, some carrying their very young children in a slendang, a long piece of colorful batik wrapped around her shoulders and hips to hold the child comfortably on her back or tightly held in the front on her chest. Older children are milling around, sometimes clutching their mother's legs. Children are a mother's constant companions. The petite, island mother, is physically equipped with flexibility and great strength to carry a basket on her head, balancing it perfectly without fear of losing the contents, indifferent to the jostling of her little ones. The laughter of the children add to the friendly atmosphere of the pasar, completing another productive day for Kasmenah.

For centuries in the Eastern culture, motherhood is considered the highest calling for a woman. If she is childless, she is pitied and mourned. Childless women are considered to have bad luck because of past deeds as society judges them harshly. In 1900's Indonesia, the woman blessed with children is expected to be supremely devoted to them, sacrificing her own needs for the sake of her family! The standard role for the female is to serve her husband and children, and her value is assessed by how well she accomplishes that role. Without ambiguity, Kasmenah's destiny in Indonesian society as wife and mother is mapped out to the end of her life and it pleases her to fulfill the calling!

The wife of Mr. Hall is barely 60 inches tall. In photographs, Christiaan towers over her and with the normal, stoic expression accepted in the culture, neither Christiaan nor Kasmenah smile for the camera. Gazing at a portrait of the family, one wonders about the life Kasmenah has lived up to that day. Her story is one with a rich past!

On the island of Sumatra, devout followers of Mohammed practice Islam adhering to more stringent rules compared to the more moderate Muslims on neighboring islands. Historians believe that because Islam arrived first on the island of Sumatra via the trade routes by overseas merchants in the middle of the 13th century, the teachings of Mohammed found fertile ground in Sumatra where the roots of Islam grew deep.

Initially from southern India and Gujarat in western India, entrepreneurs who were devout followers of Allah did not confine their activities just to business but were enthusiastic proselytizers of Islam. By the end of the 13th century, the coastal populations of northern Sumatra readily accepted the new religion as they chose their first Muslim ruler, Sultan Malik al Saleh of Pasai. Islam spreads rapidly, rising to the sultanate (the region of land ruled by a Muslim sultan) of Malacca on the peninsula of Malaysia's west coast. As a result, Malacca gains commercial and political power quickly becoming the major center in Southeast Asia influencing the way men conduct business and eventually, political enterprises.

The religion which heralds Mohammed as their prophet, who himself had multiple wives and concubines, encouraged his male followers to do the same. It is accepted that Islam considers marriage to be a civil contract, not a sacrament, which gives the man permission to marry many women as long as he is financially able to care for them. Wealthy clerics take on multiple wives and concubines. The Muslim woman is considered erotic, but empty-headed, thus she is subject to purdah (seclusion and veiling), polygyny, and concubinage or she is chosen to be part of a harem. Not a priority for their role in society, women are not taught to read or write. Bearing children and caring for the needs of the family does not require an education. If the cleric marries a woman, she receives the privilege that marriage offers in Islamic law. The wife is allowed to occupy the same space in the home as her husband. The children of that union, especially sons, are highly valued and rewarded with many birthright advantages.

Kasmenah's mother is one of three concubines obtained by a wealthy Muslin cleric living in the province of Medan who also possessed three wives. Already the household burgeoned with eight children, making Kasmenah and her mother responsible for the main load of domestic duties. Without the advantage of being a wife, the concubine is a resource mainly to provide more children to the cleric's household and she is considered not much more than a domestic servant. Concubines are sent to live in another part of the property, typically in a humble dwelling separate from the main house. Her children do not receive the status or material wealth associated with the social position of the cleric, although they are subject to attend classes to learn the ways of the Qur'an. The cleric's legitimate wives are expected to be the overseers of the concubines, enjoying many more privileges and, as in the case of Kasmenah's mother, routinely verbally and physically abuse their lowly counterparts.

The story is told of one evening, young Kasmenah abruptly awakens to see her mother wrapping their meager belongings in a sarong. The explanation from Kasmenah's mother is that the cleric is unhappy about her infertility. It has been seven years since Kasmenah's birth without a subsequent pregnancy, and the cleric is contemplating putting them away as mere outcasts.

While it is still dark outside, the two steal away into the nearby forest with the frightened mother warning Kasmenah they would face dire consequences if caught. There were many accounts of severe beatings for acts of insubordination or attempted desertion, with the violence sometimes resulting in death. Kasmenah and her mother survive by begging, living in a kampong where the poorest of society exist, able to survive in obscurity, free from scrutiny. By the time twenty-year-old Christiaan Hall marries the fifteen-year-old waif, Kasmenah's mother had already passed away.

Marriage for young, native girls at the turn of the 20th century in the Indonesian culture was not unusual. Attending school is not compulsory for females and although in 1903 one primary school opened for Indonesian girls on the island of Java, the idea of educating them is a new concept. This prevailing, unpopular sentiment at the beginning of the 1900's has no radical effect on the large, native female population. With regularity, by the time island girls reach their early teens, many are married to indigenious men or men with Eurasian ethnicity.

Island women married to men of Eurasian or European origin, result in a double standard within the family. The lowly, indigenous wife is to remain subservient to her husband, meek in behavior. That is the condition in the Hall's marriage, as Kasmenah, without question, accepts society's expectation for wives to remain focused primarily on domestic duties.

The mother of four keeps social contacts minimal. Her days are filled with caring for seven-year-old Christine, Hetty who is five, four-year-old Guus and the youngest daughter Dora at two years of age. Kasmenah is grateful for the consistent help of baboe, without whom would make the days much more challenging. Together the two women collaborate, making sure the household runs smoothly per the demands of Christiaan Hall.

Life for Christiaan is a different story. Worldly, educated and keenly aware about current affairs, his job as provider is the more relevant, important one. His social contacts are many and generally revolve around his work.

Arriving home one evening, Christiaan Hall announces he received a job promotion and cheerfully informs Kasmenah the family will relocate to the metropolis of Bandoeng (Bandung), located on the island of Java. Christine's father is thrilled with the opportunity to live in a city which is experiencing a boom in business commerce as longtime residents had begun making demands to increase Bandoeng's municipality.

Kasmenah had an announcement of her own and informs her husband that she is pregnant with their fifth child. Christiaan is not concerned. The promotion will increase the family's yearly income and the addition of another child will not be a burden. Kasmenah dutifully accepts the commitment her husband has made. She has no voice in the matter since her opinion is never a consideration in the marriage.

Leaving Medan is difficult for Kasmenah. She had established several friendships with a close community of island wives who were married with Eurasian men. The camaraderie of shared interests and common challenges secured a mutual trust among the women. Kasmenah is unhappy about the move so far away. Christiaan Hall expects his wife's response to be one of complete compliance and support. She is relieved that Christiaan presumes their long-time servant will accompany them. The baboe is a trustworthy young woman who has become a devoted companion for Kasmenah and the children.

Kasmenah Hall could not know that soon she would come to depend on her faithful maidservant more than ever before.

The Hall Family circa 1925
Oma Kasmenah, Opa Christiaan (Standing)
Christine, Hetty, Guus, baby Dora seated on baboe's lap (Left-to-Right)

chapter

5

"Fathers, do not exasperate your children, so that they will not lose heart."

Colossians 3:21 NASB

Bandoeng is a city located in the western part of Java. Sitting almost 2,600 feet above sea level, it is blessed with cooler temperatures than most of the interior areas of the island. Surrounded by volcanic mountains, Dutch colonists established tea plantations in the fertile areas bringing in trade seekers who realized the valuable desirability of tea commodities. In the late 1800's, the government built the first major railroad linking Bandoeng to the capital city of Java called Batavia to make trade in the tea business more efficient. Hundreds of Chinese immigrants converge into the city to help build the railroad and later work as servants to help the growing metropolis in the hotel and restaurant business. As commerce grows rapidly in Bandoeng, the need for governmental accounting teams increases, bringing in men like Christiaan Hall to work in compliance and support. Christiaan is proud to be one of many white- collar administrators holding a position which will launch his career, offering him opportunities to make his dream a reality.

The Hall family moves into a middle-class neighborhood similar to the one left behind in Medan, but located further away from the city. The property accommodates a house built according to the western standards using masonry and brick. Kasmenah is delighted the house has a small veranda leading up to the front door. Many evening hours, after the family is down for the night, Kasmenah is alone on the porch, enjoying the company of new neighbors including the women who bring her up to date with the latest gossip in the neighborhood. Her husband rises early before sun up, taking the bus into the city. In Medan, Christiaan was content to ride his bicycle to work, but here on the island of Java, the city of Bandoeng is too far and he is happy to use public transportation.

On Sunday mornings, the entire Hall family boards the bus to transport them to the local Lutheran church in the city. Christiaan had made it clear that the Protestant religion would be practiced in their home. Kasmenah didn't mind. She was never a follower of Islam!

Mrs. Hall with the help of her loyal maidservant is settling in. Almost immediately, the young mother fills many empty places of her garden planting several melati bushes which throw out the lovely jasmine fragrances of its tiny, star-like flowers. Her eldest daughter, Christine begs for a dog and because the child enjoys all animals, she pleads for a parrot and chickens and a cat. Kasmenah is not a fan of cats but allows a German shepherd puppy to become part of the family. Care of the animals becomes Christine's responsibility. Eventually, the children are excited that a parrot is added, joining a dozen chickens which complete the menagerie.

With her fifth pregnancy Kasmenah struggles to maintain her strength because the demands of a husband, four active children and a host of animals prevent her from getting the proper rest. Kasmenah suffers from exhaustion and is warned by the local midwife, she is risking a miscarriage.

The opportunity to rest never comes as Kasmenah wakes up one morning to the ravaged, fevered body of her husband whose labored breathing is shallow as he desperately gasps for air.

In the hospital, Christiaan is one of hundreds who dies from a deadly, contagious, typhoid epidemic which sweeps through Bandoeng and its surrounding communities. The twenty-nine-year-old husband and father does not survive to fulfill his dreams. In the Dutch East Indies, a social assistance program is not available, leaving the young widow without the advantages of European ancestry in dire, financial hardship!

The untimely passing of Christiaan brings on even more challenges for his surviving spouse. Yet at twenty-four years of age, Kasmenah understands she is young and resourceful enough to find ways to provide for her family. The young mother cannot afford the time to grieve Christiaan's sudden passing and immediately secures a space for a food stall at the pasar, enlisting Christine's help with the cooking while baboe cares for the younger children. Christine is happy to help! There is something wonderful about her mother's need for support. Yes, the death of her father was unexpected but secretly, deep in her heart, Christine does not miss him!

Nine-year-old Christine makes a promise never to reveal how her relief about the passing of Christiaan far outweighs her love for him!

Acquaintances of the Hall family characterized Christine's father as a man of brooding, moody, and easily annoyed. His reserved, impatient nature regularly clashed with the free-spirited Christine. Folks describe Christiaan as an emotionally detached individual who did not bother to make people comfortable. In his presence, conversations had to remain brief, and to the point. Yet Mr. Hall did not hesitate to reveal that he had not counted on being the parent of a spontaneous, impassioned youngster like Christine, who is full of exuberance, impulsively happy to express her feelings and struggles to maintain any self-restraint demanded by her father.

Christine is not yet ten years old as Christiaan's resentment escalates against his daughter who has brought him shame because of numerous reprimands from school teachers for disturbing other students in class. Many times, his daughter is placed outside of the classroom. While the youngster experiences the initial sting of embarrassment, within minutes Christine is heard humming a tune, much to the frustration of her instructors and amusement of fellow students!

In the home, exasperated with her constant chatter, Christiaan relies on the baboe to take Christine outdoors. There, the child's affection grows for her pets, as the animals fulfill the young girl's desperate need to be accepted, temporarily easing her intense feelings of rejection.

Unfortunately, there are times baboe is not available to remove the loquacious, energetic youngster from the house. On those occasions, Christiaan Hall takes control, forcefully placing a kicking, screaming Christine in a corner, who is instructed to squat and hold her ear lobes with opposite hands. The young girl would endure that position for hours before fainting on to the floor. Exhausted, the child lies still, not allowed to move until baboe is available to carry her to bed. That evening, Christine is not given anything to eat, while Kasmenah watches helplessly, powerless to help. Christiaan forbids Kasmenah's involvement in any disciplinary action concerning all of their children, deeming his wife incapable of properly punishing a disobedient child.

However, in one incident, Kasmenah should have stepped in.

Christiaan had remained home from work one day. His wife and baboe were preoccupied caring for the younger children. Seven-year-old Christine was playing in the courtyard with one of baboe's children, a girl of the same age. The laughter and exuberance of children at play warms the hearts of most people, but not for Christiaan Hall! Annoyed as the level of noise rises, disturbing his rest, Christiaan reprimands them, demanding absolute silence. Engrossed in the fun and frolic, it is not long before the girls forget the rebuke and the two youngsters are loudly, gleefully at play again.

Exasperated, Christiaan normally using the woody stem of a bamboo stem when applying corporal punishment, decides to cut a thick branch off a nearby rubber tree begins striking his young daughter repeatedly and mercilessly on her back, injuring Christine severely. The physician called to the home is concerned about stopping the profuse bleeding! He cannot be bothered that his imperfect stitching of the wound never heals properly, leaving the child with a lesion almost 5 inches long and a 1/2 inch deep.

The ugly scar becomes a lifetime reminder for Christine of her tumultuous relationship with her father.

After Christiaan's passing, Kasmenah continued to attend the Lutheran church with her children. Several church goers complement Kasmenah about Christine's beautiful singing voice. Not yet fully developed, the young girl's melodious delivery is described by some as angelic. Christine has found refuge in the music and message of the protestant church and is asked to join the children's choir.

Free from her father's oppressive demands, the child is heard by neighbors, joyfully filling the home of Kasmenah Hall with song and laughter, encouraging her younger siblings to join her in a favorite, American hymn she learned in church called "Amazing Grace."

chapter 6

"Beauty is in the eye of the beholder."
ENGLISH PLAYWRIGHT SIR WILLIAM SHAKESPEARE

Things greatly change in the Hall household. The financial strain has increased, forcing Kasmenah to relocate to a poorer neighborhood, farther away from the city. On December 24th, 1928, Kasmenah gives birth to her fifth child Bernard, six months after Christiaan's death. Managing with the help of her faithful servant baboe, Kasmenah reduces her expenses by giving away the family's pets. Christine and her siblings are devastated!

Several years into widowhood, Kasmenah continues to struggle putting enough food on the table for five, growing children. Ultimately, the eldest daughter of the Hall family realizes her mother needs more help! As financial pressures mount, fourteen-year-old Christine voluntarily leaves school, overjoyed to find employment at a neighborhood movie theater. Located close enough for the teenager to ride Christiaan's bike the short distance, Christine experiences unbridled freedom from the oppressive, classroom environment.

In the small, enclosed booth where Christine works, the compartment stands separate from the main building of the cinema. Her job is easy! Christine collects the fee from patrons, handing them a ticket stub in exchange. Feelings of pride and confidence begin to rise up in the young woman as she witnesses Kasmenah's relief each time Christine hands over her weekly paycheck. However, once a month, Christine believed she was justified withholding a few rupiahs to put away for personal use.

In the 1930's, on the Indonesian islands, many films from Hollywood in America have made their way to the other side of the world, thrilling audiences across Europe and eventually making their way into Southeast Asian countries. Exposed to this new form of entertainment, Christine enters a brand-new world. The young girl is captivated with the romance, mystery and adventure that movies bring. Temporarily, every film lifts her out of the loneliness which has taken over her life. Not missing the academic aspects of the classroom, but feeling the social void leaving school has produced, Christine lives for the days she reports for work.

Routinely, after hours, the manager allows theater employees to view the movie playing that day. What joy it brings the island teen as she is drawn into the scenes on the giant screen. Christine is easily enraptured with the dance of Fred Astaire and Ginger Rogers across a spacious ballroom floor, while the handsome, leading man serenades his beautiful, blonde co-star. And who could resist the heroics of John Wayne, Randolph Scott and Johnny Weissmuller, as they portray rugged, brave men who rescue the pretty damsel in distress? The audience bursts out in laughter with the hilarious comedy acts of the three Marx brothers and the series depicting the antics of poor neighborhood children called "The Little Rascals". But it's the singing, tap dancing Shirley Temple who is Christine's favorite star of them all! Christine Hall begins to use her savings to purchase monthly magazines which detail the lives of the famous actors she watches on the silver screen.

As the pictures and stories in the periodicals transport Christine into a world of excessive daydreaming, Kasmenah's growing disappointment with the influence movies has on her daughter begins to express her displeasure. Christine ignores the criticisms and surreptitiously among friends, stubbornly defends her love of the cinema. Increasingly, the teenager surrounds herself with likeminded people, spending more time with them after work, causing hostilities to escalate between Christine and her mother. Kasmenah complains to friends that Christine is becoming the main reason for her daily frustration, making their increasing, loud quarrels the latest topic of surrounding, neighborhood gossip. Desperate to avoid any confrontation, Christine tries a different approach by refusing to respond to Kasmenah's outbursts, retreating into stony silence. The island mother mistakenly believes she has made her point, trusting her teenage daughter will give up the silly notions of unrealistic, fanciful ideals.

But it's too late…Christine is hooked! Movie stars are handsome gentlemen and lovely ladies. They are sophisticated people dressed in beautiful clothes giving them elegance ordinary folk could only dream about. Life for them is filled with adventure and excitement! How could a poor girl be prevented from yearning for that kind of life? Would she deny herself of a loving, handsome prince carrying her away from the boring, predictable existence she already lives?

The entertainment business from a country a world away has begun to influence a simple, island girl with possibilities she had never considered before. Christine realizes there is adventure beyond the monotonous routine of her impoverished life, further away from the tiny house she occupies with her mother and four, younger, noisy siblings. The tedious chore of cutting out her own patterns from old newspapers to construct an ordinary sarong every woman wears with the plain, fitted blouse of the kebaya, is beginning to irritate the teenager. Perhaps she could save enough money to purchase material to construct a different type of outfit, something westerners call a dress. Traditional sarongs have grown outdated for Christine and lately, her attempts to convince Kasmenah to replace her worn out sandals for a pair of shoes with high heels, fails. Conversations about a change of hairstyle fall on deaf ears, as Kasmenah is overwhelmed with the changes in her daughter. The angry teen is convinced her ignorant, island mother does not understand the ways of the modern world!

Determined to stop the corrupt values of western entertainment from influencing her child, Kasmenah adds more restrictions to Christine's free time. As the bickering escalates, disrupting the entire family, Kasmenah is disturbed by more displays of rebellion from her ten-year-old son Guus, and twelve-year-old daughter Hetty who has been caught leaving the school grounds without permission.

Kasmenah spends sleepless nights, struggling at losing Christine to an alien world filled with delusion. A responsible mother would do all she could to protect her daughter from destructive, foreign ideas. The modest, island mother admits that her husband, Christiaan would have done a better job at managing their strong-willed, eldest child. How would he discipline a girl who is almost a woman?

With pressure mounting, Kasmenah makes a desperate decision to return Christine back to live with Christiaan's relatives in Medan on the island of Sumatra for an indefinitive amount of time.

The forced move makes Christine furious! The loss of her job, friends and independence brings on an indignation Christine has not experienced since the days when her father was alive. As weeks turn into months, the angry teenager does not answer her mother's letters, and taking her resentment against Kasmenah further, Christine cuts off her thick, long hair very short above her ears!

Christine Hall believes Kasmenah is a stumbling block she plans for the future. She views the simple, uneducated, island mother as one who not interested in the progressive culture of the West but squanders precious time with silly, antiquated practices which carry over into superstitious ideas about the afterlife.

Once a month, Kasmenah, follows the villagers' ritual of putting out bits of food near the front entrance of their small house to appease hungry "ghosts." Convinced these spirits were hungry when they died, Kasmenah believes they will not disturb the occupants of the home if they are fed regularly. Christine never wasted an opportunity to offer her opinion of the ridiculous custom but Kasmenah practiced the rite faithfully ignoring her daughter's criticisms. Christine is nothing like her mother and considers herself more enlightened than her parents' generation!

Surely the eldest daughter of Mr. Christiaan Hall is not destined to pattern a future which resembles her mother's life? Christine has more ambitious goals than just remaining another poor and dreary, village girl.

As Christine's bitterness against Kasmenah grows, the young woman fails to understand that the decision to send Christine away broke her mother's heart!

Time passes slowly on the Hall compound of Medan. By comparison, Christiaan's relatives prove to be significantly less tolerant of western, progressive ideas even more than Kasmenah. Their protestant ethics forbid Christine to pursue outside employment. According to their strict, religious precepts, it is not acceptable for women to seek work outside the bounds of domestic duties. Insisting that Christine remains inside the family compound to facilitate their baboe, Christine's uncle proves to be as harsh and controlling as Christiaan had been. Eventually, the rebellious teenager is forced to face increasing feelings of longing for Kasmenah and her siblings in Bandoeng.

Long, tedious weeks stretch into monotonous months as the rigid domestic routine begins to soften Christine's strident opinions she holds against her mother.

It takes many more months and conversations between Kasmenah and the Hall family before Christine is allowed to return home. The motivations for her return are many, but Kasmenah admits that she needed her daughter's domestic and financial help. On her own, the widow and mother of five struggled to carry the burden of their economical responsibilities. Adding to numerous, exigent challenges, Kasmenah confesses that the emotional and physical demands of the younger children was too much for her to bear alone. She is desperate for Christine help with Guus, Hetty, Dora and baby Bernard. Eagerly Christine jumps back in, happy to take control of her siblings, and with ease finds employment in the front office of a small textile manufacturer. The teenage girl is seventeen-years-old.

Seventeen and beautiful!

Blessed with the combined physical traits of her Dutch father and island mother, Christine Victorine Hall is turning heads. Bestowed with the highly valued, ivory complexion, arched brows accenting large, brown eyes, the young woman's good looks is accentuated by prominent cheekbones and full, rosy lips which surround perfect, straight teeth. With an affectionate, soft smile which reach alluring, comely eyes, Christine's, short, wavy hair easily falls around her pleasant, pretty face. Standing 5 feet 4 inches tall, Christine's slender legs hold a curvaceous figure, sporting a tiny waistline.

Well known in the surrounding villages for her vocal abilities, Kasmenah's daughter can also whistle a tune louder than most grown men. But it's Christine's reputation as an accomplished cook that is the favorite topic among the neighborhood gossip mongers. At the tender age of nine, the year of Christiaan's passing, Kasmenah began teaching her daughter the basics of preparing the complex dishes of Indonesian cuisine. Christine proves to be a fast learner and Kasmenah makes it mandatory for Christine to pass everything she has learned to her younger sisters, Hetty and Dora. Like her mother, Christine is serious about the art of cooking.

The accolades she receives from friends and family about her delicious meals, Christine makes clear, should go to Kasmenah.

Preparing homemade meals in the majority of Southeast Asian countries is typically done in a kitchen area located in a small separate building, typically, set apart from the main house. In poorer neighborhoods, rural areas or villages, residents share the common use of the "dapur". The small structure, surrounded by four walls has an opening in one or two walls half way up to the ceiling. Inside the dwelling stands either a table or counter top for food prep. Attached to the wall, made of brick, concrete or stone is the compartment called an "arang", resembling a grill, holding a mesh or wire rack used for cooking. Below, the arang is filled with wood and lit on fire. Earthen pots and iron pans are placed on the rack above it, or if desired, meat is put directly on the grill.

Theories vary as to the reason the dapur was built away from the main house. Historically, the first concern was that fires could get out of control, causing a possible hazard to the rest of the home. Another reason explained that the culinary fare of Indonesia is extremely pungent, making the separation of the dapur from the main house, a sensible solution.

Cooking the cuisine of the east requires hours of preparation with much patience needed to crush many spices and vegetables like onions, garlic, tamarind seed, coriander seeds, sereh (lemongrass), lombok (chillies), trassi (shrimp paste), laos (galangal), ginger root, just to name a few. All of this is accomplished using a tumbukan (stone mortar) with a stone pestle. The wadjan (wok) and the kukusan (rice steamer) are invaluable, necessary tools for the cook.

Preparing meals together restores Kasmenah's relationship with Christine. The bond grows quickly between mother and daughter as the two share common goals of feeding and caring for the younger children.

Like most island families, Christine and Kasmenah raise chickens to provide eggs and meat for the family. As ardent gardeners, both women grow fruit, vegetables and beautiful island flowers on their humble, small property. Much of their crop make it to Kasmenah's stand at the pasar, which brings in much needed revenue.

Appreciating more than ever before the comfort Kasmenah brings, Christine makes a commitment to be more thankful for the woman who had already suffered with many trials, motivating the teenager to become more aware of her personal selfishness.

Thankfully, tensions cease between mother and daughter and just in time as Kasmenah is faced with new challenges regarding Christine. Local boys begin to show an interest in the lovely, seventeen-year-old girl living in the Hall household. Several are brave enough to appear on Kasmenah's front door, requesting permission to "socialize" with Christine. Social engagements in the Indonesian culture of the 1930's between a young woman and man are allowed after the young man makes a formal request with the girl's father. The role of father includes chaperoning the dating couple, which leaves Kasmenah as a single parent, uncertain about her responsibility. She does not allow Christine to keep male company beyond the boundaries of their small front porch and only after her own assessment, gives each one permission to drop by and visit inside the confines of their humble home. The boys who qualify are Broertje De Wolff, brothers Piet and Schipp Schrander and a young Chinese/Indonesian man. These potential suitors, willing to suffer through the scrutiny of the stern, widowed mother, amuse Christine as her wide-eyed younger siblings join them on the porch.

Kasmenah is no fool. She has endured enough hardship to make her a wise, protective parent. The young man at her door had better be ready to give her a list of his accomplishments, beginning with his education and his standing in the community. Small town gossip is very reliable and according to Kasmenah, a young man's reputation follows close behind him.

Christine's suitors are carefully screened with Kasmenah maintaining a keen vigilance during each visit.

Life is beginning to open doors for the lovely Christine Victorine, with many more western influences via film and magazines coming across the ocean. One trend especially objectionable for Kasmenah is the trend which persuades the younger generation to use their middle name in place of the first name! Christine's friends begin calling her Vicky, short for Victorine. Kasmenah barely tolerates the practice, continues to call Christine by her first name and forbids Christine's younger siblings to address her as Vicky.

But some things even Kasmenah is forced to compromise with. Well in her late teen years, on special occasions, Christine is now allowed to wear western type dresses which she constructs herself cutting up used newspaper for patterns. Her friends are wearing high heels and Christine squeals with delight the day Kasmenah permits her daughter to purchase a pair.

Kasmenah has begun to accept that many Western influences will remain in her beloved country and reluctantly releases some control of her first-born child. With four other children who occupy her concern, Kasmenah joins hundreds of island mothers who feel pressured to consider that before long, all their children will be greatly impacted by the culture of the west.

Unaware of the major economic and political shifts occurring around the world, Kasmenah Hall could not know that before long, the remaining control she has of her family will be violently ripped away!

chapter 7

"Heaven, I'm in heaven, and my heart beats so that I can hardly speak, and I seem to find the happiness I seek, when we're out together dancing cheek to cheek!"

RUSSIAN-AMERICAN COMPOSER IRVING BERLIN

For centuries, the arts in Indonesia emanated from many civilizations and religions. The religions of Hinduism, Buddhism and Islam, plus the civilizations of the Southeast Asian, Polynesian, Chinese, Arabic, Portuguese and European cultures influenced not just the food, social, economic, architectural and political arenas of the country. Literature, art, music and dance are major reflections of thousands of years in the history of the archipelago. Westerners have a difficult time relating to the complex, diverse and rich heritage those elements bring. Indonesia's diverse expressions of beliefs, native tradition and social mores found many outlets of expression through the arts.

In music, the gamelan is a drum and gong orchestra best known in Indonesia's classical music forms. The orchestra includes gongs, xylophones and bronze kettles on a horizontal frame and can also include a flute and zithers, a two-stringed bowed instrument. The gamelan performs in instrumental form, solo, or in a supportive role for dance and puppet performances.

Wayang kulit, shadow puppets have been the core of Javanese theater for more than 1,000 years. In wayang kulit, the puppeteer manipulates the leather or flat wooden puppets so that their shadows dance across a white screen. Performances in the poorer sections of town were done outdoors in the late evening after sundown upon a white piece of material, traversed from one palm tree to another.

Indonesia is home to many traditional dance styles. The most significant are Javanese court dances of bedaja and serimpi. Slow and restrained, women dancers move solemnly using delicate hand gestures to the accompaniment of the gamelan, telling various tales of tragic love, war or ancient history. Typically, beautiful, sentimental music of the "krontjong" would accompany the dancers as well. The western ear would find krontjong similar to the style and tempo of music from the islands of Hawaii. The braguinha guitar, sharing its roots from ancient Portuguese musicians akin to the Hawaiian ukulele and mandolin, is backed by the percussion instrument of the xylophone. All of these instruments brought into many island nations of the Pacific by Portuguese explorers.

This cultural entertainment reinforces the ancestral tales most native Indonesians relate to.

However, for the western influenced, younger generation, the world has introduced much more thrilling, stimulating forms of recreation. A film in the movie theater is only one of the new, exciting ways the West introduce their type of entertainment to the east side of the globe.

Industrialization at the turn of the 20th century changes the economic landscape of the Indonesia. Dutch colonists a century before, had introduced cocoa, rubber trees, coffee, sugar and tobacco to the islands, causing a boom in business and trade. As progress expands so do the needs of the growing population. There is a demand to bring in manufacturers who want to produce items in the archipelagoes that range from textiles and wood products to motor vehicle parts and electrical appliances for export. The opportunity for jobs explodes and even the native men from the local villages are trained to work at the assembly line garnering new hope for the poorer areas of the island. As the west encroaches more and more inland, it brings the latest gadgets too.

And young people everywhere discover the "gramophone!"

The gramophone is a wooden box holding a turntable, which turns round and around when the operator winds a key. On top of the box sits a cylinder out of which sounds emit as a needle on a steel arm comes into contact with a round, black disk. And what a sound it makes!

Music which is loud, and boisterous, not like the slow, serene music of the islands, no! These are sounds made by different types of instruments with swift rhythms and a rapid pulse. In dancing, Westerners take partners of the opposite gender and both move their legs in accelerated, fast paced motions. At times, the man holds the woman around her waist making some islanders blush.

The popularity of western music takes the youth of the Dutch East Indies by storm. Aghast, their elders sit back nervously and watch. It seems the younger generation has ceased listening to warnings that current cultural standards will not accept this peculiar social behavior. Reluctantly, parents all over the islands admit that western entertainment has taken over!

Opportunistic businessmen begin to pursue this popular, rising industry and it is not long before local organizers assemble gatherings, which involve the lively music, dancing and food. Dozens of young people attend, some walking, others riding bicycles and still many attending from miles away using public transportation. Every social function is chaperoned by fathers of the young people in attendance.

In every local village near Bandoeng, news spreads quickly of a community dance scheduled to be held not too far from Vicky's neighborhood. Kasmenah allows her daughter to go as long as one of the Schrander brothers accompanies her but Vicky refuses, instead suggesting that she will attend the dance with her choice of friends. She does not want the control or attention from one boy.

While Christine Victorine Hall basks in the regular attention from Broertje, the Schrander brothers and the Chinese lad however, she has no intention of becoming serious with any of them. Keeping company with the well-mannered lads on the little veranda is enough to boost any young lady's ego, but Vicky's view is that they are not sophisticated enough to take her to the gala.

In all fairness, there is nothing to criticize about any of them.

Not only sensible and straight forward, Broertje is handsome, whose smile reaches big, brown, friendly eyes. Broertje loves the outdoors and encourages Vicky to consider accompanying him on his hiking trips in the rugged, volcanic terrain near Bandoeng. She is amused, but not interested. If Vicky Hall is going to spend hours outdoors, the teenager would rather be cultivating her flowers, fruit trees and caring for her animals at home.

Besides, a girl can't wear high heels on a hike and lately, Kasmenah has allowed Vicky to wear lipstick. The priority of wearing lipstick is even greater on the days the Schrander brothers come to call. Tall, blonde and blue-eyed, Piet and Schipp inherited their father's Dutch features, and benefitting from a good education, the two brothers are very ambitious yet lucky to possess their island mother's sensibility and sense of humor. Each time they visit, Vicky is happy in their company.

Unfortunately, Vicky keeps them on the string too long with Schipp losing interest and eventually, Piet marries her younger sister, Dora.

The young man who is Kasmenah's favorite and her choice for Christine is the Chinese boy. Several years older than her daughter, Kasmenah believes Christine would have a comfortable life with him. The island mother does not wish to see any of her children struggle in ways that life has required of her.

Intelligent and focused on a future in his career as a scientist, the Asian man had earned his graduate degree in physics from the prestigious Bandoeng Institute of Technology. Established in 1920, the institute is regarded as one of Indonesia's elite educational institutions. To Kasmenah's disappointment and in spite of her strong appeals, Vicky is not attracted to the serious, humorless, Chinese gentleman.

Keeping her options open, Vicky continues to dream of the perfect man who will sweep her off her feet!

Every girl treasures private thoughts of romance linked to a lifelong partner who would feel the same. Vicky has endured much disappointment already and partnership with a wonderful young man will fill the empty spaces of her life.

For the fatherless young woman, affection for the lifelong partner would be given over to him completely, without any hesitation which would produce the greatest joy she has ever known!

Vicky's starry-eyed list of priorities for the man of her dreams is a long one.

Her hero will never be angry with her for extraneous, irrelevant, or petty reasons. His arms would keep her safe. He will always be true, faithful, honest, kind, fair, and tolerant while maintaining an incredible sense of humor. Yes, he would make her laugh as they both enjoy the lighter side of life. Vicky would reassure him that she did not desire diamonds, a fancy house, or lots of money because she has outgrown her desire for objects that are far out of reach for an ordinary, island girl.

No, all she desires is someone loyal. A young man with a big heart!

And what a life Vicky is prepared to give in return! Kasmenah was a good example and to make her mother proud, the young woman will serve her own family in precisely the same manner. With joy, Vicky will prepare the most glorious meals for her husband, launder his clothes, clean house, work in the garden and if he allows, she will raise her own chickens! The young man will brag to others how thrifty his wife is and that she is conscientious of the family's finances, always happy to stay within their budget. Kasmenah has raised a no- nonsense individual and taught Vicky to be frugal, using her talents to make the best of limited resources. The eldest daughter of Mr. and Mrs. Christiaan Hall put that principle to practice when she earned her own income.

Regularly updating her checklist, the young, island girl dreams of days when she will engage in the intimate conversations with her husband after the children are tucked in bed. Vicky imagines nights they will confide in each other with respectful communication and both enjoying transparency, free from criticism or judgment. The man Vicky chooses to marry will be a good listener and will intuitively understand what brings her joy or makes her fearful. But most importantly, he will agree to have lots of children. Yes, many babies!

Marriage is in the young woman's plan, but only with the right man!

The year is 1939 and Vicky is twenty-years-old.

On the afternoon of the dance, Christine Victorine Hall is wearing a brand-new dress. With money saved from her weekly paychecks, she had purchased two yards of polka dotted, white organza material and made a dress with short, puffed sleeves, a cinched waist and a flared skirt which slightly covered her knees. A black belt accents her small waistline and white, open-toed high heels accentuate her slender legs. Vicky's raven hair is pulled back at the sides and she is wearing red lipstick! The movie magazines are filled with black and white photographs but writers describe red as the popular color on the lips of famous actresses. Vicky contentedly strolls down the path, watching friends chatter about the latest trends in western music and fashion. Kasmenah's daughter walks a few steps behind because she would rather hum or whistle a tune instead of engaging in conversation. Observing the discrepancy between the modest dwellings of her neighborhood in contrast to the buildings and community as they enter the busier district of town, Vicky is struck by a sudden jolt of emotion. She is painfully aware that Kasmenah had never enjoyed an opportunity to feel so buoyant or carefree.

Yet the pretty young woman, walking at the rear of the group couldn't be happier! A beautiful blue sky above is dotted with large, billowy clouds as the warm island breezes produce a gentle rustle of the surrounding tropical trees adding a heavenly fragrance from the sweet melati blooms. How blessed Vicky feels to live in such a glorious paradise! God must have known she was meant to live in the warm, balmy climate of the lovely Indonesian islands.

No wonder those early explorers chose to stay in her country! Vicky believes she would never leave this beautiful land of her birth. With a skip in her step, she whistles a tune from the latest Astaire/Rogers film as the group approaches the town hall.

Upon entering the large building, Vicky takes note that walls are decorated with colorful, bright wallpaper. Tables, at least forty of them, are tastefully covered with beautiful cloths of batik. Each table holds a vase filled with exotic flowers, which fills the expansive room with sweet-scented fragrances. Against each vase sits a number. Many people are already in attendance and it is easy to spot the fathers who are in attendance solely for chaperoning duty. They are seated far across the room next to a very large, empty space reserved for dancing. In a distant corner, Vicky recognizes a group of military men wearing the traditional summer white uniform of the Royal Dutch Air Force, but a young lady is to be on guard, uses restraint and stops staring. Following Miel and Dirk to their assigned table of number 19, Vicky is glad to see krupuk, dried shrimp chips accompanied by the spicy sambal Manis, already placed at each setting. Comfortably seated at their table, the thirsty travelers enjoy glasses of tjendol, the sweet, delicious rose water syrup filled with tiny cornstarch tendrils. On the opposite side of the building, Vicky spots an enclosure where food is prepared by domestic servants hired to set out the evening meal which would be served later.

The music has not yet begun as more patrons enter the building, but soon a gentleman, dressed in a formal dinner jacket, climbs up the podium welcoming the guests with a lengthy speech explaining this is the first of many dances to come. Surprised that her heart skips a beat, Vicky grows excited these functions could present an opportunity for her and Kasmenah to earn an income if they are hired to provide food for all the events.

Finally, the announcer introduces the music of an American bandleader named Glenn Miller. Standing next to a table holding a box Vicky recognizes as a gramophone, the man winds up a key and lifts the arm of the machine making a strange, scratchy sound as the needle first hits the black disc. Fortunately, the music is loud enough to cover the imperfection. The rhythm and movement of the first song is captivating and Vicky finds herself tapping her fingers on the table. Miel and Dirk get up to dance, leaving Vicky with her female companions. Soon each one of them is requested to be a dance partner by other boys, leaving Vicky alone at the table. She is happy to sit and enjoy the music. Vicky's few attempts to dance at home were futile, leaving her content to watch other patrons awkwardly trying out the steps. The music is appealing, permeated with fast-paced-rhythms and many more couples fill up the dance floor as the evening flies into full swing.

Glenn Miller, known globally as one of several, American "big-band" leaders in 1939, conducts a large orchestra which includes percussive, woodwind, brass and string instruments. Miller's type of music has its roots in early jazz and blues also earning its reputation as the precursor to rock and roll, yet big-band music also contains elements of rhythms which are slow, romantic, later making crooners such as Frank Sinatra, Perry Como, Doris Day, Rosemary Clooney, Bing Crosby and Nat King Cole, famous. Monthly, movie magazines are eventually joined by weekly periodicals which highlight the music scene in the United States, and soon, village girls and boys on far away Southeast Asian islands, like the Indonesian archipelago are purchasing the publications, drifting away in romantic lyrics.

Before long, one young man in uniform approaches the young lady sitting alone at table number 19. He had noticed her immediately when she entered the room keeping his eye on her until it was clear, she was not spoken for. The lovely girl had his undivided attention along with his companions who had noticed her too. He enlightened them all that he saw her first, and being gentlemen of the uniform, each one of his companions had reluctantly capitulated, surrendering any chance they may have had of securing Vicky's company.

With head bowed, discreetly peeking out of the corner of one eye, Vicky is aware a young man is approaching her. He is not tall or blonde like the Schrander brothers, certainly not as handsome as Broertje De Wolff and unfortunately, is already showing signs of a receding hairline. Before he reaches the table, Vicky has already made a decision to be uninterested!

Standing in front of the pretty girl, the serviceman holds his hand out and introduces himself as Air Force Sergeant Harry Meijer. Vicky is not impressed but finds herself drawn to his pleasant smile. The young woman does not return his handshake but Harry is not dissuaded and promptly sits down. Making himself comfortable without invitation irks Vicky, who refuses his request for a dance. As her gaze returns to the dance floor, she hopes her friends can rescue her from this awkward situation.

The announcer keeps the music playing as Vicky spies her friends, Dirk and Miel, lost in each other's arms on the dance floor. It is obvious they will not be returning to their table in time! Annoyed with this stranger who sits uninvited at their table, Vicky excuses herself and makes her way to the water closet. The toilet, located outside of the building is separated by a dirt alleyway which is difficult to navigate in the dark for a young woman wearing high heels. The pretty shoes now annoy her! Harry follows her, explaining that she needs his protection. Feeling uncomfortably grateful to a man she has just met, Vicky allows Harry to escort her as he holds her gently by the arm. She is unaware that Harry has determined not to take his eyes off the lovely young woman and he is willing to go to great lengths to impress her, wasting no time to share information about himself, his family and current station in life. By the time the couple return to table 19, Vicky finds herself responding to Harry's charming overtures.

Not discouraged by Vicky's mixed signals, Harry makes another request for a dance and this time Vicky says yes. For the timid, island girl, dancing feels awkward but Harry holds her firmly around her tiny waist, and with a self-confidence he has nurtured since the days he courageously opposed his father, Harry guides his dance partner with ease. Pleasantly surprised, she is relaxed in his company, Vicky allows Harry Meijer to be the companion she keeps for the rest of the evening. Miel and Dirk rejoin them when the music stops for the dinner break and the two couples discover they have much to talk about. Harry explains that he works as a mechanic at Andir, the military base in Bandoeng commissioned with the Sixth Reconnaissance Group of the Royal Dutch Air Force. Finding they have much in common, Dirk does not hesitate to exchange his address with Harry.

However, Harry's dance partner is not ready to give him any personal information and it would take many more weeks and several more organized dance party events before Vicky offers up Harry her home address.

The social aspect of the occasion inspires Vicky to become involved in arranging future dances which as she had hoped, opens opportunities for the Hall women to make a small income preparing food for the events. Harry attends each one.

Eventually, patience and persistence wins! Vicky gives Harry the information he desires. Within a week, dressed in full, military uniform, the Air Force Sergeant arrives on Kasmenah's doorstep requesting permission to visit with her daughter. Kasmenah is easily smitten with Harry's charm and his calm disposition, but Vicky's mother is nobody's fool! She interrogates this worldly stranger, who is more mature than Vicky's previous suitors. Harry is comfortable answering every probing question Kasmenah asks of him. He is relieved the steely-eyed mother missed one fundamental question about his life because he is not ready to disclose it yet. It is unnecessary to reveal information about a private episode which Harry had decided is no one's business.

Harry calls on Vicky weekly, and with every visit to the Hall residence, his arms are loaded with goodies from the pasar.

Many photos portray Kasmenah's stoic demeanor conventional for the era in 1930's Indonesian society. But the typical, neutral expression on Kasmenah's face changes significantly when photographed with Harry. In addition, with a look of obvious delight, one photograph shows Kasmenah with her arm affectionately wrapped around his waist! Vicky is aware that her mother is taken with the charismatic Harry Meijer, however in her private thoughts, she is reserved about this man who is unconditionally accepted by her entire family.

Kasmenah's eldest daughter has learned well the boundaries a young woman must maintain for making wise choices. Vicky does not hesitate to inform Harry that she still desires to continue her friendships with the other young men in her life, but is unaware that Kasmenah and Harry have teamed up by applying pressure surreptitiously to any young man interested in Vicky while Kasmenah reminds her daughter that at twenty years of age, she is still single. Most of her friends are married, including Miel Pies who became Mrs. Dirk Wildeboer just a few weeks before. But Vicky is aware of the manipulation and becomes angry when her friends end their visits. To her dismay, Harry Meijer becomes her only, potential suitor. Christine's frustration rekindles the past of her troubled relationship with Kasmenah and doubles down on her refusal to meet with Harry, making some afternoons the sergeant and Kasmenah are the only people seated on the porch. Ultimately many weeks of Harry's regular visits pays off! He has successfully used his wit and charm to win over the widow Hall, and he is convinced her stubborn daughter will relent and welcome his company once again.

Parental approval in life-changing choices their children make is important in eastern cultures. With many important decisions, including marriage, society respects the endorsement of parents and grandparents. In spite of disagreements on minor issues, Vicky ultimately desires her mother's blessings for future plans she makes. The young woman has witnessed her island mother to be prudent in the most challenging circumstances of life, and Kasmenah's opinion could be trusted. Vicky is forced to agree that Harry has proven to be kind, hardworking and reasonably successful. With a new perspective, Vicky accepts Harry's proposal of marriage and a few months later, on the 23rd of October, before major monsoon storms arrive, the young couple marry.

Smiling in their wedding photo, Harry wears a black tuxedo even though Vicky preferred the winter dress military uniform. As an accomplished seamstress, Vicky loved the winter uniform for the Royal Dutch Air Force, made of a fine gabardine wool and striking in its formal black color. The jacket showcasing straight shoulder boards above a row of seven gilt buttons, forming a column from top to bottom is what Vicky would have chosen but Harry and his future mother-in-law preferred the tux. It should have been a foreshadowing of things to come yet Vicky could not be bothered by the extraneous irritation!

The bride had more important priorities to deal with. Vicky was concentrating on making her wedding dress. The beautiful, floor length gown of her own creation, Vicky constructs the train long enough to trail onto the floor, with a veil made up of lace organza. On the day of their wedding, Vicky holds a beautiful bouquet of white oriental lilies picked from her mother's garden. The weather is perfect the day Sgt. Harry Meijer and Christine Victorine Hall marry, unaware that around the world, storm clouds have been gathering.

This young couple celebrating a newfound love, culminating within the bounds of marriage, would soon discover that everything in their future together is about to be tested beyond their wildest imagination.

Harry and Vicky engaged circa 1939

chapter 8

"Marriage was God's idea... between one man and one woman."
Pastor/ Theologian/Author - Alistair Begg

Sergeant and Mrs. Harry Meijer begin their life together in military housing provided for married couples on the Andir Air Force Base, in Bandoeng. Vicky plunges into her role as wife with enthusiasm. She is grateful her mother and younger siblings live a short distance away. With a quick trip on public transportation provided by city buses, she visits them as much as possible. Not long into the marriage, Harry asks Kasmenah to make the journey to their home because Vicky is with child.

The pregnancy proves to be difficult for Vicky because of frequent fainting spells. The physician in charge advises her to get as much rest as possible. Not until much later in the pregnancy does the doctor learn that his stubborn patient mistakenly equates rest with laziness. Inactivity is not allowed in Vicky's worldview as she approaches household duties with fervor.

Early in the marriage, the happy bride learns that her husband enjoys her cooking, increasing her desire to please him more each day. Harry has his favorite dishes: soto ayam, a spicy chicken soup, ayam panggang Sumatra, an Indonesian version of fried chicken, sajur asem, a popular sour soup, made with tamarindo and lots of vegetables, and the most favored of all, gado-gado with sate, the peanut sauce poured on top of marinated, skewered barbequed meats which are reserved for the weekend company who visit regularly, including a host of Harry's military, bachelor friends, Vicky's friends Dirk and Miel Wildenboer, Broertje De Wolff and the Schrander brothers.

Vicky is in her element! Excited about the baby, happily preparing for child's arrival, the newly wed concentrates on her marriage. She works extra hard to build relationships with her father- law Johann Meijer and Harry's four siblings. Vicky has many questions about their childhood years. There is a mutual understanding of the loss they all share related to Christiaan's unfortunate passing and Mineoh's untimely death. Vicky enjoys her new sister-in- law Ida who received an undergraduate degree, masters seven languages and continues on to graduate school. Ellie, Harry's youngest sister has interests in animal husbandry, attending a local school nearby. But Vicky is partial to one member of the family who is Harry's favorite too. Rudy is their youngest brother and liked immediately by everyone who meets him. Different in personality from his older brother Harry, Rudy is reserved, yet kind. When he speaks, his tone is gentle, using words that are charitable. Tall, handsome and self-assured without a hint of arrogance, Rudy is an accomplished pilot who receives a special assignment to become a test pilot for the Royal Dutch Air Force. He spends many afternoons with Harry and Vicky explaining to them the rigors of specialized training and the mental discipline required for the task of flying planes with experimental technology on board.

Military life is challenging for Vicky. Living on the Andir Air Force Base in the little bungalow is comfortable enough, plus Vicky enjoys the camaraderie of friendly neighbors. However, Vicky takes issue with some of the mandates of living on federal property. As the wife of a non-commissioned officer, she is expected to attend meetings with other military wives to be familiarized with the rules and expectations of families living on base. Before the marriage, Vicky's evenings were spent visiting with friends and taking long, leisurely walks. Life on the base makes those evenings a thing of the past. Each family member is held to strict rules of curfew at 1900 hours. In the archipelago's way of life, that is considered too early.

The young bride adjusts quickly and works hard to adapt her role as wife. Confined to sitting outdoors in the common area of the base reserved for non-commissioned officers and their families, Vicky enjoys the company of other military members and their wives. The neighbors exchange stories and experiences which enables to Vicky understand they all have many challenges in common. The older wives tell her to be prepared for long separations, late nights and last-minute scheduling changes.

In the months since her wedding day, Vicky struggles with familiar feelings of loneliness, making her wonder if marital bliss truly did exist. She was expecting those dreadful, negative emotions of abandonment to disappear. Perhaps the intensity is brought on because of the little life growing inside her.

The desire for her mother's reassuring words, comforting touch and good cooking has increased in Vicky's mind, disrupting feelings of joy about married life.

The physician assigned to Mrs. Harry Meijer has reassured her that the baby is growing at a normal rate.

The initial movements of the child felt foreign at first, but after a few weeks, they are welcomed! Vicky wonders who the child will resemble. Will it be a boy or girl? It doesn't matter. The privilege of carrying a human being inside her own body is a wonderful experience. The thought of caring for a helpless, precious, human being warms her heart and the thrill of facing a future with many more babies like this one seems like a miracle!

Daily, Vicky is reminded of the goodness of God. The amazing God that the Lutheran pastor preached about years ago when she was a little girl. The same God who comforted her every time she was forced into a dark, lonely corner by her dictatorial father. Vicky vaguely remembers the words of songs about God and His Son, Jesus Christ. Something about His sacrifice on a cross. If only she could remember the words accurately, because the message of an old, rugged cross comes across her mind and then frustratingly, fades away.

The increased activity in her womb makes Vicky commit to be the best mother in the world! Vicky considers what mother could not delight in the sweet smell of soft, supple, baby skin? The gentle cooing of baby sounds and the touch of tiny fingers and toes can make the most hardened heart melt with benevolence. Babies are the hope of the world. All the miracles of life are wrapped in a little bundle of flesh, and can be caressed in the crook of an arm. Every girl's dream comes alive with the gift of a beautiful, vulnerable infant. The essence of motherhood increases deep in Vicky's heart as the feeling of that familiar loneliness is abated for a while, jogging her memory about years past.

In Sunday school, Vicky had learned about the indescribable wonder of creation and the magnificence of a Creator who made it all possible. She realizes that she believed it primarily because of babies! In her mind there could not be any way these amazing, tiny, human beings were the result of accidental spores flying across one area of space to another. The island girl had not experienced much schooling, but she felt sorry for any person who found that strange theory plausible, and hoped that individual would examine his poor, destitute soul!

Finding pleasure at the end of a busy day is never difficult for a girl like Vicky. While her husband spent his time relaxing with the current newspaper, she contentedly knits baby items. She could not be bothered with the movie magazines anymore which juvenile and trivial now. Nothing is more important than being a wife and mother as the baby grows inside her body.

January in the archipelagos of Indonesia is typically wet with monsoon rains drenching everything on its lush, green topography. On the 21st of that month in the year 1941, ten days before her 22nd birthday, Vicky gives birth to a baby boy. The child is robust and healthy!

As the mid-wife presents Johny Diederich Meijer to his father, Harry's thoughts take him to another child he held not so long ago.

chapter 9

"Marriage does not make problems, it reveals them."
Pastor/ Evangelist Santana Acuna

Since the beginning of the twentieth century, family counselors, therapists, doctors and pastors have written hundreds of books offering advice on marriage. All couples agree within the first few weeks, little "surprises" begin to appear in the relationship. Whether the issue concerns something small and insignificant or is considered overwhelming, depends largely on the individuals involved. It is common knowledge that the health of the relationship is not only determined by the action of one person, but vastly impacted by the reaction of the other.

Shortly after their wedding, Harry tells his new bride about a child who lives in a nearby regency, called a "kabupaten." The regency in which the child resides is a town called Cirebon located a far distance from Andir Airforce Base. Vicky demands that her husband takes her to meet this child immediately!

The story is that several years before Vicky Hall entered his life, Harry had been involved in an intimate relationship with a civilian employed by the Royal Dutch Air Force. The lady was married to a man, reportedly, an invalid confined to a wheelchair. Harry's relationship with her resulted in a pregnancy with both in agreement that Harry would be financially responsible for the baby until the child reached adulthood. Sadly, the woman dies in childbirth, however, the baby boy survives and is raised by his maternal grandparents, Frank and Esme Ries.

Harry understands that this story of his past could have made his wife angry but the opposite happens! Vicky makes immediate plans to include the little boy in their lives. They must go, she says, and fetch the child, not wasting another minute! Vicky's pregnancy does not deter her from traveling the long distance on the cramped and often crowded bus to meet three-year-old Walter Antoine Meijer.

Amazingly, overnight, Vicky's world grows bigger and brighter!

The initial meeting of Walter's grandparents is cordial. They had agreed to allow Vicky to make the acquaintance of their grandson with a few provisions, including a verbal agreement the Meijers would never wage a custody battle with them. At first, Vicky agrees but furtively, her mind is changed the instant she meets Walter!

The handsome, little boy is an instantaneous delight for Harry's wife. Vicky is taken by Walter's mischievous grin which lights up his large, brown eyes framed by unusually long eyelashes. The young child's plump, round cheeks resemble a baby's face rather than a toddler. Thick black, wavy hair complements his fair complexion. Vicky is smitten!

For the meeting, Oma Ries has dressed Walter in dark slacks and a white, collared shirt, enclosed at the nape of his neck with a bow tie. Just three years of age, it is evident that Walter's grandparents have taught him proper etiquette as he extends his little hand towards Vicky. Frank and Esme have informed Walter that the woman is Harry's wife and would become a significant person in his life.

Immediately, without restraint Vicky happily embraces her role as the doting stepmother. She loves Walter and makes considerable effort to visit him often! On days Harry cannot accompany her because of work restraints, Vicky Meijer makes the long, increasingly challenging trip on public transportation even as she enters the last trimester of her pregnancy, mindless of her own comfort. With every visit, Vicky's affection grows for Harry's son, escalating the heartache she experiences when it is time to leave.

Sleepless nights increase causing Vicky to make a risky decision.

The headstrong wife of Harry Meijer will bring up the subject of Walter's custody!

On the next visit without her husband present, Vicky carefully broaches the subject with Walter's grandfather. Frank is not surprised! He and Esme feared that Vicky Meijer might become aggressive in pursuing custody of their grandson as they notice Vicky's growing interest in Walter. The grandparents regret that the rudimentary agreement made between them was verbal, not in writing. Frank is annoyed by Vicky's request and accuses her of violating a promise she had made. The woman Harry has brought into Walter's life has become a problem and is now insisting that Walter belongs with his father. Panic-stricken but resolute, the grandparents refuse to discuss the matter escorting Vicky to the front door. In spite of tears blinding the long walk back to the bus depot, Vicky is even more determined to pursue Walter's custody. With every passing day, the strong-willed, young woman takes on the challenge which affirms what she has accepted since childhood. In Vicky's world view, she believes that greater the opposition, the more satisfying are the eventual victories!

Immediately Vicky Meijer places more pressure on her husband with demands that he obtain an attorney. Harry angrily disagrees, remaining firm that he will not disrupt young Walter's living arrangement, reminding his wife that he had given his word to the grandparents to not pursue custody of their grandchild!

While Vicky is furious, her anger is trumped by fears that her marriage is in trouble. She must make sure that the fragile state of her marriage is not jeopardized by selfish motives but how could the welfare of a vulnerable, little boy be considered selfish?

Harry remains resolute in his decision as the issue begins to fracture the couple's ability to communicate. Neither one notices the breakdown in respect and civility in their marriage. Vicky is bent on saving Walter while Harry insists he will not interfere with the life of the Ries family. Not dissuaded, Vicky makes an attempt to solicit support from Kasmenah. Her mother had an exceptionally close relationship with Harry and Vicky pleads with Kasmenah to leverage the influence she has with her son-in-law to change his mind, but Kasmenah declines to get involved, adamant that ripping a three-year-old from the only home he knows would be cruel!

And for a while, Vicky lays the matter to rest as the birth of her own, newborn son gives her a welcome distraction.

Becoming a mother ignites in Vicky a joy and passion she has never felt before. With Johny's birth, Vicky thrives in the routine of regular scheduled feeding times, nap times and play time with him. She happily discovers that breast feeding is easy because the new mother is blessed with more than enough breast milk to keep him full. If Johny is fussy or having a difficult time falling asleep, Vicky doesn't mind because she takes the opportunity to sing lullabies and hymns she learned in Sunday school. Vicky's favorite melody is "Nina Bobo," the popular, krontjong lullaby which soothes many babies to sleep. The neighbors in nearby bungalows overhear the beautiful voice of Vicky Meijer and make requests for the young mother to sing for special occasions.

As Vicky settles into the wonderful world of motherhood, Johny's birth causes Kasmenah's status as grandmother to increase in the local community.

The strength of the family in the Eastern culture includes the value and respect grandmothers are given to impart their knowledge, years of experience and opinions on the younger generation. Culturally, older women are given the honor within the family, to exert much influence about child rearing more than any other member. Grandmothers are valued for their unconditional love and young parents welcome "Oma" to be involved with the care of their children. The expectation for grandmother to be available at all times, daily if needed, is never questioned.

One strict mandate many island grandmothers agree on is that a newborn cannot be exposed to strangers or the outdoors too soon. Conventional wisdom dictates that a baby's immune system does not have the ability to ward off uncommon germs. Oma Kasmenah admonishes her daughter, she must wait until Johny is at least twelve weeks old before the child is taken to visit friends and neighbors. Vicky agrees wholeheartedly!

The weather is beautiful in April and offers Vicky an opportunity to visit her neighbors around the base, pushing her newborn, baby son in the pram (baby-carriage). The monsoons have ceased and the stale air is replaced by the freshness of gentle breezes once again giving Vicky an opportunity to show off her little boy! Even daily shopping trips at the nearby pasar are more thrilling with Johny in her slendang. It brings her great pleasure to hear friends exclaim what a beautiful boy he is, alert and already smiling. Johny is a happy infant, which is a good reflection on his mother! The gossip around town and on the Andir Air Force base substantiates that Harry and Kasmenah can be proud of her. Vicky is immersed with the lives of her child and husband which keeps the young mother busy.

Daily, Vicky works hard, focusing on the care and concern for the family. Her own mother is a perfect example of devoted motherhood and Vicky is committed to be the same. As days slip into weeks and weeks quickly turn into months, the new mother begins to realize that her role as wife is much more demanding. The baby is predictable. Vicky meets her son's needs when he is hungry, requires a nap and instinctively understands why he might be uncomfortable.

In marriage the challenge is different!

Harry is a good provider and when at home, assists Vicky with the care of the baby. Harry is not reluctant to change baby's diaper or help with heavier household duties but the hope Vicky once had about open and honest communication in marriage is more difficult than she had anticipated.

Candor has not accomplished the results the young woman was hoping for. In the midst of a disagreement or dispute, Harry retorts defensively, frustrating his wife until both plunge into an abyss of a tug of wills, with the louder, more vocal partner feeling victorious. Each is reluctant to admit that measured, indifferent responses are dishonest. The couple does acknowledge that resentment is growing. They agree to work harder to treat each other with respect, and Vicky does not want to criticize Harry that lately, her husband placates her with mechanical retorts. Yes, she has learned that marriage requires a lot of compromise!

And things have changed in the Meijer household. Lately, Harry is not content to spend the evenings at home and with disturbing stories coming from overseas, reading the newspaper had become depressing for him. Instead, Vicky's husband chooses to spend much of his leisure time at the military lounge playing carom billiards, a game Harry had become proficient at.

Carom billiards is a game played on a large, felt covered table similar to the size of a pool table, although in billiards, the table is typically ten feet long by five feet wide. Unlike the game of pool, a carom billiards table has no pockets. The indoor version Harry plays is called the "Diamond System." Holding a cue stick, the object is to hit three sides before striking the opponent's balls thus creating a diamond pattern. Running combinations result in adding up the scores. The game which is extremely technical and precise requires much skill. Vicky hears testimonies from

Harry's billiards partners that he is a master player, brilliantly disciplined in the game.

Vicky is not alarmed at her husband's absences. She finds great comfort with Johny who occupies all of her time. In free moments while the infant sleeps, after the dinner dishes are washed and the laundry is put away, Vicky rests with knitting or crocheting more baby clothes. Many evenings she spends preparing dessert for Harry's return home, and lately, Harry brings along two or three, hungry, billiard companions.

The young family has settled into a comfortable routine. Every weekday, Harry leaves for work on the base. He is not happy in his job as a mechanic because it leaves his hands and clothes soiled. The gloves and overalls he wears do not adequately protect him from getting dirty. Vicky had discovered early in the marriage that Harry's notion of clean really means sanitary and spotless! She was challenged by his need to have everything in its proper place, neat and tidy. With a newborn and household duties taking up most of the fourteen-hour days, Vicky's priorities did not include satisfying Harry's need to have their home organized the way her husband desired. Over time, small disagreements about Vicky's lack of orderliness increase.

Thankfully, Harry's request to begin training for flight engineer school is granted. The air force uniform flight engineers are required to wear suits him better than the unsightly overalls of a mechanic. Harry revels in the boost it gives his morale.

The weekends are extra special. Baby Johny is seven months old, which allow Harry and Vicky to visit Walter more often. Every week, the four-year-old eagerly anticipates their arrival. However, Vicky is aware that the strain in the relationship between her and Walter's grandparents have become untenable yet her concern for Walter's future overrides any uncomfortable feelings she has about the grandparents. Doggedly, Vicky confronts them again about the child's custody. The conversation becomes tense immediately as the grandparents react defensively, voicing their concern about the little boy bonding too closely with his new family. They explain that at every departure, the toddler demands to know why he is not allowed to stay with his daddy. Vicky takes the opportunity to make the argument that Walter indeed belongs with his father and new baby brother. Desperate to make them understand, she asks the elderly couple to consider Walter's future, launching into an emotional rant.

Do they grasp that it is natural for the child to desire a relationship with his father and little brother? Who could expect a youngster to be happy raised by elderly folks as an only child? Surely these people are aware of the little boy's need to grow up with a family which includes his father, a mother and his baby brother. Walter's Oma interrupts and bitterly responds. Esme is offended by Vicky's false narrative and her failure to understand their point of view. The birth of their grandchild resulted in the loss of their only daughter. The elderly woman is vehement and declares loudly that Walter belongs with them! The fifty-five-year-old grandmother reiterates that in the four years since Walter's birth there had never been a dispute between them and Harry. As Oma Ries looks toward Harry, she raises her voice another decibel and tells him that he married a trouble maker!

Frank steps forward placing himself between the two women turns to Vicky with dark eyes menacingly fixed on her and calmly states he will retain a lawyer if the young couple insist on pursuing custody. But Vicky does not hear him. Unyielding, determined to stand her ground, Vicky continues her criticism of the grandparents, calling them selfish, narrow-minded people. She argues that the welfare of the child should be everyone's first consideration and every reasonable, clear-thinking individual would instinctively understand that Walter belongs with his father.

With clenched jaw and furrowed brow, the grandfather demands the couple leave. Frank Ries will not tolerate any more disrespect in his home! Desperate, Vicky looks to her husband for support but she stands alone as Harry makes no attempt to support her. The elderly gentleman insists the Meijer family reduce their appointed times with Walter to one day a month, threatening to stop their visits altogether.

Walter is sobbing uncontrollably as his father, Vicky and his baby brother are escorted out of the front door.

The painful exchange makes the journey home for the couple even longer and between searing, hot tears, spilling down her cheeks, Vicky somehow manages to find words, begging Harry to fight for his son. She pleads with her husband to make Walter a priority. Does she need to remind him that Walter is his flesh and blood making it Harry's responsibility to raise his son, giving Walter the opportunity to grow up with his little brother? If they seek legal advice, Vicky is convinced Harry's parental rights would win! After all, the grandparents are elderly and Walter needs his younger, more able parents to raise him. Vicky implores her husband to consider consultation with a lawyer trained in family law, she knows the air force has the service available at no cost! But Vicky's attempts to wear Harry down with many logical arguments and a flood of tears, are in vain.

Vicky's impassioned pleas fall on deaf ears as Harry ignores his wife, staring straight ahead, stoic, silent, holding Johny on his lap. As the crowded transit bus carries the Meijer family along the bustling, narrow roadway, Vicky realizes for the first time the depth of resentment she feels for her husband. It frightens the young woman because lately, feelings of regret in her marriage with him have increased. All the disappointments she has experienced in their relationship seem to culminate with the heart-wrenching issue about Walter. For Vicky, Walter deserves to be raised with them as their son and Johny's big brother! She will never accept that an active, four-year-old boy is best to live with his grandparents alone. Vicky finds Harry's reluctance reprehensible and is not surprised by the disrespect she feels for a man who would give up his son so easily!

In the midst of turmoil about one child, Vicky has not informed her husband that she is pregnant with another.

chapter 10

"A speaker of truth has no friends."
AFRICAN PROVERB

In the Dutch East Indies of September 1941, disturbing news has widely spread across the country that a bloody, two-year conflict in Europe is beginning to impact other nations around the world. News that Germany was stepping up its aggression against its neighbors, with Italy joining forces, is a growing concern among all of the western nations. Fascist dictators Adolph Hitler of Germany and Benito Mussolini of Italy are determined to conquer all of Northern, Western and Eastern Europe, including the British Isles. Their radical form of authoritarian nationalism is criticized politically worldwide and the intergovernmental League of Nations attempts to impose sanctions on both dictators. Popular notions in their own countries claim they wished to be worshipped like gods. One Italian newspaper called Mussolini to be transfigured "like a god." No, no, said another newspaper, "he is a god!"

The League of Nations, founded after World War I with the ideal that its principal mission of collective security and disarmament could maintain world peace and prevent future wars, turns out to be grossly ineffective. The ideology is noble and considered grand to believe that settling international disputes through negotiations and arbitration would stop hostilities between countries and their leaders. By the 1930's, it is clear that the organization fails in its primary purpose as Germany, Italy, Spain and Japan blatantly, without justification or explanation, withdraw their memberships. And in late 1939, Hitler had successfully convinced the citizens of his country that complete national authority would make them the greatest and most powerful republic in the history of postmodern time. Methodically and with meticulous precision, Hitler begins the eradication of "enemies of the State." While the rest of world turns a blind eye, the maniacal chancellor of Germany successfully advances a campaign of torture and inevitably destroys more than six million innocent, German citizens. Men, women and children of Jewish heritage are systematically starved, slaughtered or gassed to death. Included are those who risk their own lives to help the Jewish families. The Nazi government confiscates millions of dollars in property, businesses, homes, personal possessions, furniture and jewelry, anything of value taken from those thrown into the death camps.

At the beginning of 1940, the surrounding leaders of Europe are forced to take notice of Hitler's intentions to commit the same crimes in their countries as he invades France, Belgium, and the tiny nation of the Netherlands.

Hitler proves to be a formidable enemy but the Dutch fight bravely, fierce about defending their country. As the Dutch monarchy is primarily concerned with fighting the Germans in their own country, she hopelessly neglects her colonies including the Dutch East Indies, naively believing they would be spared any conflict.

But by the end of the summer of 1941, the Dutch military intelligence realize they had taken too much for granted, and without any joint plans with their allies and only 400 marines on the ground, the allied forces of the Royal Netherlands East Indies Army (KNIL), under the command of Commander Hein ter Poorten, calls to active duty 25,000 well-armed but poorly trained troops to defend the archipelagos of the Dutch East Indies.

Tragically, the Dutch had forgotten about another aggressor from the Northeast and the beautiful islands, vulnerable and unprepared, are dealt a severe blow.

While the German/Italian war machines build up their military arsenal, the Northeast Asian country of Japan had been spreading its tentacles to the west of their own country, invading Manchuria in Northern China as early as 1931. China bravely fights to fend the off the aggressor for almost a decade. Russia aligns with China in full scale fighting but in less than one year, Japan captures the major Chinese province of Hankow, advancing up the Yangtze River in early 1939. More than 500,000 Chinese civilians are killed as Japan commences the beginning of war in the Pacific.

The United States wanting to remain uninvolved militarily finds the Japanese aggression inexcusable and announces its withdrawal from their commercial treaty in the spring of 1941. By August, the United States of America, which supplied 80% of Japanese imports, initiates a complete oil embargo. Not any of these actions deter the Japanese leadership and they are emboldened to invade all of Southeast Asia, including the Dutch/British controlled island of Borneo.

By October of 1941, all of the Dutch East Indies' military is put on immediate high alert and thousands of the Royal Dutch Navy, Army, and Air Force personnel, including Vicky's husband Sgt. Harry Meijer depart to fight the Japanese, who continue their aggressive, island invasions and are now already occupying Northern Java. In the previous short weeks before the men on base are deployed, military officials meet with the families to inform them that the Dutch government has declared war on the Japanese. What the Dutch/Indonesian community finds difficult to believe is that radical Indonesians, including Sukarno and his co-hort Mohammed Hatta made political and military alliances with the Japanese to assist them with the invasion of their own, beloved country.

Receiving support from thousands of islanders, Sukarno and Hatta give the Japanese invaders carte blanche in establishing military rule in the Dutch East Indies. Since the late 1920's, Sukarno and Hatta and their supporters have waited patiently for the best opportunity to overthrow the Dutch. Cultivating the existing animosity and distrust between the European population and the islanders, the two Communist leaders are successful in building confidence and credibility among many of the Indonesian people. Solidifying an alliance with the powerful and wealthy nation of Japan, Sukarno and Hatta see their dreams realized as the Emperor Hirohito and the Prime Minister of Japan, Hideki Tojo, each sign treaties with the PNI to plan the invasion of the Dutch East Indies. Promising Sukarno and Hatta, they will assist them in liberating the islands, Japan sends thousands of soldiers to the northern shores of Java, along with a battery full of military arsenal and financial support.

The beginning of autumn in 1941, the archipelago of the Dutch East Indies is forever changed.

The Netherlands declare war on Japan and seek the assistance of the American-British-Dutch-Australian Command (ABDACOM) to form a coordinating group of allied forces in South East Asia under the command of General Archibald Wavell. In the weeks leading up to the invasion, senior Dutch government officials retreat into exile taking family members and personal staff to safety in nearby Australia. Before the arrival of Japanese troops, internal conflicts arise as rival Indonesian groups with different alliances for and against the Japanese, begin fighting one another. The Indonesian islanders who are the most pro-allied supporters, assisting the Dutch in underground resistance operations are the Ambonese and Menadonese. Caught in the middle of these conflicts are citizens of Chinese and Dutch descent whose properties are ransacked, with many innocent, non-combatant land owners murdered, or go into hiding. Within weeks, the Japanese invade the beautiful islands of the Dutch East Indies, with the fiercest fighting occurring in Ambon, Timor, in Kalimantan and on the Java Sea. On the island of Bali, where there are no Dutch troops, the Japanese experience no resistance.

In four, short months, the Japanese army have occupied and triumphantly take full control of the entire Dutch Indonesian archipelago. The occupation is easy as many in governmental and military authority who were complacent on the war in faraway places, erroneously believed the conflict would never reach their shores. In March of 1942, the Dutch Governor-General A.W.L. Stachouwer, Commander ter Poorten and Major Jacob Pesman surrender the islands of the Dutch East Indies to the Japanese Commander-in-chief Lieutenant General Hitoshi Imamura.

On the Andir Royal Dutch Air Force Base, Harry and Vicky Meijer lay their differences aside about Walter, spending quiet nights together, finding comfort in each other's arms once again. Recognizing the need to remain in harmony together for the safety and protection of their baby Johny, little Walter and extended family members, Vicky informs her husband that she is pregnant again.

Two weeks before their third anniversary, Vicky and other military wives, are saying tearful goodbyes to beloved husbands. Upon return to their bungalows, Vicky faints, falling hard onto the pavement, sending her to the base hospital for observation. She reminds the doctor that fainting spells have regularly plagued her during pregnancy and refuses the doctor's recommendation to remain in the hospital.

Suddenly, life changes for Vicky, her friends, her neighbors. Although the base commander briefs them every week, unsubstantiated rumors and conjecture fill their days with dismay. Locals are unaware that the invasion of the Japanese has advanced in Batavia, one hundred miles away in northern Java with the assistance of revolutionary islanders. Many of the Dutch/Indonesian public become suspicious of their island neighbors as the archipelago country experiences nationwide, political division. The combination of fear and distrust dominate conversations among family and friends. Vicky is greatly disturbed by their collective hostilities including ambiguous statements repudiating islands neighbors. Vicky reminds them they are the offspring of island mothers and all have in common island family members. But her anger quickly focuses on the negligence of political leaders who fail to accurately communicate the invasion of enemy troops on the archipelagoes to their citizens.

Telephones are not available for the average family in the Dutch East Indies of the early 1940's. Communication is conducted by mail or word of mouth as family members and friends pass information back and forth. Unofficially, news has come to Vicky that the Japanese have taken over other military compounds in the north, east and west of the islands and are advancing quickly to the south. The wife of Sgt. Harry Meijer becomes aggressive about confronting the Dutch military personnel, who deny the reports. Vicky's frustration about the lack of military transparency in news reports motivates her to investigate other outlets for information.

The level of stress grows collectively on the base. Many wives left without the companionship of their husbands, feel the urgency to remain in constant contact with extended family members. Vicky is among those who needs the support of her family. Concerned for the safety of Johny, Kasmenah and her younger siblings, Vicky makes a request to move them all into base housing. Base regulations do not allow it so Vicky makes a difficult decision to return to her mother's house.

The family welcomes Vicky and Johny in Kasmenah's modest home. Vicky Meijer is happy to be surrounded by people who trust her. Village residents have been reduced to women, children and the elderly. Most of the men and boys over the age of sixteen have been deployed, including Vicky's brother Guus and other male relatives of Vicky's family, including both of Harry's brothers, Rudy and Jan. Left under her care are thirteen-year-old Bernard, who was born five months after Christiaan's passing, and another, younger brother named Fentje, who was born six years later. Fentje was born as the result of a relationship Kasmenah had with one of Christiaan's acquaintances years after she was widowed. The village gossip at the time claimed he was married. Kasmenah never disclosed the name of the man involved and Vicky was unsuccessful in her search for Fentje's father.

Vicky's concern grows about her two younger sisters, Hetty and Dora who had also married. Both their husbands were sent out to duty and the sisters decide to join Kasmenah and their siblings. Vicky is relieved to have them near her as news of horrific, but unsubstantiated stories about Indonesian soldiers and Japanese troops raping young women, circulate around the villages. Vicky feels the pressure but welcomes the responsibility to keep everyone safe, including the new baby growing inside her. More than ever before she entreats God for help.

Newspaper circulations still occur in pockets of large cities, while surrounding villages are dependent on second hand information. The unconfirmed reports about the ongoing Japanese occupation in the northern parts of Java, concerns everyone in Vicky's local community causing a disruption among the neighbors who begin defending opposing sides of the conflict. Adding to the family's stress are federal mandate notices of injunctions imposed upon each resident. Government authorities send flyers around to all villages and local neighborhoods, announcing that water will be rationed, demanding that citizens be frugal in their consumption of food and daily use of commodities of gas and electricity.

Already, Vicky and her mother have noticed a lack of food in their visits to the pasar. Sadly, the aura in the pasar has changed. An increase in hostilities pervade from the usual, friendly island merchants as they exorbitantly drive up their prices. Mothers are no longer bringing their children to the marketplace and the once easy going, happy atmosphere has been replaced with impatient, angry voices as smiles have disappeared from customers replaced by antagonistic, suspicious glances.

Daily, Vicky experiences indescribable physical pain which travels from her chest into her stomach, accompanied by severe headaches. Losing her appetite during her pregnancy with Johny did not impact his health but she is aware that a limitation of good fruits and vegetables could jeopardize the child she is carrying now. At night she succumbs to exhaustion and in the cramped, small dwelling the entire Hall family occupies, Vicky sleeps on a cot next to Johny. Weeping is a luxury she cannot afford because it could wake and possibly frighten the child. She will have to save her tears for another day.

There is no time for self-pity!

Everything about life has changed. Even the daily routine of cleaning and washing is limited because of necessary water rationing. Vicky and Kasmenah have put out receptacles, including buckets to catch rain water.

The two women are grateful that their chickens sustain them with eggs, but in the garden, exotic lilies, gladiolus, chrysanthemums and Vicky's favorite flower, the melati: a fragrant, delicate, white blossoms have all suffered from the lack of care. Neglect of everyone's gardens has changed the appearance of the neighborhood.

Lately, the serenity of the community is greatly disturbed by the regular appearance and noisy rumble of military vehicles.

Every other week, Vicky makes the journey to Andir to collect the wages earned by her husband. Although the amount is greatly reduced from the usual pay, Vicky manages to feed her household which includes the entire family of Kasmenah's baboe. Travel to the base is more difficult since most of the public transportation has ceased in the outskirts of the cities, and even the operators of the pedi cabs are demanding exorbitant prices for their service. Whenever possible, Vicky makes the journey on foot, walking for miles, resting to stop long enough to sit on the side of the road, finding shade under a large tree. If she is fortunate enough, a banana or mango tree growing outside private property, bearing fruit, offers her enough sustenance to continue.

Sadly, the landscape of the beautiful island seems different. The sky is not so blue anymore and once billowy clouds seem menacing somehow. Vicky senses a pervading fear has changed the atmosphere of everything surrounding her world. Accepting the loss of all things past, Vicky Meijer remains vigilant in the present, keenly aware that the trips to Andir will become challenging as the baby inside her, grows. Bernard and Fentje are too young to run the errand for her. Vicky will have to trust God to make a way.

Evenings continue to be the young mother's favorite time of the day. Vicky spends them on the porch with Kasmenah as they whisper about the uncertainty of their future including the responsibility both carry for the safety and well-being of the family. Amid the tension of current events, Vicky has made great effort to build a new relationship with Kasmenah. Lately, communication between them is comfortable and easy, in the way close friends confide in each other. Grateful she is able to openly express her fears, Vicky finds comfort in the older woman's words of wisdom. They agree not to separate the family. Many friends and neighbors have sent their younger children away hoping they will be safer elsewhere but Kasmenah and Vicky choose to keep the family intact. The disturbing news that the Japanese are rapidly advancing over all the major islands make mother and daughter more determined to keep their loved ones together. Their family alliance helps to encourage each member.

The main challenge the two women face is lack of information about Harry. Vicky is reduced to relying on local town gossip because mail delivery has stopped and newspapers are no longer distributed. She is told that a distant neighbor has still possession of his illegal short-wave radio, but the location of her husband's regiment would not necessarily be available. The entire community had been informed that anyone owning any type of illegal communication device is subject to arrest.

The authorities believe no one is above suspicion in aiding the enemy.

Vicky collaborates with a handful of neighbors to keep one another informed of the latest developments. Understanding the times have become dangerous, alliances are made with people they trust, reminding one another to remain neutral in public. Making public statements of dissent directed at the government, increased the risk of becoming the target of unwanted, official scrutiny. A close friend of Broertje De Wolf narrowly escapes arrest, and now is on the run as a fugitive for initiating protests.

How strange life is for Vicky and her family! The wonderful, carefree days of days past seem unreal and dreams she had for the future have turned into terrifying nightmares making Vicky feel she has become an alien in her own country. Dominated by increasing fears about her husband is mentally exhausting, but spurns her frustration into action as

Vicky joins with the wives and mothers and compose a letter addressed to the top military official at Andir Air Force Base demanding information about their men. It is agreed that one of the wives would make the journey to deliver the correspondence in person. It will not be Vicky Meijer because she is more than five months pregnant.

For weeks the small group patiently wait for a reply from their Dutch officials. Weeks pass with no response! Vicky and her friends are reduced to hearing fragments of news regarding the terrible fate of citizens in some parts of Europe, but it isn't until rumors swirl around stories about the invasion of northern Java that causes Vicky panic.

Then one day, while rocking baby Johny to sleep, Vicky observes a man dressed in uniform exit a military vehicle with a telegram in his hand.

Mrs. Harry Meijer is about to receive the answers to all her inquiries concerning her husband, Sergeant Harry Meijer.

chapter

11

*"When we meet with suffering – often intense suffering –
our knees wobble and our hearts melt within us."*

PASTOR/THEOLOGIAN/AUTHOR - GREG HARRIS

Located more than 4,000 miles north/east of the island of Java, across the vast Pacific Ocean lies the island nation of Imperial Japan. Consisting of more than 2,000 tiny islands, the main, four, large landmasses include the islands of Hokkaido, Honshu, Shikoku and Kyushu. Influenced as early as the 7th Century by the nearby countries of China and Korea; the history of Japan is one of internal and external wars and struggle. The beginning of its historical records tell of Japan's fight to keep invaders from China and Korea out of their country for centuries. The constant need for defense began to grow a society and military culture always ready for war but there was even more internal conflict between local lords and feuding families.

Following the Chinese model of a permanent seat in government, the Japanese institute the office of Emperor. Given the highest authority in the country, the emperor utilizes all of the national resources and finances to maintain law and order. By the 11th century it is clear that the vast areas out of his reach cannot end the internal wars between the dissident lords or defiant families and the role of the emperor changes into a ceremonial one. The beginning of the 13th century witnesses the military taking center stage of governmental duties under the leadership of the Shogun, the general of the Japanese Imperial Army. Created primarily to stop the internal feuding, the Shogun is given all necessary resources, including the compulsory enrollment and training of thousands of young men to maintain civil law and order. The discipline exacted from the young soldiers' rivals that of their contemporaries and their enemies. Special Forces existing within the Imperial Army are the Samurai warriors, a formidable match against the persistent Chinese Mongols who make numerous attempts to invade Japan.

Appealing to these powerful Samurais is the religion of Zen Buddhism, which embraces austerity and self-discipline. Thus, the existential, empirical philosophy combined with the aesthetic values of simplicity enhances a warrior's belief that salvation is obtained through Buddha via the Pure Land of Japan into Nirvana. Yet in the realm of spiritual beliefs, the people differ about which strand of Buddhism to follow and it is evident, Buddhism does not stop the centuries of internal friction between the various factions of hundreds of warlords including the Shogun, feuding families and the governmental interference of the military. Over many decades, violent, internal wars result in the deaths of hundreds of thousands Japanese citizens.

Desperate for unity, the Japanese follow the examples of the way the British governs with different heads of state. The internal conflicts are greatly reduced when the Japanese create the office of Prime Minister is in 1885. As the head of government, the PM exercises control and supervision over the executive branch and fulfills the role as commander and chief of the Japan Self- defense Forces. For the first time in its rivaling history, the country settles in uniting politically, militarily, financially and philosophically.

As Japan increases in sovereignty and might, the global community of the 20th Century is forced to acknowledge her ascendancy in strength and power.

A world away in the tiny village near the city of Bandoeng, Indonesia, a young mother's heart is beating fast and hard against her chest afraid to face the man standing on the porch. Gently placing her baby on his cot, she resists the feeling to faint. Cautiously, Vicky answers the door. The gentleman standing on the veranda looks too old to be serving in active, military service, but he is kind as he introduces himself and hands the telegram over to Vicky. With trembling hands and tears streaming down her cheeks, the words blur as Vicky is officially informed by the Royal Dutch Air Force that her husband, Sgt. Harry Antoine Diederich Meijer has been captured by enemy forces along with the rest of his unit of the

Sixth Reconnaissance Group. No other information is offered and she stares into the man's sympathetic eyes. Politely, he salutes her and returns back to his vehicle, leaving her numb, unable to move.

Within minutes, Vicky is surrounded by her mother and two sisters, holding on to her, fearing that letting go might cause Vicky to fall. Before the young mother has time to digest the news, several friends and neighbors arrive to show the telegrams they received with the same information about their loved ones. Kasmenah requests for them to stay for the noontime meal and before the lunch is finished, they choose the person who, when nighttime falls, will go and seek help from the man said to own a short-wave radio.

Desperate for more information, Vicky volunteers in spite of Kasmenah protests, citing her daughter's condition but Vicky insists. Sending everyone back to their homes, the pregnant mother waits patiently until late into the evening. The last rays of sunshine had disappeared behind the horizon hours before as Vicky quietly slips out the back door. She is annoyed that the neighbor's dog had begun barking, but making the exit through the backyard gate is the wisest move. The young woman is covered in goose bumps even though the night air is warm. Vicky's heart has begun to beat rapidly and the infant inside her is moving as if to concur with Kasmenah's objection. Silently Vicky offers the child an apology and sends up a prayer.

The neighbor with the short-wave radio lives almost a half mile down the road. Several dogs barking in the area could alert authorities that Vicky Meijer is violating the rules of curfew and could be arrested but she had considered the risk if it results in obtaining any news at all. Being careful not to kick up any pebbles, Vicky is amazed at the change in the neighborhood. Windows usually left open on balmy nights are now covered with cotton cloths or batik. Doors are locked and no one is sitting on their verandas enjoying the beautiful nighttime air. Memories flood back of the wonderful times spent with her friends and loved ones. The ache in Vicky's heart matches the pain she feels in her head but she quietly presses on. Suddenly, one her favorite Sunday school hymns overcomes her thoughts, giving her a familiar comfort. Even for just a few minutes, Vicky feels lighter.

Finally, safely, she reaches her destination.

The neighbor, a kind, elderly gentleman had already turned on the radio. Using the lowest possible volume, he and Vicky crouch on the floor to listen intently. The news is alarming causing Vicky Meijer, wife of Sergeant Harry Meijer to clasp both hands tightly on her mouth to silence desperate cries of despair

chapter

12

"For nation shall rise against nation and kingdom against kingdom..."

JESUS CHRIST IN MATTHEW 24:7 KJV

The history of World War II has had its share of ubiquitous scrutiny over the last 75 years. With historians, analysts, biographers, journalists, authors and reporters from different points of references, citing sources which may have been accurate, exaggerated or skewed, the debate continues over the winner verses the loser, the aggressors against the victims and many shallow justifications for this global holocaust. The rhetoric endures for decades in speeches from the public square, argued in the classrooms of higher learning, debated in the halls of famous think tanks, preached behind the pulpit in churches and discussed at the family dinner table.

Yet two cold, hard facts are indisputable: war is hell and the majority of its victims are innocent, non-combatant men, women and children!

The past records centuries of man's inhumanity to his fellow man, proving that he prefers to be the aggressor. Sadly, postmodern man in spite his technological capabilities, medical and scientific advances has no answer for the devastation his own, selfish desires cause!

Encompassing most of the world, including the Middle East, the northern countries of Africa and territories in north/eastern South America, World War II is fought on two major fronts later identified as the European Theater and the Asian/ Pacific Theater. The aggressors, namely Germany, Italy and Japan are labeled as the trio in the Rome-Berlin Axis. Identical in their lust for world domination, Germany and Italy concentrate their efforts in the western and northern hemispheres, while Japan focuses her attention on capturing the hemisphere nations of the south and east.

Beginning in 1932, the nation of Japan flexes her military muscle for the following decade, invading their neighbor to the west, winning major victories in the cities and regions of China, which included Shanghai, Nanking, Soochow, Paoting, Huschow, Chunking, Changsha, Kweilin, and hundreds of small villages, inflicting devastating destruction and killing an estimated 10 – 25 million Chinese civilians. By the autumn of 1941, Japan continues her campaign of terror, besieging the countries of Korea, Hong Kong, Cambodia, Laos, Vietnam, the Philippines, Thailand, Burma, eastern India, Malaysia, Singapore, Timor, New Guinea, the Pacific and Indian Ocean Islands and the Dutch East Indies. The Japanese war machine methodically forces the subjection, rape, torture and deaths of millions of civilian men, women and children in these southeast nations while the rest of the free world looks the other way. Not until they are brazen enough to bomb Pearl Harbor, Hawaii on December 7, 1941, does the United States step in and declare war with all the members and allies of the Roman/Berlin Axis.

The unverified news stories Vicky and her elderly neighbor hear on the short-wave radio about the invasion of Japanese troops on the islands of Sumatra and Java, sound implausible for the two listeners. The speaker repeats stories of hundreds of Dutch, Eurasian and Indonesian citizens, primarily in the north, rounded up and taken to large areas where land has been confiscated, cleared, and surrounded by barbed wire and bamboo fences. Women, children and the elderly men are forced into these "camps" against their will and named "political prisoners" under the control of the Japanese military. The man talking into the microphone is speaking rapidly, with haste and repeats the same information over and over again. He also describes the capture of thousands of pro-Dutch military troops and explains that survivors of combat are taken as prisoners onto Japanese cargo ships. No one knows of their fate.

Vicky is in shock to learn that the enemy was advancing on the archipelagoes so quickly. It didn't make sense! Where was the defense of the Dutch military who were supposed to prevent invasion and keep them safe?

Suddenly, the radio goes silent! The pregnant mother is trembling and finds it difficult to rise up from the floor. She feels faint and her knees wobble as the elderly neighbor offers the young woman something to eat. Vicky politely refuses, needing to return home immediately. Grateful for his help, Vicky leaves a few rupiahs on the table as she exists out of the back door.

The walk home is difficult, and in the grip of fear, Vicky battles an intense desire to scream.

The informant on the short-wave radio had been correct! Fighting on the northern shores of Java did not last long. The Japanese with the assistance of sympathetic Indonesians win major victories which commence with the capture of thousands Dutch/Indonesian military personnel.

Vicky's husband is one of more than 2,000 troops captured less than a hundred miles north of Bandoeng, detained in several large buildings originally used as batik factories. Thousands more are captured along the upper, northern Java shores. Vicky and her family are unaware that Harry's fate lay in the hands of a foreign, dangerous adversary. The Japanese swiftly demonstrate needless brutality in apprehending their hostages and after capture, deny them food and water.

Earlier news stories concerning the Japanese treatment of captured civilians had been inaccurate, biased and limited by reporters who blindly leaned towards sympathetic for the invaders.

Sergeant Harry Meijer and his colleagues witness firsthand the cruelty of their captors against the troops loyal to the Dutch government. Any resistance resulted in immediate, on the spot execution. Adding to the tension is the collective anger of Dutch/Indonesian troops as they observe Indonesian soldiers stand in solidarity with the enemy. Major news headlines had proclaimed Japan would assist the Indonesian nationalists in securing their long, sought independence from the Dutch government and her monarchy.

Harry Meijer finds himself seated on cold, cement flooring, with other prisoners, in groups of twenty or more, chained together as one common series of metal links on the wrists and ankles, makes it impossible to move. Taken at gunpoint on the day of his captivity, Harry stared at the austere, Japanese faces and realized he had never taken much notice of their physical features before. A person of Japanese ethnicity was never part of Harry's social circle, although he recalls one day meeting a gentleman from

Japan who was employed at the same company where his father worked but the introduction was brief and unmemorable.

Reflecting back to the last few months brings Harry considerable grief. Sent to work on the aircraft engines, while surrounded by a daily barrage of artillery fire, Harry and his colleagues had worked extended, pressure-filled, sixteen-hour days, keenly aware the lives of the pilots and crews depended upon his expertise as a mechanic and flight engineer. Harry had always been proud to perform his best when the job demanded of him his utmost proficiency. The men who labored alongside him agree.

Some of them included British and Australian soldiers. Harry is amused with the differences between them. Both come from English roots, but the Brits remain reserved and formal, different from the Aussies, who display a mellow, relaxed approach. Harry had enjoyed their infectious amiability and sense of humor.

Only ten months had passed before the Japanese invasion stopped Harry's work. His desire to make a difference to defend his beloved country has failed. The serviceman struggles with the bitter pill of defeat as the reality overwhelms him!

Now seated alongside many of his fellow soldiers, Harry joins them as he battles mortifying shame, suffering the humiliation of defeat by an enemy bent on destroying them.

Their Japanese captors use various methods in keeping the large number of prisoners subdued. Conversation among the detainees is prohibited. A violation results in a blow from the back end of a bayonet coupled with fierce shrieking of the Japanese guard applying the punch. The volume and intensity of shouting from the enemy soldiers jolts Harry Meijer, but he understands it is meant to further intimidate their prisoners.

Surrounded by hundreds of dejected, defeated comrades, Harry is forced to face the truth of the dire, frightening circumstances he finds himself in. As his young wife comes to mind, Harry calculates that Vicky must have given birth to their new baby. He imagines her beautiful voice singing the island lullabies yet steels himself not to weep. His Japanese captors do not tolerate any sign of emotion.

It has been two days since the capture of Harry's regiment, causing the restless stirring among his fellow prisoners to increase. Several become desperate enough to demand food and water. The Japanese guards use an

Indonesian soldier to translate, but the discrepancies between the Malayan, Dutch and Japanese languages cause a breakdown in communication exacerbating the existing anger and frustration between the captured troops and their subjugators.

Abruptly, several feet away from Harry's position along the chain-linked shackles, an officer of the Royal Dutch Army bravely stands without permission, making demands. Harry faintly makes out his words as the officer makes a case about the captors violating the League of Nations Treaty about the treatment of prisoners. A Japanese soldier near him bellows raucously and slams the butt of his bayonet directly into the officer's face. Harry's line of vision prevents him from seeing the officer drop but hears the rattle of the chains as he falls on top of fellow prisoners who are secured alongside him. The entire string of prisoners stir up in response as a brawl ensues with chained captives attempting to lunge towards the nearest Japanese guard. Quickly the milieu is quelled by the firing of a gun in the air. Harry is shocked that the gun was not pointed at any of the protesters. The attempted revolt would have been a justifiable excuse for the Japanese soldiers to execute the entire platoon. Harry believes they are lucky to be alive one more day as each hour drags agonizingly, slowly on.

The surrounding buildings on the compound hold hundreds of prisoners in addition to the multitude occupying the building where Harry is held captive. Sergeant Meijer is amused that the enemy seems unprepared, even overwhelmed with the burden of so many prisoners. Another Dutch soldier courageously stands and begs to use the outdoors for the men to relieve themselves. He makes the case that the buildings are surrounded by vast regions of ferns, low lying grasses, and acres of palm trees where the duty could be accomplished.

Harry is grateful to hear one Japanese officer agree.

Instead of releasing each man individually, the Japanese escort their prisoners by groups of twenty. Every man has to relieve himself the best way possible, keeping in mind the man on each side. It requires a simple form of acrobatics but Harry is grateful their hands are chained in front making it easier for each man to remove his own trousers. It dawns on the air force sergeant that he has to become more grateful for every, small convenience.

Being outdoors offers the Harry the blessing of stretching his legs which had become numb. The sight of the Indonesian landscape and blue sky above helps recharge his mind, and renews his resolve to remain alert. With hundreds of prisoners filing outdoors, the process of toilet breaks take hours to complete, and in spite of the humility required to perform such a private act in public, the air force sergeant appreciates the opportunity be a comfortable distance away from the Japanese guards. Taking advantage of the situation, he is able to quietly, cautiously say a few words to the men chained next to him, grateful to exchange a few smiles.

That evening Harry reflects upon the irony in life. In the midst of his captivity, surrounded by strangers in the same situation, he discovers the deep ties of common humanity and the dependence which bind one human being to another.

Cargo Ship Junyo Maru - Frost, Walter E.

chapter

13

"Silent tears hold the loudest pain!"

ANONYMOUS

In the European and Asian/Pacific Theater of war, arsenal on land consisted of the infantry soldiers on foot with rifles, automatic fire weapons and support with artillery machines, which were cannons that caused the greater number of casualties. Tanks, motorcars and horses provide most of the transportation on land. In the air, warplanes drone on incessantly. War on the seas, with naval operations in place uses warships, aircraft carriers, cargo ships and submarines.

In sporadic but accurate news stories, Japanese ships sailing from Java to Japan are freighters described as "hell ships." It is on one of those cargo ships that Harry, along with dozens other prisoners of war are forced to board one week after being captured. Originally built to carry cargo for import and export shipment, during the war, the ships are utilized to transport thousands of prisoners from the Dutch East Indies, the Philippines, Hong Kong and other Asian ports to prison camps in Japan. The typical cargo ship was 430-500 feet long with a beam measurement of 56 feet wide. Most of them ran on a triple expansion steam engine averaging 14 to 19 knots an hour. Not equipped to carry passengers, the prisoners are thrown down below in little compartments meant to hold freight. Some of the enclosures are less than five feet wide and ten feet long. Men are forcibly cramped into these cells with no ventilation or light. Harry had spent the previous week preparing his heart about the possibility that the Japanese would line up their prisoners and kill them. After 24 hours in the cargo hold, he wished they would have!

The ship prisoners occupy is in a serious state of disrepair. Rust had set in, with pieces of metal protruding and dangerously exposed near the areas where the men are thrust onto the floor. Driven to the bottom of the ship, Harry approximates they are about twenty feet below the top deck. In that short distance the temperature has risen at least ten degrees.

Left without food and water for periods extending more than 24 hours, men begin to suffer from dehydration, dysentery, diarrhea, sea-sickness, with many contracting pneumonia. On the occasion when their captors bring them food, it is a handful of rice, rife with vermin droppings and the water they are given is cloudy, tasting of metal. Unable to recline in the damp, cramped space, men doze sitting up, sometimes slouching over one another. For Harry Meijer, the physical discomfort is minute compared to the mental anguish. Like the rest of his fellow prisoners, Harry is gravely concerned about his wife, children and the rest of his family.

Their Japanese tormentors are physically abusive but the psychological torture they employ is worse. Repeatedly, on loud speakers, in harsh, loud tones, instructions and commands are repeated hourly, all day and throughout the night, making it impossible for their prisoners to sleep.

The conditions are grim in the cargo holds causing the Japanese soldiers to toss the plastic containers of rice and water down the narrow openings. The stench from the lack of bathroom facilities is too much for the captors to bear.

With coldhearted indifference, over a period of the following 24 months, 150,000 allied prisoners suffer in the holds of more than 200 Japanese hell ships. Twenty thousand prisoners perish on vessels as the result of allied bombings which sink ships meant to cripple the Japanese navy, unaware that thousands of their comrades are on board!

But even in the bowels of hell, Harry manages to find a ray of sunshine. Several of the men seated near him remain hopeful, using the opportunity to encourage one another. Harry begins by sharing his personal story of meeting Vicky, and becoming the father of two little boys. Other men do the same, keeping their voices low. Two British soldiers and one, an Australian officer with the Royal Australian Air Force, explain to Harry that all countries of the British Empire, including Canada had declared war on the trio of Germany, Italy and Japan as early as September 1939 when Germany and Italy began invading its neighbors and allies of the British Isles. The cordial sharing of personal information comforts Harry. Time passes faster with the conversations taking his mind off the filthy conditions surrounding them. At times when one soldier becomes angry, discouraged or grows silent, others find the opportunity to speak words of hope and encouragement.

There are moments Harry feels like a hypocrite. Speaking words of optimism to men who are on death's door, Harry risks sounding hollow but men, filled with anguish, express gratitude for any word of reassurance. Collectively they agree, hope is all they possess!

During quiet times, Harry observes each man is greatly despairing, yet each one understands they had already considered the cost when they enlisted for military service. Harry knows that the physical pain inside his chest must be similar for them too. One of the Australians crouched near him is a young soldier, just nineteen years old. As Harry spots tears silently streaming down the boy's cheeks, the cramped conditions limit him to reach out and pat his shoulder.

Thus, hundreds of men including one frightened teenager, expected to give the ultimate sacrifice for the sake of country, spend two, horrific weeks on an enemy's cargo ship, bound for an alien land and an uncertain future.

chapter 14

"The corpse of an enemy always smells sweet."
FRENCH GENERAL NAPOLEON BONAPARTE

Every country the Japanese military successfully invades and ultimately controls is accomplished by applying efficient, intimidating procedures. The military's campaigning is resourceful, cleverly utilizing the very people they hold captive to achieve their own goals. Not concerned about a prisoner's well-being, the Japanese commanders extract out of him in the way of work and labor, and when the captive has nothing left to give, he is discarded in a heap, joining others who were either dead or dying. With regularity the smallest infraction would be reason enough for the Japanese soldier to shoot his prisoner in the head or in his back. Nonchalant when delivering the fatal blow, the executioner walks away, expecting other prisoners to remove the corpse. Individuals in captivity who witness the murder in horror, quickly become submissive.

The successful, Japanese occupation of the entire Dutch East Indies archipelago transpires within weeks. Fearing the Dutch Allied counter attacks and concerns about losing Indonesian resources, particularly petroleum, the Japanese regime initiates extreme, repressive injunctions on the Indonesian citizens. They force tens of thousands of men, women and children into conscripted labor camps.

Locally, rumors and eyewitness testimonies about the Japanese occupation send shock waves throughout suburban and village communities. Before Vicky and her family have time to consider what routes there could be in the way of escape, Indonesian authorities using bull horns, riding in the back of government, utility vehicles, inform surrounding neighborhoods that all residents are under house arrest.

Overtaking her fear is Vicky's seething anger, challenging her ability to remain rational.

How could their Dutch government have been so irresponsible? What more should they have done to keep their citizens safe? Surely, someone is going to come and rescue them from these insane, vile individuals. She has heard stories about the great nations of America and Russia possessing massive weapons which could wipe these malignant pariahs off the map. With little effort, couldn't those powerful countries rescue and rid her beloved land of these foreign, slant-eyed bullies? Inflaming her increasing feelings of disgust, is the inconceivable betrayal of thousands of her island citizens. How could they possibly trust these foreign aliens to secure Indonesian independence from the Dutch?

The regulations of the lockdown include that occupants are not allowed to leave their homes unless given special permission and accompanied by military escort. Because the time for the delivery of her baby will be soon, Vicky makes plans to find help. Giving birth at home is not unusual in the native communities, but Vicky questions if the new restrictions would allow a midwife to assist her?

Making requests of any kind proves to be daunting. Although Vicky and her family had not seen any Japanese military, the Indonesian military is lock-step in reinforcing the mandates from Japanese authorities. Communication with any government official is required to be in a formal setting in the town's civic building on specific days of the week, which to Vicky's frustration, changes daily. Vicky is desperate to make the trip before the birth of her baby. God answers her prayer and the young mother is escorted by an Indonesian soldier to address the local authorities.

Surprisingly, the officer in charge is sympathetic and gives Vicky permission to summon the same midwife who helped when Johny was born.

Early in the morning of Thursday, April 23, 1942, Vicky wakes up abruptly with a sharp pain. Less than four hours later, with the help of the midwife, Kasmenah and their baboe, Vicky's second son, Rene Ludwig Meijer, enters the world, healthy and well.

The birth of another baby in the Meijer/Hall household is a wonderful reason for celebration, and under normal circumstances would have been a time of inviting friends, neighbors and relatives for "rijstafel", the island tradition of preparing dozens of delicious dishes of food, served banquet-style but not this time! Although she is sad that Rene's birth cannot be commemorated, Vicky is grateful he seems strong and robust. She is blessed with enough breast milk to help him thrive. Little Johny is happy to be a big brother. The baby's presence has caused Johny to stop asking his mother about his brother, Walter.

Fluctuating directives from the civil authorities concern Vicky about her family's safety. Almost daily, sanctions on the citizens of Bandoeng are continuously changing, causing a noticeable unrest in the Meijer/Hall household. The small dwelling is cramped with four adult women, two teenage boys, a toddler and an infant, making Bernard and Fentje angry enough to sneak outdoors, putting the family's safety in jeopardy. The boys' defiant behavior puts the entire family at risk of being arrested! Vicky encourages Kasmenah and her siblings to cooperate with the authorities who make regular visits to all the residents in the neighborhood and nearby communities. But Bernard and Fentje resist, offering unrealistic suggestions about dealing with the "foreign devils." More restrictive injunctions follow causing an uproar with local young people. Dozens are arrested during a protest and Vicky is relieved Bernard and Fentje are not among them!

In the weeks that follow, the entire Meijer/Hall family is growing accustomed to the routine of remaining inside the confines of their tiny home and yard. Johny, who is walking now, takes great delight in his baby brother, which help Vicky and Kasmenah remain hopeful for the future. Children give the two women the courage they need when the future looks bleak. Johny has been saying more words and his gestures of blowing a kiss, have thrilled his mother and grandmother. Watching the toddler grow has helped alleviate some of the fear the family experiences every day.

Once a week, the rationing and distribution of groceries is done by the Indonesian military which has occupied the city of Bandoeng. Vicky has learned to be even more conservative and creative with the small quantity allotted to them. Although at times the stress of Harry's fate is overwhelming, the young mother continues in hope everyone will survive. She thinks of Rudy, Guus, Broertje, Schipp, Piet and young Walter, adding to the daily anguish of the lack of news about her friends including, Dirk and Miel Wildenboer. The ache in her heart threatens to wear her down every minute of every day, but she must choose to remain resolute in the face of the ever-changing circumstances! Two, innocent little boys and the rest of the family depend on her.

However, Vicky is not surprised that the little bit of freedom is short-lived. Authorities that every occupant over the age of eighteen is required to register and update their personal information and with military police escort, have to make their way to the same civic building where weeks earlier, Vicky had made a request for a midwife. Filled with frustration because the order leaves Bernard and Fentje alone in charge at home, responsible for her two sons, Vicky grows weary with ongoing fury and rage!

What knuckleheads these moronic fools are! No consideration for children! Instantly, the hatred ramps up inside her chest, increasing the physical pain.

Following orders, Vicky enters the building along with her mother, sisters and many others, some she recognized from her neighborhood. As they stand to wait their turn to file into a large room, Vicky stands on her toes to see if she can spot a familiar, friendly face. The young mother would feel much better if she could see Mrs. Pies or Miel. But the room fills quickly and each person is instructed to stand in rows according to age. Being separated from her mother and sisters makes Vicky uneasy as she sees the fear on the faces of her younger siblings. Offering them a quick smile, she mouths the words, "Saya sayang awak," I love you.

As Vicky's turn in line comes, she is informed by a female government worker to relinquish her identification papers. The woman stamps the papers with a seal and instructs Vicky to make her way to another door. Upon entering, Vicky is relieved to be reunited with her mother, who is calm but very sad. Kasmenah has aged, looking older than her 39 years. Thankfully, Hetty and Dora join them and the space fills up quickly with many more detainees while an official of the Indonesian military stands upon a platform accompanied by a foreign soldier.

For the first time, Vicky lays her eyes upon a Japanese individual and decides that his alien appearance seem menacing, just as people have described. Immediately, Vicky is aware her teeth have been clenched for hours making the pounding in her head worse. An Indonesian official delivers a short message giving concise, instructions presented with veritable hostility.

Thankfully, the group is dismissed but with a warning that some residents would be interviewed in greater length at home. Vicky understands the more accurate word is "interrogation." Hopefully, gossip in her neighborhood had not leaked about her meeting with the elderly neighbor. Earlier in the week he had been arrested for possession of the radio.

The long walk home is quiet, even though the Hall women are accompanied by dozens of their fellow neighbors and town folk. Surrounded by the usual, tropical noises of the evening made by the reverberation of fluttering wings of cicadas, the collective chirping of crickets, including the incessant whistle of local parrots, Vicky's mind is swirling about new civil ordinances placed on all Bandoeng residents. Her pondering is interrupted as somewhere in the crowd, Vicky hears the desperate, yet muffled sounds of someone's sorrowful weeping. As her thoughts turn to her little boys who have been left alone with their young uncles, Vicky steps up the pace, but is forcibly slowed down as one of the Indonesian soldiers escorting the group lays a strong hand on her shoulder. It is another harsh reminder that her life is no longer her own.

A sick, unfamiliar feeling of defeat washes over Vicky, threatening to snuff out the little bit of optimism left in her body. The mother of Johny and Rene, Mrs. Harry Meijer is determined to renew her strength as she reaches for Kasmenah's hand, locking arms with Hetty and Dora. Without words they make a commitment never to be separated! Vicky is proud of her courageous mother and younger sisters. They will face the future together, determined to stand against the face of the evil closing in. These vile intruders can steal the people's freedom, while not one is capable of robbing a person's soul! Vicky Meijer finds comfort in the thought.

Somehow the mood of the crowd changes as the weeping ceases and silently everyone continues to walk a little taller taking brisk, determined steps of hope!

chapter 15

"For we wrestle not against flesh and blood, but against principalities, against powers, against the rulers of the darkness of this world, against spiritual wickedness in high places."

Ephesians 6:12 KJV

Before World War II ends, the Empire of Japan would have more than 200 Prisoner of War camps on the islands of Japan and hundreds more POW camps combined in the occupied countries of the Philippines, Malaysia, Singapore, Formosa (now Taiwan), North Borneo, China, Sarawak, Manchuria, Dutch East Indies, Thailand, Burma, New Guinea and Korea. The conditions of the camps were in violation of the terms of the Geneva Convention which stipulated the humanitarian conditions required of detainees. Of the more than 150,000 prisoners kept in custody by the Japanese, 1 in 3 died of starvation, disease or severe punishment. Each camp is operated by the code and conduct of its camp commandant, who makes up the rules according to his own personal criteria. The majority of the prisoners, men of 19 to 40 years of age are put to work in coal mines, fields, shipyards, factories and on railway lines.

The Japanese take advantage of the production an able-bodied man could deliver to continue feeding the war machine and to keep their own country functioning in spite of wartime conditions. In the fields men plant and harvest fruit, vegetables and rice. Those kept in factories are forced to help the Japanese produce warheads, machinery and arsenal to be used to continue the war. The prisoners chosen to work on the railways endure hours in hostile weather conditions. In the shipyards, prisoners work on all the naval and ground equipment to be used in combat. The coal extracted by captives working in the mines, is used to generate electricity, heat and other forms of energy. Referred to as "black gold," coal was also liquefied into fuel.

Arriving in the evening on the island of Kyushu, Harry and his comrades are marched over to Camp Miyata Machi in the Kurate district of Fukuoka municipality #9, located 28 miles southeast from the large, well-populated, port city of Nagasaki. Harry learns that he and prisoners from the same cargo ship are assigned to work in the coalmines. Considering himself an individual who is well read, Harry admits to his fellow inmates the only thing he knows about mining is the danger involved. Everyone within hearing distance concur, including two British soldiers whose relatives were miners in Ireland. But fear of working in the mine is the last thing on Harry's mind. Two weeks in the hole of the ship has left him weak and shaky, with his hearing compromised because of the continuous, deafening clangor of the ship's engines! Less than two hours on land and already he had witnessed the brutal beating of one prisoner for not responding fast enough to the commands of a Japanese guard as they were being processed into the prison camp. The soldier had been one of the British men seated near Harry in the bowels of the tanker. Silently, Harry hoped the poor fellow survived.

While exiting the ship, prisoners were chained together once more, in groups of thirty to forty and instructed to stand at attention as a large, industrial hose, is used to wash them simultaneously. Harry is grateful! The water feels wonderful, washing most of the filth away and Harry opens his mouth to drink in as much as he is able. Dripping wet, the detainees are escorted to barracks, long and narrow, ramshackle, wooden buildings thrown together with a hammer and nails. Improperly built, without any foundation, the shacks look as though a slight, meandering wind could easily topple them over. Twenty men are led to barrack number "ni, san, Hachi," 238. Inside, dozens of thin bamboo mats, 4 feet in length by 2 feet wide, lie side by side on a dirt floor which are the sleeping accommodations for each prisoner. Suffering from exhaustion and hunger, most of the men fall asleep within minutes but Harry remains wide-awake. Perhaps the discomfort of wet clothes prevents him from sleep or maybe it's his concern about Vicky and the children but too soon, a Japanese guard is bellowing commands for all prisoners to get up! Shackled together with chains again, the prisoners are taken outside and for the first time, Harry sees Camp Miyata Machi in daylight fixing his gaze as far as his eye can see, on hundreds of rows of long, narrow wooden buildings encompassing the entire region. Immediately, Sergeant Harry Meijer calculates that the position of the sun tells him it must be six o'clock in the morning.

Taking advantage of the few moments the Japanese guard has taken his eyes off their group, the air force sergeant uses his military training to assess the physical parameters of the camp and its surrounding areas. From Harry's vantage point, he looks beyond the buildings to see land surrounded by low-lying foothills. Obsessed with the idea of escape since his capture, Harry is well aware that it would require a miracle to set him free! Forced to be objective about his immediate environs bring on more feelings of discouragement, and Harry knows, he is encircled by hundreds of men experiencing the same despair.

Several standing near him cannot prevent tears from streaming down their hollow cheeks. But unchecked tears of emotion are not tolerated by the guards of Camp Miyata Machi as another Japanese guard is demanding their attention!

The prisoners are instructed to "yumi," bow facing north in the direction where they are told the great emperor of Japan resides. The soldier in charge of Harry's group has returned his attention back to them, yelling additional demands, but Harry has become numb to the sound. The excruciating pain of hunger makes it difficult to concentrate as his knees threaten to buckle underneath him. Harry wonders if their Japanese captors are going to feed them.

Not until hours later, each prisoner is handed a small bowl of rice and a piece of dried fish, swimming in seaweed broth. Harry is wise in consuming it slowly. The chains around his wrists could cause him to drop the food and he cannot afford to lose one kernel of rice! Everyone is still standing as they eat, some of them shaking from hunger or fear and just as abruptly they are given food, another guard rudely snatches the plastic bowls from each prisoner, grunting something in Japanese. Harry is slightly amused because the muttering sounds remind him of a frustrated dog snarling with a muzzle on its snout but the air force sergeant must try harder to maintain an austere look on his face because a smile could result in dire consequences.

The rest of Harry Meijer's first day in Camp Miyata Machi is spent appreciating the warm sunshine as instructions are shouted out about camp procedures. Midday, the prisoners are told to remove their clothing, with each man given a gray uniform which resemble cheap, poorly constructed pajamas. The material looks like cotton, but is rough to the touch. Harry doesn't mind, at least it is clean. The striped shirt of each uniform has a number sewn on the back which the prisoner is required to commit to memory.

Sergeant Meijer is assigned "hyak, san, juu, yon" (100, 3, 10, 4), a number he will remember for the rest of his life.

chapter

16

"For I consider that the sufferings of this present time are not worthy to be compared with the glory that is to be revealed to us."
ROMANS 8:8 NASB

The Japanese military, adept at war, use prescribed methods of administrative and logistic procedures assuring them victory in the country they occupy. One strategy is the imprisonment of civilians of all occupied countries which successfully works to subjugate the residents and ferret out those who might be involved in clandestine or guerrilla activity. Military operations of surrounding all cities, towns, villages, and includes confiscating finances, property, valuable possessions, from all citizens, enabling the Japanese to render their enemy completely powerless.

Establishing hundreds of "interment camps" all over the Southeast Asian continent, prisons used to detain non-combatant citizens, Japanese officials ensure their control over every archipelago country including the Dutch East Indies.

On the three largest islands of Indonesia, "political prisoners" are housed in buildings originally used for schools, warehouses, universities, prisons and hospitals. Japanese troops have taken control of the government infrastructure and governmental services such as port and postal services. Indonesian nationalists and politicians cooperating with the Japanese, also colluded with them to supply Japanese industries and armed forces. Because of Indonesian support, the Japanese military rapidly secure the archipelago's waterways, using the islands as defense posts against British, Dutch and Australian attacks.

More than 200,000 Indonesian civilians are interred in various camps on the islands with another 270,000 used as slave laborers sent out to work at other Japanese-held areas. In his book, A *History of Modern Indonesia*, author M.C. Ricklefs states: "Japanese ordered the recruitment of 'volunteer labourers' (romusha), primarily peasants drafted from their villages in Java and put to work wherever the Japanese needed them, even as far away as Burma and Siam. It is not known how many were involved, but estimates are at least 200,000 men and may have been as many as half a million, of whom not more than 70,000 could be found alive at the end of the war. Families are left behind to fend for themselves in pitiable conditions. At the same time, the Japanese introduces new regulations for the compulsory sale of rice to the government at low prices in effect of requisitioning to supply the Japanese military. Those Indonesian officials involved in the romusha recruitment and rice requisitioning earn much hatred from the villagers."

In Bandoeng, the Japanese implementation of new, civil ordinances intended to enslave all residents makes Vicky vex with renewed outrage. It is difficult to follow her own advice to harness the anger, as the lack of sleep, frustrations and anxieties grow, mesh into one, bringing on overwhelming waves of fear. Every civilian is given instruction to pack one suitcase for each member of the family with a list of items that are not permitted. Each family must ready to leave their homes within twenty-four hours. The authorities in charge explain nothing further but Vicky has already heard stories of residents being led into compounds to be detained. With tears spilling onto her kebaya, Vicky realizes the wretchedness of the situation, as she prays for someone, anyone, to deliver them from the inevitable.

Help does not come and before twenty-four hours are up, the Hall/Meijer family members, along with their neighbors, are forced from their homes. Dozens of Indonesian soldiers, brusquely shouting instructions, push citizens into lines facing the rear end of the same armored vehicles which had been disturbing the peace of villages for weeks. Vicky reluctantly climbs into the large, transport truck, clutching onto Johny's little hand and clinging tightly on baby Rene in the slendang across her chest. Odors from the engine fuel send waves of nausea causing Vicky to stumble. Miraculously the young mother recovers her balance, finds a space to sit with the baby on her lap as Johny rapidly positions himself at her feet. The cold she feels is not caused by the metal of the rig's undercarriage, instead

Vicky recognized the familiar chill of despair! It's a small annoyance compared to the fear gripping her heart now!

However, Christine Victorine Meijer purposed in her to never lose hope! Instantly, scoldings from her father flood into the young woman's memory reminding her, she is not a victim while hot tears threaten to contradict Vicky's resolve to defy her enemies! It is the enemy fiercely ripping Vicky away from the life and freedoms she once had.

The crowded, government vehicle jostles all the occupants inside, making the bumpy ride uncomfortable as the dark, green canvas above them flaps noisily in the wind. Rene begins to whimper with hints that the three-month-old is hungry! Less than ten minutes in public, Vicky has lost valued privacy to nurse her baby. Thankfully, the slendang used to cradle Rene makes an adequate cover and Vicky uses it to feed her infant son, battling waves of fear and panic. Vicky worries how her precious, innocent children, passengers in a noxious smelling, over-crowded military vehicle, will survive? Involuntarily, as tears annoyingly fall again, Vicky steels herself, pulling young Johny closer to her side.

The toddler is frightened. Forced to leave familiar surroundings by bad tempered, hostile soldiers dressed in combat gear, clenching large assault rifles while shouting menacing instructions fills the child's face with horror. Johny is old enough to understand the soldiers were using bad words his mother had forbid him to repeat. Nervously looking up at the family members surrounding him, the lad senses their collective dread and begins to weep. This little boy had tried so hard to be brave for his mother's sake! Gently, Vicky attempts to wipe away Johny's tears but to no avail as more course down his cheeks.

Softly Johny and Rene's mother sings a lullaby as Bernard and Fentje press closer to Hettie and Dora. The entire group of passengers inside the truck remain quiet while Vicky stares at Kasmenah whose eyes are closed with grief. Her beloved mother is a kind, generous and gentle soul Vicky will never doubt again! In the midst of this forced captivity, Vicky Meijer wonders what will happen to Kasmenah? Is this nightmare even real? Will Vicky Meijer wake up and find herself back in the little bungalow she shared with her husband? Perhaps the nausea is causing brain fog and robbing her of all mental clarity.

The horror of the previous months has culminated into the reality of a missing husband, the loss of home and all worldly possessions, the forced displacement of family, friends, entire communities and neighborhoods. All has been replaced with the terror of an uncertain future!

The journey in the military transport truck lasts less than an hour to reach a site situated near the port of Bandoeng. Other similar transport vehicles have been following in a convoy, suddenly come to a halt, begin to unload the passengers as Christine Victorine Meijer-Hall becomes one of hundreds of women with children and elderly parents led into a large expanse surrounded by tall enclosures of cement walls covered on top with rolls of barbed wire.

Flanked by dozens of military personnel carrying rifles, Vicky joins the citizens of the Dutch East Indies who are swallowed up past large iron gates. Grasping tightly on Johny's hand and firmly pressing baby Rene deeper into the safety of her bosom, Vicky attempts to appear unscathed by keeping a scowl on her face!

No one needs to know about the pure terror causing the pounding of her heart inside her chest.

The lines for processing are long and the wait grows unbearable for the youngest citizens. Numerous children begin crying including Johny who clutches on to his mother. Vicky bends down close to her little boy's ear, softly sings "Terang Bulan," the beautiful, krontjong melody loved on the islands. Thankfully, Rene is asleep on her chest as Vicky's singing brings comfort to bystanders who well up with tears, including the Indonesian soldier escorting them into the compound.

Eventually, it is the Meijer/Hall family's turn to enter the office where Vicky and Kasmenah are informed they could be separated. As a full blood Indonesian, Kasmenah qualifies to be interred at a less restricted detention camp located ten miles further north. Citizens of more than 30 percent European ethnicity have to remain. Kasmenah begs the officer to allow her to stay. The official warns her that life would be much more difficult in Kamp Bandoeng if she chooses to settle in with family members but Kasmenah makes it clear, she did not want to be separated from her children and grandchildren. The officer relents reluctantly. He has been conflicted by hundreds of island mothers who refuse to leave their Eurasian children.

With a sigh of relief, the Meijer/Hall family are pushed along with the rest of the crowd to an area which looks as if it had been the courtyard for a school. Suddenly, Bernard and Fentje are violently pulled from the line by several guards! Instantly, Kasmenah frantically grabs the boys back but is thrust to the side as she wails in protest along with all the mothers whose teenage sons are ripped from their arms. The collective cries pierce the hearts of everyone around them. Vicky and her sisters' efforts to comfort their mother fail as Kasmenah crumples to the ground, sobbing uncontrollably. Agonizing wails of grieving mothers fill the compound. The Indonesian guards dare not show any sympathy, though many identify with the island mothers, as they continue to bark out commands to keep the large number of detainees moving!

Pushing ahead with the rest of the crowd, the Meijer/Hall family is directed into a large area which Vicky recognizes to be what once may have been a series of classrooms. Now with walls removed, the expanse stretched into one, long, space already occupied by numerous women and children, all of whom remain huddled in small, separate groups. The frightened looks on their faces resonates with Vicky and she makes a mental note to consider what she could do to help.

Directed by their military escort to sit down near a window, another guard points to a spot reserved for the Meijer/ Hall family. The space encompasses less than ten square feet as he outlines the area for another family standing directly behind them. Vicky is alarmed and speaking in Malay, exclaims that the space is too small for them to accommodate sleeping arrangements. Kasmenah, who recovers from her moment of grief, nervously gives her daughter a look of warning but Vicky ignores her mother and risking the antagonism of the Indonesian soldier, insisting on a bigger space. Without a word the guard relents, gives the spot to the family behind them and directs the Meijer/Hall family to a larger expanse in the corner of the room.

As the guard turns to leave, Vicky makes a request for food. He responds sympathetically and asks her, "Siapakah nama awak?" 'What is your name?' Vicky offers up her complete name of Christine Victorine Meijer-Hall, which distressed Kasmenah as the guard makes a notation in a small notebook who leaves without answering Vicky's request for food. Vicky reassures her mother that his entry will result in their family receiving favor.

Kasmenah is not so sure!

chapter 17

"A man's courage will sustain him, but when hope dies, his wounded heart stops beating."

PROVERBS 18: 14 NIV

Historically, mining for gold, diamonds, copper, iron ore and coal has been deemed one of the most dangerous occupation a man could choose to make a living. Fatalities occur typically from blasting accidents, falling machinery and collapsing roofs. But for Sgt. Harry Meijer and hundreds of his fellow prisoners, there is no choice.

After 'tenko', the roll call naming each prisoner by his Japanese number, Harry's group is led to a staging area where a guard bellows further instructions in Japanese. Harry explains to those standing near him that their detainers use this method to force prisoners to learn the commands given in the Japanese language. Within minutes internees are marched over in single file to a fleet of military trucks loading prisoners one at a time. Harry is grateful the same men he had encouraged earlier are placed in the truck with him. Like him, they are stressed about the perils of mining but Harry reminds them that their captors are to be feared much more!

The convoy travels for many miles, blessing the sergeant with a small window of silence as he reflects about the possible fate of his family. Harry renews his determination to remain strong in mind and body, although he is aware that he has lost a significant amount of weight. The sergeant noticed many days ago that his stomach had stopped rumbling. It amuses him that he does not think about food any more. Maybe he is hungry, perhaps not. Last night their captors must have forgotten to feed them because the evening broth and rice never came.

The trucks come to a halt and the prisoners disembark at the commands of the Japanese guards. Equipped with rifles which hold bayonets on the end of each weapon, the guards pose an intimidating stance. Each prisoner keeps his head down in submission to the Japanese instructions. In single file they are led to the large, imposing entrance of a cavern. While the black hole looked menacing, it is the sudden, strong odor of sulphur which takes Harry by surprise and he braces himself by holding his breath. It occurs to him that the deprivation of food, coupled with his lack of sleep has brought him to this weakened state and now the foul smell reminds Harry of a natural gas leak which had occurred on the air base in Bandoeng. It is obvious other prisoners are overcome as one falls to the ground. Harry responds by helping the young man up, but a Japanese soldier pounds him with a blow at the back of his neck. Sergeant Meijer immediately understands that he should let go but holds on until his fellow prisoner is standing upright. The guard continues the tirade while Harry stares blankly back at him. If he can pretend he did not understand the instruction maybe the ill-natured fool will turn his attention back to the other men who continue down the embankment. The blow on Harry's neck has left him in great pain but is not unbearable.

Slowly, the group of prisoners and guards travel the steep pathway which grows more narrow and darker with each step making it difficult to see. Harry estimates they have gone at least twenty feet underground and feels the temperature has dropped significantly. Thankfully the cooler air has caused the emanation of sulphur to subside. It must be safe to breathe the air because the Japanese guards are not wearing masks. Suddenly, under foot, dozens of squealing cave rats scurry away.

The cavern where the men have stopped is less than six feet high. It is the first time in Harry's life he appreciates not being tall. A smile comes to him as he recalls conversations he had with his mother addressing his concern about his height. She advised Harry to be grateful for his muscular build, blessed with strong arms and solid, athletic legs. Thinking about Mineoh sends a wave of painful nostalgia over him. Apparently the group stopped too soon because one of the Japanese guards yells at the prisoners to keep walking a few feet further when Harry notices water slowly yet steadily, dripping in tiny rivulets down the sides of the cavern walls. The ability to see is made possible by torches made with dried cow's dung, burning brightly, spaced every six or seven feet apart. He is thankful for the little bit of heat to help eliminate the heavy moisture in the air. The prisoners are instructed to stand along the wall as guards hand them each a small pick and hammer. Demonstrating how to excavate the coal by one guard, other guards hold out their bayonets.

The captors recognize that every prisoner is in possession of what could be two, potential weapons.

Each man is given instruction to fill a large metal bucket with coal then to be taken to a common area where small carts wait on a railway track. Finally, they begin the work but Harry is overcome by severe pangs of hunger. Maybe the hollow feelings from lack of food will disappear if he concentrates hard enough! The scurry of another rat across his boot sends chills up Harry's spine.

Soon the sound of hammering and picks ring inside the cavern. Oddly, it lifts Harry's spirit and he is content to work. For a while the acrid voices yelling incessantly of the Japanese guards fades allowing his mind to drift away. Here Harry's thoughts can freely flow without interruption.

His memory reaches back to the little bungalow he shared with his beautiful wife and their young son, Johny. Harry wonders about the new infant. Vicky never discussed a name because the opportunity never came but he longed to know if he had another son or maybe, a daughter.

Harry's thoughts drift to young Walter, regrettably wishing he had taken Vicky's advice about his child's custody. In contemplation, his father's fate and siblings concern him too. The sergeant finds himself uttering a prayer and it occurs to him that until now, Harry has never said a prayer.

Excavating the coal proves to be slow, arduous work but the exercise will help keep Harry's body strong and his mind clear. Required to fill up his own lorry, which is the cart assigned to each prisoner used to dispense the coal outside, each man given an allotted amount of time. Those who do not meet the quota are warned they will be punished severely yet today, as the long hours pass without incident, even the guards appear calm. Thankfully, every day is the same without any disconcerting surprises.

Towards the end of each day, overcome with a physical weakness he knows is caused by severe hunger and sleep deprivation, Harry says another prayer to continue without fainting. Not soon enough, one guard blows a whistle and yells a command in Japanese. It is required that all the prisoners place the chains back onto their ankles. Led back to the entrance of the cave, their tools of picks and hammers are left behind.

Grateful to be outside, Harry is surprised that evening has fallen and in the dark, sees how much the black coal has covered the uniforms and faces of his fellow workers. Returning in the trucks which had delivered them, the men are hungry and exhausted, each caked in coal dust, making them virtually indistinguishable. It would be wonderful to bathe, but neither water for bathing or drinking come their way.

Escorted back to the barracks by guards who at the end of each work day are more irritable and impatient, the prisoners are returned to the shacks where on each mat is the familiar small, plastic bowl containing rice and seaweed broth. The soup must have been sitting for hours because trails of ants had made their way to several of the bowls. Attempts to rid themselves of the pests proves to be futile and one prisoner jokingly asserts the insects will provide added protein. Suffering from exhaustion, the prisoners of Camp Miyata Machi silently drink their meager portion. As he stares at his companions, imprisoned by their musty, drafty barracks, Harry wonders how much longer any one of them can tolerate the evil human beings inflict on one another.

Thankfully, sleep overtakes them all except Sgt. Harry Meijer, the latest arrival in Camp Miyata Machi, whose tears pour down his coal-blackened cheeks, as he battles to keep from sinking into the abyss of despair.

That night, Harry's dreams are filled with visions of Vicky, Walter and Johny.

chapter 18

"The problem is not in dying for a friend, but in finding a friend worth dying for."

AMERICAN HUMORIST/ AUTHOR MARK TWAIN

The first evening spent on the concrete floor in the internment camp finds Vicky immersed in exasperation. Johny cried the entire night, like most of the children in the compound. Generally, Johny is an agreeable child, pleasant and docile but the hard stone ground, the endless noise of people wailing and unfamiliar surroundings have changed Vicky's usual, happy little boy. Finding ways to get comfortable on thin bamboo mats is difficult for every youngster, who are also restless and hungry! Anxious mothers try to comfort their children as the stress and panic of long-term imprisonment overwhelms everyone incarcerated in Kamp Bandoeng. Hours pass with the persistent weeping of the children increasing, leaving Vicky more frustrated than fearful and without further thought, violates one of many rules imposed on the detainees making her way towards an open door. One major directive prohibits a detainee from leaving her designated area without permission.

The frustrated mother risks severe retribution.

Immediately, the guard stops her at the entrance. With a pleasant smile, Vicky greets him with "selamat pagi," 'good morning.' The soldier does not return the greeting, demanding she returns to her designated space. But Vicky ignores him, pushing past him and demands to talk to the official in charge. Mrs. Meijer couldn't be bothered with cruel mandates which left innocent children hungry! Chagrined, the soldier is curiously amused by the spunk of the pretty, young woman. He had taken note of her obstinate ways when the group first arrived. In his estimation, her stubborn attitude makes her even more attractive and he finds himself following her to the building of the official headquarters. Upon reaching their destination, Vicky's escort jumps in front of her, opens the door, then gently taking the prisoner by the arm explains that he needs to enter while she waits outside. Reluctantly, Vicky steps aside but insists that he hurry!

Impatiently pacing across the narrow walkway, Vicky knows what the conversation will be with the officer in charge. Vicky Meijer could care less!

Several minutes pass before the soldier returns and leads her into an office and immediately, Vicky recognizes the familiar aroma of katjang ijo, the delicious, sweet soup served at breakfast time prepared with coconut milk, fresh ginger root, mung beans and palm sugar. The official behind the desk does not look up from his bowl and is noticeably irritated with the interruption of his morning meal, however, Vicky is not concerned about his displeasure as she launches into a tirade, scolding him for his neglect of the hundreds of children detained against their will! The officer is moved by the defiance of the woman standing in front of him, looks up from his bowl and stares into the face of an attractive, obviously Eurasian female. Setting his breakfast aside, he commands her to identify herself.

And for the second time in less than 12 hours Vicky tells an official her full name. He makes a notation in a book, reassuring Vicky that food will be brought soon. Believing he is sincere, Vicky proceeds to give him directions how best to handle the children with suggestions to make the children comfortable. Vicky Meijer bows respectfully with "terima kasih," 'thank you.' Amused, the official returns to his soup surprised that he is considering the young woman's requests.

As Vicky makes her way back to her assigned building, she is taken aback by the crowded conditions in the camp. While the majority of inhabitants are placed inside the brick buildings, hundreds more are left outside to take up living spaces on the ground. Bandoeng's climate is mild year round but Vicky worries about the outdoor occupants when the monsoons can send a deluge of rain for days on end.

Crushed by the endless sound of children crying, coupled with frustrated mothers pleading or scolding them, Vicky instinctively knows that a handful of Indonesian military personnel cannot maintain order for hundreds of people. Vicky's thoughts run rampant with ideas about ways to improve their dire living conditions. She must present them to the same official she met today. He seems like a reasonable man.

The following day, women forty years and older are instructed to make their way to a staging area. The location where the women are corralled is outdoors overlooking a large expanse surrounded by hundreds of tropical ferns, with towering palm trees dwarfing the women standing below them. Not yet forty, Kasmenah joins the group anyway, grateful to be outdoors and the opportunity to stretch her legs.

The women are told they will be responsible for the supervision of children when the large, metal gong is struck to signal for internees to line up for the one and only, daily distribution of food. These same women will also be required to provide haircuts for the children and elderly men. Women over sixty will be the caretakers for children ten years old and younger. These older internees are instructed to keep youngsters under control, occupied and out of the way of the daily ministrations of prisoner life. The assembly of women is dismissed with a reminder to keep the young occupants calm because any agitation is dealt with immediate consequences.

The day before, an uprising of several older females occurred including their demands to be released, violating the strict protocols of the prison camp. All of them were escorted away and not seen again.

Every day at noon the food comes but Vicky is enraged with the portions and content! How dare they think that children can exist on a small bowl of rice and a meager piece of dried fish! For the second time she makes her way back to the headquarters of the camp official and without permission, enters his office unannounced.

Vicky pleads with him for fruit, vegetables and coconut milk. Entertained by the perseverance of the pretty lady on the previous day, the officer informs Vicky she will be in charge of the meal prep in the kitchen. Not allowed to accept or protest, the woman prisoner silently submits.

The officer himself escorts her to another building, and Vicky is shocked at what she sees! Along the walls of the large space, Vicky's attention is drawn to dozens of receptacles which look as if they might have once been used as washtubs. Several women are bending down in front of them, stirring rice and water, some using wooden ladles, others using sticks made from bamboo. Scattered around the middle of the room, hundreds of opened canvas bags filled with fruit and vegetables are lying in disarray as flies, gnats and various other insects swirl around them.

Instantly, Vicky responds to the scene by scolding the woman standing near her. "Tutup beg itu dengan segera," 'close up those bags!' Without hesitation, the women close the sacks while Vicky uses a nearby "sapu lidih," the broom made from coconut reeds, effectively swatting away the bugs. The officer leads Vicky to another building resembling a large dapur with the arang stretching more than twenty feet along one wall. Vicky tells him it is a fire hazard but the official retorts rudely, telling Vicky there are more than five hundred internees to be fed every day. It will be her job to oversee the preparation and distribution of all food.

Vicky Meijer will begin immediately!

Hastening back to the family, Vicky wraps baby Rene in her slendang, grateful to hold Johny in her arms, under the watchful care of Kasmenah. Hetty and Dora, her mother explains, have been sent off to work in nearby fields to dig ditches. In the internment camp of Bandoeng, women and older children are required to hollow out ditches, mend fences, collect garbage and clean out septic tanks.

Returning to the dapur, Vicky organizes rice, produce, and fish with the women in attendance, assigning them specific responsibilities. Between the nursing schedules of baby Rene, she freely walks back and forth between the building of their assigned, family space and the building where the cooking begins. Vicky is happy to apply her cooking skills with the limited resources, feeling a vitality and urgency she has not had in months!

Her life has a purpose once again!

Several days later, the same officer comes to observe her at work, commending her for being industrious, even eager. The man has not yet discovered what a hard-working Eurasian woman Vicky Meijer is! In fact, she seizes the opportunity to tell him that the camp needs more meat and dairy products for the children. Boldly she tells him about an area in the compound that could be used to raise chickens where the children in the camp would learn how to care for the animals.

Detailing her vision, Vicky explains that raising chickens is simple and would serve the dual purpose of providing eggs and meat for consumption. The project would be a big undertaking in the beginning, but Vicky assures the officer, she will gladly oversee the project. The man in charge of Kamp Bandoeng is surprised to hear himself say that he will get her a chicken coop!

Overjoyed, Vicky returns to her kitchen duties, content to be working with what she loves most. Singing as she cooks, the other women join her in song and the atmosphere in the dapur becomes one of hope and possibility. With renewed enthusiasm, Vicky returns to her family, encouraging Hettie, Dora and Kasmenah with hopeful assurances that everything will turn out all right!

However, in the building the Meijer/Hall family members occupy, several, ailing, young mothers die and fate will require from Vicky immeasurably more love and compassion than life has ever demanded from her before.

chapter

19

"The measure of a man's character is what he would do if he knew he would never be found out."

ENGLISH POLITICIAN/ESSAYIST - THOMAS B. MACAULAY

In the culture of Japan, young men inducted for Japanese military service are routinely punished and beaten to make them physically and mentally "strong and resilient." While the majority of Japanese inductees are young men in their late teens and early twenties, the military machine of Japan consistently used brutal tactics in their training. Japanese historians record that severe, corporal punishment was used as part of intense discipline required for all of Japanese Imperial Army military personnel. "No soldier is made without beatings" is the code trainees learned early in their military experience.

To be weak was considered shameful, vastly shunned and collectively not tolerated.

Also, deep in their ancient culture is the repulsion of capture and imprisonment. The point is made clear in the Japanese Military Field Code of 1941: "Rather than live and bear the shame of imprisonment, the soldier must die and avoid leaving a dishonorable shame."

The utter revulsion most Japanese soldiers toward those who surrender was demonstrated against the prisoners every hour of every day in Miyata Machi prison.

Japanese historian, Yuri Tanaka explains that the punishment of the POW was based on the standard discipline written in the Japanese military code. Officers reprimanded their own men by slapping them hard across the face as Japanese soldiers accept the slap with a bow and thank you. Likewise, POWs quickly learn how to take a beating by keeping a passive stare and avoiding eye contact.

In the Japanese armed forces, it is the guards who are brazen in their contempt for all prisoners of war! Guards hold a special hatred for enemy officers who had been successful in civilian life, including commanders, physicians, business men, teachers, and chaplains. The men reduced to guard duty are, typically, soldiers who were considered too incompetent for regular military life and could not function in even the most menial jobs. Labeled the dregs of the military by their peers, guard duty offers downtrodden soldiers a platform to unleash unbridled power over the enemy. Without any restraint and no accountability, many of these demeaned recruits enjoyed inflicting injury with murderous intent upon their helpless captives.

In Camp Miyata Machi, Harry and his colleagues learn the rules of the camp quickly. Every detail of life is controlled by their captors, which include falling into line for the morning roll call, "tenko," learning the precise method of rolling up their mats, knowing the exact formation required before entering and exiting the mine, the timing of each step he takes or the way the he lifts his bowl to his mouth to consume the rice. Every movement is monitored and each activity is conducted with prisoners keeping their heads bowed and eyes directed downward at all times. Men are beaten for unintentionally looking up.

Routinely, Harry witnesses vicious thrashings of men who did not respond "quickly enough" to a command. Guards maintain menacing postures as they yell unintelligible orders, picking random days when prisoners are made to exercise until they collapse. For the hostage who could not recover, a beating or kicking would ensue, injuring him further. Men are pommeled savagely until their injuries prevent them from moving or communicating,

Brain injuries are a specialty the guards save exclusively for prisoner of war officers.

The majority of punishment takes place in front of other prisoners, leaving them helpless to assist their comrades. Captives who make any attempts to help injured victims are attacked themselves and typically receive a more violent beating. Breaking noses, smashing jaws, fracturing windpipes, rupturing eardrums, shattering teeth, tearing ears completely off, breaking fingers and smashing toes, leaving men unconscious where they lay, many succumb to the exposure of extreme heat or cold. Humiliation using profanities in the prisoner's native language and intentionally giving them orders to break a camp rule, only to attack them for the violation, are some of the tormenting measures inflicted upon their victims.

Open sores are the leading symptom of beriberi, the disease of malnutrition. Prisoners sit naked in the sun to dry out and hopefully heal their skin. If discovered by a guard, these men are inflicted with merciless lashings and whippings, anything to open the wounds afresh. Punishments for folding arms, changing positions while sitting down or standing, for talking in their sleep, snoring, for leaning against a wall, scratching their heads, or yawning without permission, are reasons enough for the Japanese guards to dole out more evil tyranny against their enemy.

Morally abhorrent to the captives is the practice of making prisoners fight against each other. If the detainee reveals any reluctance, he is forced to stand still, hands tied behind his back while the remaining prisoners are commanded to punch the victim in his face. The psychological effects of forcing a prisoner to hurt his powerless ally, is a tactic the Japanese believe would further break their prisoners' will. Sadistic guards relish the amount of power they have over their demoralized victims, transferring their own ineptitude against those they hate.

One afternoon, Harry and all of his fellow prisoners are made to witness the execution of two Australian brothers who were caught attempting to escape. Facing the firing squad, Japanese guards tauntingly jeer and mock them before they are shot. Harry feels sick to his stomach on behalf of the two young men and afterwards, vomits in the back of his barracks. The following day, ten more prisoners chosen at random are executed to "pay for the violations" of those who attempted to break free.

Every detainee learns that attempts to escape results in the immediate execution of dozens more!

As prisoners of war, most captives quickly come to the conclusion that survival largely depends on their will to live. Although each man is at the mercy of his enemy captors, a prisoner's will to endure is the strength he needs to be galvanized against all odds. To eventually find that strength varies and the coping methods used is as individual as the person himself. Harry tries to apply mentally what he is able to survive.

In times of great distress and struggle, the mind and heart of a person have been known to "detach" from the body, making the experience less painful. Harry has discovered that day dreams have successfully taken away some trauma, even if for a few minutes. Greater relief comes in the involuntary dreams at night, when the body undergoes deep sleep and a person is magically transported to a different time, a better place, surrounded by people he knows and the family he loves. However, dreams can be a double- edged sword. If the ethereal world of dreams could be captured, lived over and over again making dreams of times past are more desirable than the reality of present circumstances, Harry is tempted to return back to sleep with high hopes never to wake again.

"Okiagaru!" and with a jolt, Harry is forcibly roused from a dream about Vicky, Walter, and Johny. The Japanese shout of "get up!" ends his reverie and reluctantly returns to his deplorable, present situation! It is another day and having no access to a calendar, Harry and fellow inmates guess from weather patterns and the position of the sun that perhaps a year or more has passed since their arrival at Camp Miyata Machi.

Life for a man in prison under the Japanese-controlled military is measured in minutes. The initial gratitude Harry felt for the ability to work wore out months before. Deprivation of nutritious food, much needed sleep and no daylight, result in the illnesses and deaths of many companions, some he had grown to appreciate in friendship. Every day has become routine for Sergeant Harry Meijer. Entering the cave at dawn, before sun up and exiting in the late evening, working fourteen to sixteen hours a day, kills weaker, older, ill prone prisoner within the first few months. Dozens throughout the camp perish from preventable illnesses like dysentery, influenza, and whooping cough. Hunger becomes a constant enemy, relentlessly stalking them. In the early months, some of the men were lucky enough to catch a cave rat, save it and consume it after finding a way to roast it on an open fire.

As time passes, extreme hunger motivates them to become adept at seizing a rat and eating it raw!

The cave in which Harry was assigned, has expanded in height and depth as a result of the yearlong excavation, leaving more water on the cavern floor where the men had to work. Lately they have been using blasting powder, which made the job more dangerous. Coal lamps have replaced the torches and buckets were no longer adequate, so designated prisoners are used to push fully loaded coal cars up the same steep slope to the entrance of the mine. Harry is one of them. Considered to be one of the stronger prisoners, Harry and 'healthy' prisoners like him, are required to perform more burdensome tasks. The hard work is not his greatest concern; Harry's anxiety grows about inhaling the coal dust. For many weeks the Japanese troops keeping watch over them have begun wearing protective masks with no such provision made available for the prisoners.

With every passing day, each detainee has come to understand the reality of his circumstances. His captors have no interest in keeping prisoners safe or healthy. Hostages are treated like animals confirming Harry's long held conclusion that Japanese leadership strongly believed their captives to be less than human. The cruel physical and psychological torture each POW experiences, has begun to make Harry feel less human too. In the evenings, when few hours of sleep is allowed, some of his companions remain awake to unburden their hearts. Several have come up with nicknames for their Japanese guards. "Brutal Benny" and "Cross-eyed Charley" help remind them that their captors are fragile and human too. But Harry and his fellow inmates acknowledge their future is bleak unless a miracle occurs.

Many months into captivity, the prisoners learn of the motivations surrounding their enemy's tenets and moral codes for conquering other nations.

Culturally, the Japanese people are indoctrinated with the belief that Japan was chosen before time began to be the "Land of the Gods," making their enemies burdensome impediments and annoying hindrances to the Japanese cause of world domination! This value systematically deems the Japanese military justified in stamping out any opposition and using whatever means necessary to accomplish the sovereign mandate of global governance. In the military, Japanese troops are trained to believe they are fighting for a divine cause. To defeat and then subjugate the enemy is the saintly duty for every soldier! The adversary needs to be crushed into submission, and keeping him alive is merely a means to use him until he was no longer necessary. At the end of each day, prisoners are commanded to bow in front of the Japanese flag and forced to learn and then repeat back the story of its significance. Word for word in Japanese, the captives are compelled to recite the story of the bright red sun on the Japanese flag, placed there because the gods have chosen Japan above all other nations on earth, making them the superior race!

Nationally, citizens of Japan accept the sovereign idea that their Majesty, the Emperor, Michinomiya Hirohito and his family are direct descendants of the sun goddess, "Amaterasu." Publically, any resident is not allowed to question the supremacy of the emperor and his heirs! Their Emperor is free to rule with an iron fist, using the Imperial Armies of Japan to do his majesty's bidding as their command! No one dares to question the Emperor or his authority, including members of his own family!

In the camps, daily, all prisoners of war are reminded he is allowed to survive one more day at the behest of "the Sovereign One," Emperor Hirohito. The captive of Camp Miyata Machi is under no illusion that every move he makes is determined by the commands of their subjugators. If a prisoner is foolish enough to oppose a directive, the consequence includes torture and ultimately, a possible death sentence.

Harry is no fool…he understands his life is not his own!

Some months later, several prisoners arrive transferred from Fukuoka District #3. Harry routinely made a point to become acquainted with transferees hoping they could provide new revelations about ongoing conflicts anywhere. He is disappointed to learn that most prisoners did not possess current, verifiable information about the status of the war but one man, a pilot, was willing to share with Harry several, tragic circumstances he experienced at Fukuoka #3.

A pilot with the Royal New Zealand Air Force, captured off the coast of northern Java, Flight Lieutenant Benjamin Guyton was transported to the island of Kyushu on a cargo ship, along with 300 New Zealand army troops assigned to Fukuoka district #3. Early on, Guyton had heard stories about the Japanese commandant in charge systematically applying extreme brutality and torture. He tells of witnessing one unfortunate prisoner, an Australian, who was beaten and savagely beheaded in front of everyone in the camp by a guard the prisoners nicknamed "the beast." The reason given was "hanko;" insubordination.

Over many weeks, officer Guyton shares more anecdotal, horrific accounts with Harry.

In Fukuoka #3 one morning, after "tenko," all captives of the camp are ordered to remain at attention. Random numbers were called out as a Japanese soldier pulled slips of paper out of a plastic bowl. Each prisoner, whose number corresponded, was ordered to make his way to the front of the staging area. This particular morning, twelve names were called. The New Zealander feels his heart beating fast. By now, Guyton knew the methods used by the guards to demoralize their captives. As prisoners are lined up, without warning, six Japanese soldiers make their way less than fifteen feet across from twelve chosen prisoners and begin shooting. The gunfire was deafening and commenced for almost five minutes while the rest of the prisoners watch in horror.

No explanation was given and for the New Zealander, the message was loud and clear! Their captors were free to use any method to physically or mentally torture their prisoners! Prisoners who witness the bloodshed were commanded to pick up the bleeding corpses, while remaining POWs were loaded on to utility vehicles to be driven to the mines.

Officer Guyton said he heard stories of Japanese troops, burying prisoners alive, practiced with chemical experiments on other POWs, as other prisoners were forced to witness the Japanese guards torturing their fellow inmates and while some victims are still alive, cutting thighs, buttocks and waistlines to perform abominable acts of cannibalism. In another example he tells of the mine in which he worked while waist-deep in water, making the burden of excavating the coal insurmountable. Requests to drain the water were ignored, causing several men to protest and stop working. They were taken away, never to be seen again.

Benjamin Guyton and Harry become friends in prison camp #9. The officers' prison quarters at Miyata Machi were filled to capacity, so Guyton is assigned to barracks number 238 joining the noncommissioned officers. Whenever possible, Harry and his new friend encourage each other, working closely together inside the mine. It is good to have a mate to confide in, someone trustworthy. Ben is a sympathetic listener allowing Harry to vent! Together both men agree that their captors are misanthropic, dangerous individuals but each man understands that the horrors of captivity cannot overtake the desire to survive! Harry doesn't mind admitting to his new friend that three years in the horrific circumstances of imprisonment, he has battled numerous bouts of extreme depression.

Harry is heartsick! He is beyond exasperation and outrage. Their captors derive great pleasure in the psychological and physical torment of the prisoners. In the middle of the night, sirens would begin to blare all over the camp to keep the men awake, other times, randomly chosen prisoners, would be required to stand still all day in the blazing sun, or freezing cold. The deplorable conditions of prison life including lack of proper sanitation facilities, insufficient dietary provisions and the inadequate supply of clean water cause rampant dehydration, dysentery, and diarrhea. The only relief Harry Meijer experiences is on the rare days when the prisoners are permitted a day off. He takes the opportunity to walk around an enclosure, the area of 30 x 60 feet allowed as free space. There prisoners are be able to congregate and Harry uses the opportunity to engage them in conversations about freedom, justice, love of family and loves to share his dream of one day, moving to the great country, United States of America! Enthusiastically, he tells them about George Washington, Thomas Jefferson, and Abraham Lincoln, and everything he remembers about the United States Constitution. Harry passionately declares that one day, he hopes to visit Washington D.C.!

In his fervor, Harry forgets his audience is dejected and inconsolable! Many call him a dreamer, walk away angry and accuse him of spreading false hope. Harry's only cheerleader is his friend, flight lieutenant Benjamin Guyton. The majority of fellow prisoners are realists, convinced they will not survive another beating and live through endless days of forced starvation or endure another winter. But Harry is not dissuaded. He is convinced all he had read about that wonderful country is true! Perhaps one day, he and his beloved family will be able to live in America! While he has breath, Harry will cling on to the hope of seeing his loved ones again and taking them to the United States of America!

As the long, dreadful months in the concentration camp of Miyata Machi, on the island of Kyushu, turn into another brutal winter, the gaps between the floor and wall boards, and doors of the crumbling buildings, allow the chilling cold winds and rain to seep into the ramshackle structures where the POWs reside. Hundreds more prisoners suffer from respiratory ailments of colds, pneumonia, bronchitis, the flu, pleurisy, and whooping cough. Illnesses are ignored and unattended by medical staff. Many suffer from convulsions and delirium brought on by high fevers. Harry witness many fall to their deaths while working inside the mine, or standing during tenko or in the evenings, helplessly observing those who are ill, slip peaceably to sleep, never to wake again.

Numerous times, their remains are left for days.

Testimonies from other prisoners tell Harry their job is to assist the guards to dispose of dead bodies by systematically cremating them at a makeshift crematorium behind the foothills. Guards mock the dead by bragging to the captives there are no records kept of those cremated because the enemy is no better than dogs.

Yet Harry is one of the few who is grateful for cold weather. Winter months on the island Kyushu offers him relief from the hundreds of flies, mosquitoes and lice, which breed during the warmer months in the stagnant pool areas near the unsanitary conditions of the latrines. On a rotating schedule, Harry along with other prisoners, is required to clean the filth of the communal toilets using a small plastic bowl. Once, Harry caused a guard to laugh in derision when he asked for a pair of gloves.

The callous disregard for human life from his Japanese captors Harry has grown accustomed to but the archenemy he faces every day is the one inside him head! And his fellow inmates agree!

Despair is the common adversary. The majority of them had given up any hope to be rescued and Harry is beginning to believe it too. Receiving no information about the world outside of the penitentiary gates, prisoners have no news. Even a tidbit of information about possible victories with allied nations could bring life into their miserable existence. The black hole of misery Harry encounters daily, is exacerbated by the lack of news about his world beyond the high walls, razor wire, guard towers and armed soldiers.

Tragically, Harry witnesses time and time again, many prisoners perish within days of giving up hope. Like a bird of ill omen, his own mind taunts him, threatening to lead him into a pit of hopelessness from which there would be no escape!

Yet, Harry Meijer, husband of Vicky Meijer and father of three, is determined to beat down the anguish of his circumstances, renewing the vow he made to his wife that one day he would return!

chapter 20

"You will find as you look back upon your life that the moments when you have really lived, are the moments when you have done things in the spirit of love."

SCOTTISH EVANGELIST/ SCIENTIST/ MATHEMATICIAN - HENRY DRUMMOND

Life in the Japanese-run internment camps in Indonesia become more difficult with each passing year. By the end of the war, of the 200,000 civilians kept in custody, more than 45,000 would perish. Starvation, dehydration, communicable diseases and injuries resulting from beatings, rapes and torture would destroy the lives of innocent, non-combatant women, children and the elderly. Each camp is ruled according to the auspices and preponderance of the official in charge.

In Kamp Bandoeng, Vicky Meijer appreciates the empathy of the official in charge who demonstrated kindness towards his detainees. Horror stories of other camps are not intrinsic of the way he ruled. For the internees of Kamp Bandoeng, Vicky becomes the irrepressible advocate for improved sleeping arrangements, clean water and better food. She has found favor with the officer in charge of the camp! He is aware of her tireless energy, desire to help and in spite of the circumstances, maintains a positive disposition. In many ways, the Dutch/Indonesian woman has made his job easier. Not only had she been successful in organizing the distribution of food, she had a natural talent to galvanize others to cooperate and when he discovered her excellent cooking abilities, he chose her to prepare the meals for him and his staff.

This is a joy for Vicky because she is given special ingredients not available for the general population. Every week, she manages to pilfer and hide ginger root, garlic, extra onions and the pricey "trassi" shrimp paste, in her sarong to use the components for the food she and her assistants prepare for the massive population in the camp. Vicky is grateful that the official is a man of his word. Not only did he provide small cots for many of the elderly internees. In less than a month, he had several of his troops bring in all the necessary wood, hardware and fencing for the construction of several, large enclosure for the chickens Vicky had requested.

Vicky drew up the plans for the Indonesian guards to follow in constructing each shelter containing one open and one closed quadrant. She explains to them that chickens like to nest in the dark and lay their eggs in an enclosed space. Also, for chickens to remain healthy, the animals need a perch. With the specifications outlined by Christine Victorine Meijer-Hall, Kamp Bandoeng had the joy of three 16 ft x 24 ft chicken coops and within two months, more than thirty chickens were laying delicious, nutritious eggs. Kasmenah is delighted. The young children in her charge brighten up with encouragement, learning to care for the animals. The chicken coops bring renewed optimism for everyone and the guards of the internment camp seem less surly. For a while, a ray of happiness mitigates even the most ill-tempered officials in the encampment.

The joy however, is short lived as the population of the camp increases. Daily, new internees are brought in and the lack of clean water for drinking and bathing cause head and body lice to multiply, especially among the children, disrupting the daily routine of prison life. Many of the guards blame the chickens and Vicky is powerless to convince them the problem with lice had nothing to do with the animals. One day, she is informed that the chickens must go. Internees watch in despair as the coops are dismantled. The children watch and wail in horror, as they witness the slaughter of the animals behind the dapur. Vicky's attempts to comfort them is ineffective with many of their mothers laying blame with Mrs. Meijer for not preventing the destruction.

The sad chain of events offers up a temptation to give in to a renewed spirit of despair but Vicky cannot afford such a luxury because a new threat has entered the internment camp!

Disposing of waste in the rapidly growing, overcrowded conditions has become an increasing, more serious issue! If not discarded quickly, unattended waste becomes the breeding ground for the anopheles mosquitoes spreading the deadly disease of malaria in the Bandoeng Internment Camp. Vicky and her family are gravely concerned because most of its victims are young children. A group of women in charge of the nursing detail, try desperately to keep cold, wet towels available for those with high fevers, caring for the ill patients. Vicky's heart breaks for the youngsters who lay suffering and eventually die a painful, slow death. For months, the physicians who visit the camp, work to dispense quinine to bring down the fevers of the malaria victims and depend on the stronger, younger women of the camp to help. Vicky assists in organizing the schedules as doctors, nurses and volunteers work around the clock to save as many victims as possible. She is grateful young Johny or Rene have not been infected by the mosquitoes.

Months have turned into years, as the inescapable confinement and crowded conditions begin to wear down Vicky's initial enthusiasm. She is sad to witness Johny and many like him, limited in the space where they cannot run, jump and play. For hours, her little boy would be staring longingly beyond the barbed-wire fence. And now baby Rene joins him. Although Vicky is still breastfeeding, Rene is more interested in accompanying his big brother. Johny is kind and slows down the pace because Rene's pudgy, little legs cannot take big steps.

Vicky grieves daily for the normal life her sons will never experience.

Exhibiting characteristics including his keen sense of observation, Johny is beginning to make comments about their incarceration. Vicky and Kasmenah with the help of Hetty and Dora try to convince the toddler that their circumstances are temporary but the little boy doesn't accept their explanations! He has been entrapped in a confined space his entire life! Their imprisonment does not make sense to him and Johny continues to ask for Bernard and Fentje. There is no explanation for the curious child as the women continue to despair about the fate of the two brothers.

It is a daily challenge for Vicky to find something-no matter how minute-to be thankful for. One thing she is thankful for are the elderly men of the camp, who whittle small, wooden toys for the children which help occupy them for hours. And there are other blessings for which she is grateful.

Bandoeng is a beautiful city. Located in the higher elevations of Java,

Bandoeng's temperature remains at a comfortable seventy-five degrees year-round. The internment camp is situated near the famous Citarum River, and looking beyond the barbed wire fencing, Vicky could see the tops of the majestic, volcanic mountains surrounding the area. She is grateful the ground battle is being waged on the island more in the northern territory of Java which does not impact Bandoeng too much. Reliable news of the conflict claims that many of the battles occur near the shore lines and major shipping yards in the north. However, the sound of bombings and gun fire keep the anxiety level of the young woman high.

One day, the official in charge orders Vicky into his office. He makes a request which is confusing. Typically, he made demands but this time he gives her the option to refuse and if she did not want to comply, she would not be punished. He tells Vicky about two women, both residing in Vicky's building, who are very ill and had recently given birth. Vicky is aware of the two women because Kasmenah had assisted in both deliveries. The officer asks Vicky if she would consider being a "wet" nurse for both babies. It was a strange request, making her very uncomfortable. Vicky hesitatingly asks her mother for advice but Kasmenah did not give Vicky an answer. Instead, Kasmenah leads her daughter to the two infants, placing the frail, crying babies in Vicky's arms and replies, "Christine, melakukan apa yang hati anda memberitahu anda," do what your heart tells you.

Kasmenah's daughter did not give it another thought and before the day over, Vicky is breast feeding baby Rene along with two, tiny, vulnerable infants. Before the end of their third year in Kamp Bandoeng because of her indomitable spirit and unselfishness, Vicky continues to nurse six additional babies helping them survive as she becomes the inspiration for other lactating mothers to help many newborns at risk.

In the midst of her reality, Vicky struggles to make sense of her incarceration. Considering the challenges of overcrowding, the lack of privacy, experiencing conditions of many personal discomforts, she is grateful for the friendships formed with other women in the camp, especially from mothers who thankful for Vicky's willingness to nurse their babies, keeping them alive. Maybe, the war will end soon and she will be free once more!

Does she dare hold on to hope that her husband may still be alive? That would be a miracle indeed! But destiny has a different plan which could crush her fragile spirit and will impact the rest of Vicky Meijer's life.

chapter 21

"No man is such a fool to hold onto that which he cannot keep and give up what he can never lose."

American Missionary/Martyr - Jim Elliot

Most Americans know something about WWII in Europe. Some may claim knowledge about the war in the Pacific regarding the naval defeats and victories. However, the majority of Americans were taught little about the Great War in Southeast Asia.

Author and historian Werner Gruhl in his book *Imperial Japan's World War Two* makes the case that imperialistic Japan caused the great Asian-Pacific "Crescent of Pain" which impacted many hundreds of millions of people from China, Southeast Asia, and all of the numerous island nations in the Pacific and Indian Oceans, including South Korea, Vietnam, Cambodia, Thailand, the Philippines, the Wake Islands and the vast archipelago of the Dutch East Indies. Those severely affected included the wounded, maimed, raped, tortured, forced labor, starved, forced prostitution (comfort women), which result in millions of desperate, homeless, refugees, war orphans and war widows. The count of the dead when added to the number severely impacted and traumatized equaled the total population of the United States at the time with much of the Japanese Imperial Army killing done in cold blood. As the winds of war shift, Japan's Imperial Emperor Hirohito, encourages his army to step up the brutalization and killing of all POWs defined as political prisoners.

In August of 1944, his "kill all" rule goes into effect.

The prisoners in camp #9 are aware that something has changed. The expected routine of the daily roll call and work in the mines during daylight hours have been eliminated. In the middle of the night the men are ordered to get up and are transported to the mine to work extra-long hours under the cover of darkness. Other days after roll call in the mornings, they are returned to the barracks where they remain for days. While some POWs assume it is more psychological torture, others view it with a glimmer of hope, including prisoner of war, Harry Meijer. He is convinced it is a sign that the direction of the war may have changed in their favor.

But the varying interpretations do not help the men deal with their tormenting hunger and psychological pain. Harry does not allow his thoughts to stray from one theory to another. Sergeant Meijer needs to concentrate on staying alive! The horrific months of captivity have turned into years as the cruel, sadistic captors increase the ongoing, inhumane treatment of their prisoners. If fate decides that the Japanese will succeed to destroy him, Harry resolves to fight back until he draws his last breath. Daily, his resolution to remain strong in body and mind is sorely tested. In the beginning Harry had purposed in his heart not to be defeated, however, years of facing hopelessness and giving up the expectation of a miraculous rescue makes the struggle to survive more challenging.

Even clinging on to hope proves to be exhausting!

Random feeding times, inconsistent sleeping schedules and longer work details have made every captive more rankled than usual, including Harry Meijer. The relentless bullying, scathing, and repetitious shouting wears down his resolve to remain focused minute by minute. The guards' continuous harassment, fraught with their piercing shrills as the intensity of physical force increases when shoving inmates into lines, kicking them to the ground, propelling them downhill, adds to the degradation Harry battles every day. He thinks the maliciousness is accelerating because the Japanese captors are tired of prison life too. Quickly, Harry reconsiders this silly notion. What he believes about the enemy is irrelevant. But prisoner "hyak san, juu, yon" is disturbed that his desire to retaliate grows stronger every day! He works hard at self-discipline and not to lose control. On occasion, Harry proudly displays his restraint, mocking the guards with a smile as they bully him.

Inevitably the day arrives when unexpectedly, a provocation blows the lid of burning hatred inside Harry Meijer and he explodes!

A freezing cold, winter morning began with the routine tenko, however, this day Harry and his colleagues instantly notice a great number of prisoners missing. Risking their personal safety, many swarm their captors, demanding answers. The collective rage startles several guards who violently pull the shackles harder to restrain the movement of the prisoners. Harry's friend, New Zealander Flight Lieutenant Benjamin Guyton stumbles over the chains secured at his ankles. A guard near him slams the back end of his bayonet into the side of Benjamin's face causing him to bleed profusely. As the guard continues to assault Guyton, the prisoner falls to the ground, while another guard uses the heel of his boot to kick the lieutenant in the head. Impulsively, Harry, who is chained alongside his friend, swiftly begins to use the chain links around his wrists to punch the guard in return, sending the Japanese soldier to the pavement. Strengthened by the sudden release of adrenaline, Harry wraps the chain at his ankles around his adversary's neck but another guard grabs Harry from behind shouting profanities in Japanese! Instantly, a piercing, excruciating blow to the prisoner's head sends Harry reeling to the ground finding himself face to face with his New Zealander friend. Time stands still as brothers in arms exchange a quick glance, with the pilot offering Harry a look of gratitude.

In a flash, Harry realizes that his actions will be dealt with severely, yet strangely, is not concerned. Years of imprisonment and long-suffering need to come to an end and Harry is strangely relieved to go out fighting! Fear is gone, replaced by a strange warmth of peace. Life flashes by in the twinkling of an eye and Harry is prepared for the consequences of his actions!

Forcefully yanked to his feet, Sgt. Harry Meijer is pushed by the butt end of a guard's rifle towards the building of the commandant in charge. Looking back, Harry watches as Flight Lieutenant Benjamin Guyton is ushered in the opposite direction.

As he is led into the large building of the headquarters, Harry is sickened by the familiar scent of barbequed meat but takes a deep breath inhaling the familiar, delicious aroma of chicken soup. Of course, he knew the Japanese ate well, intensifying his resentment. The structure they enter is well-built, and comfortably warm in extreme contrast to the shabby dwellings he and his companions have occupied for more than four years. The thirty-year-old prisoner steels himself for the possibility that he will be beaten first and then, executed. The injury on the back of his head is painful but Harry is not bleeding.

Inside the office of Commander Yuhichi Sakamoto, Sergeant Meijer is reprimanded by an officer he has not seen before or could he be mistaken? Lately all of his Japanese tormentors look the same. Suddenly, the prisoner receives another blow from behind. The guard is screaming at him to keep his head down but Harry has already noticed the clenched fists of Commandant Sakamoto, whose flared nostrils and cold, sharp stare, Harry assumes is the precursor to a death sentence.

Surprising himself again, he is markedly numb, notably indifferent.

For a split second, it seems his mind or perhaps, his soul has left his body? As the sergeant remains staring down at the floor, droplets of blood from the second blow fall to fall, enraging the guard standing behind him. Sakamoto's voice which has risen to the level of rage, quells the guard's protest of the bloody puddle on the floor. Harry is amused that the frustrated commander is struggling to use Malayan words to describe his personal administrations of punishment against any prisoner he chooses, using his fists, open hand, clubs and swords. Yet, Sgt. Harry Meijer of the Royal Dutch Air Force is no longer listening.

Harry's mind journeys back to the dreadful years of suffering he and his fellow prisoners have endured. His thoughts are far above his circumstances, making today a special day he is proud to have served with so many, courageous, resilient heroes. Harry is strengthened by the thought of their collective patriotism and every man's perseverance in hope that they might survive to see their families again. In this vulnerable moment, Harry is grateful for their comradery, friendship and willingness to work together in the most challenging, seemingly hopeless situation. The majority of the POWs, regardless what part of the world they came from, demonstrated kindness to one another, glad to share the burden and in most instances, without complaint. At the end of a day full of difficult labor, intense bullying, constant harassment or severe beatings by their captors it was not unusual for prisoners to acknowledge one another with a smile or touch on the shoulder.

In the midst of these harrowing circumstances, it did not matter that one prisoner could not speak the same language of another. They are comrades, brothers suffering collectively! For Harry is honored to be among heroic prisoners of Camp Miyata Machi. Whatever happens to him now is incomparable to the admiration Harry feels for his brothers in arms.

Commander Sakamoto completes his lengthy, denunciatory speech and directs prisoner hyak, san, juu, yon back to his barracks. Harry is stunned! Lesser offenses have landed prisoners in solitary confinement, resulted in a severe beating and even execution.

That evening, Harry Meijer is glad to be alive, but feels great pain as he sees that the mat usually occupied by his New Zealander friend, Benjamin Guyton, is empty.

chapter

22

*"Those who died yesterday had plans this morning and
those who died this morning had plans for tonight."*

Anonymous

By the end of December, 1944 the Japanese-controlled internment camps in the Southeast-Asian/Pacific Axis are filled with more than two hundred thousand women, children and the elderly, all of them innocent citizens confined and cruelly treated as guilty, hostile enemies.

At the beginning of the Japanese occupation in the Dutch East Indies, the Japanese government allowed Indonesian officials to rule over each camp according to their own capabilities but those sentiments begin to change after the third year of occupation. As the Japanese military begin to take control of the internment camps on the island of Java, reports of increased beatings and torture including head shavings begin to circulate among internees.

Vicky and her mother discuss the small, yet notable shift in the guards' attitudes in Kamp Bandoeng. Both mother and daughter grow anxious about the meaning of the changes. The kind official of the camp no longer called on Vicky to prepare the meals for officers and he had stopped visiting her in the kitchen. Still working in the dapur, Vicky noticed the amount of food diminishing but didn't feel comfortable to complain anymore and she worried about rumors that he had been replaced. Vicky hoped the information was incorrect, reassuring her family that everything would all be alright. In her heart, she doesn't believe her own lies.

Putting up a brave front works for a little while yet the stress makes

Vicky feel much older than her twenty-four years. She is not looking forward to her twenty-fifth birthday the following month.

Soon, unverified stories turn out to be accurate on a day when the sound of the gong is heard unusually early one morning. With heart beating rapidly as Vicky Meijer carries baby Rene firmly gripping Johny's little hand, Vicky makes her way along with hundreds of other occupants to an area where the chicken coups once stood. The entire assembly of women look concerned, Vicky smiles and tells them not to be afraid.

Expecting to see the Indonesian official standing on the platform, Vicky is dismayed to see a Japanese officer occupying the platform. In broken Malayan, the Japanese official informs the crowd that staff has been changed and introduces a different administrator as the new Indonesian official in charge of Kamp Bandoeng. Standing stiff, at attention, the Japanese officer is bellowing instructions at the top of his voice. Vicky steels herself clutching her sons even tighter. Staring at the foreigner helps Vicky not to fear him. The strange man is short in stature with a noticeable, rotund belly. His struggle with the Malay language is humorous, oddly reducing her fear.

Vicky knows to fake a show of respect for the authority.

Menacing in his tone, the pudgy little man lays out more restrictive rules. The familiar, overwhelming anger, burns in her chest. The official continues to ramble on about the good fortune Kamp Bandoeng internees have to live in such a beautiful city. The affectation does not last long as suddenly, his voice changes in pitch and bellowing loudly, the rotund, little man begins haranguing about gratitude, reprimanding his audience about their selfishness. Vicky and her mother are in disbelief at the arrogance of the diminutive, Japanese official as he drones on. Indifferent to fragility of his audience and the whimpering of children, the narcissist appears to be in a trance during his speech. Vicky is convinced he is mentally ill.

After an interminable length of time, the weary members of the Meijer/Hall family return to their designated area, as Kasmenah and Vicky whisper in desperate tones what other changes will take place. That evening, neither of them sleep and the feelings of despair wrap their tentacles around Vicky's heart once again. She hears the quiet, desperate sobs of other women who are awake too and like Vicky Meijer, believe the worst is yet to come!

Daily, the newly inducted, Indonesian official of the Kamp Bandoeng requires all internees to attend his early morning assemblies. After several speeches, Vicky and Kasmenah realize his talks are meant to indoctrinate internees into sympathy with the Japanese effort to take rid the Southeast Asian nations of their colonists' governments.

The lengthy tirades continue for weeks. It is proof for Vicky and Kasmenah that the radical shift in leadership implies life will become even more challenging. Sadly, they are right!

For every survivor in Kamp Bandoeng, the overhaul and extreme modifications in the rules have made captivity even more unbearable. Impacting hundreds of occupants is the radical restriction in movement! No longer are they free to roam the open areas of the camp. The younger children, unable to understand the changes, become unruly making it harder for mothers to console them. Older siblings previously involved in caring for the chickens, have begun sulking, with several setting into motion a campaign of silent treatment against their mothers, mistakenly holding them responsible, standing together in solidarity for the betrayal of adults they trusted.

The majority of youngsters are inconsolable, adding to Vicky's grief! Mentally and physically exhausted, and tempted to give up hope, Vicky's sleepless nights weaken her more, making it difficult to manage her emotions during the waking hours. It is essential to remain focused on her mission and figure out how to help the multitude of discouraged children in Kamp Bandoeng.

Christine Victorine Meijer-Hall joins thousands of mothers in war-torn nations around the globe struggling to survive amid the ruin of family, country and hope.

chapter 23

"Don't walk behind me; I may not lead. Don't walk in front of me; I may not follow. Just walk beside me and be my friend."

French philosopher Albert Camus

In his book, *Hidden Horrors: Japanese War Crimes in World War II*, Japanese historian Yuri Tanaka makes clear that the forced enslavement of women for the sexual pleasure for Japanese soldiers could be considered one of the most serious war crimes in history.

According to hundreds of testimonies, girls as young as ten and women the age of sixty and even older were taken from countries under Japanese control and used as "comfort women." Thousands of girls and women from China, South Korea, the Philippines, Taiwan, and Indonesia were forced to give over their bodies to be used for pleasure or game by the Japanese military and their allies. Threatened with torture or death, the coercive method includes threats against family members and loved ones. Vulnerable young girls and women are kidnapped from their homes or taken from internment camps and against their will, compelled to yield to the demands of Japanese and Indonesian military commanders.

The term comfort women is used by the Japanese government to justify the perpetration of thousands of innocent females. The justification places the soldier as a battle-worn hero who requires to be comforted at the end of an exhausting day. Women are told to submit in order to prove unwavering national loyalty and are instructed to view the responsibility as their patriotic duty. According to author George Hicks in his book *The Comfort Women*, groups of girls and women were divided by their comeliness, with the best-looking ones destined for use by officers and all others to service the enlisted men.

Historically, sexual abuse during wartime was not uncommon. Every country participating in war carries the widespread, collective guilt of forcing millions of blameless girls and women into sexual slavery.

In the Japanese-controlled Dutch East Indies during World War II, Japanese and Indonesian military leaders take full advantage of the vulnerable, female citizens of the Indonesian islands and one ill-fated day, Kasmenah's daughter Christine Victorine Meijer/Hall, Johny and Rene's mother, detainee in Kamp Bandoeng becomes the latest of innocent victims on a day she will never forget!

In spite of discernible, major changes, Vicky is still allowed to maintain the job of organizing the dapur for mealtime, but the number of provisions has been greatly reduced! The internees who arrive late in line quickly discover there is no more food available. Feeling responsible and carrying the burden for those who go hungry, Vicky pilfers extra cooked rice and fish, concealing it under her sarong and under the cover of darkness looks for mothers and children who have not received anything to eat. Vicky understands the risks involved but she is driven by something stronger than fear. The burden rests on her to help everyone survive!

While organizing the women in the dapur this particular morning, beginning the usual preparation for the noon meal, Vicky is summoned to the official's office by an Indonesian guard who escorts her to the building. She is troubled. This officer in charge is not to be trusted. Since the weeks he has taken over leadership in Kamp Bandoeng, it is apparent he is a sympathizer with the Japanese cause to take over her beloved Indonesia. Familiar feelings of despair quicken the beating of her heart, making Vicky dizzy. Up to now she had observed the officer from a distance and always as she stood in the midst of many women and children.

This face-to-face confrontation will be different.

As the young woman is led into the building, she recalls the time she met with the first Indonesian official in charge, and the obvious change in the surrounding atmosphere frightens her. Instructed by the guard to sit on a stool located near the administrator's entrance Vicky sees the Japanese and Indonesian flags standing side by side makes her nauseous. The guard returns with a dozen more women, some approximately Vicky's age, others who are younger. Several women she recognizes from her building. Fear etched on their faces and like Vicky, all are visibly trembling.

Expecting to be called inside the office one at a time, Vicky is relieved they are beckoned into the room together. This new officer in charge is shorter in stature than she originally assumed. Vicky had only viewed him on the platform in the staging area. Here Vicky finds herself standing eye-to-eye with him. Frightened, yet slightly amused at his diminutive height, Vicky understands the full authority he represents. Without warning, the official's face turns red and with furrowed brow demands they bow! Vicky prays she has lowered her head enough but sheer panic grips her as she hears him articulate his demands.

Lecturing the women about patriotism, insisting that females were given the responsibility to demonstrate charity and generosity, the portly tyrant informs them they have been chosen to service the best, bravest and elitist of the Japanese and Indonesian military, the women are told they should feel privileged to be handpicked and favored above all the female population in Kamp Bandoeng!

Understanding she is in a dangerous situation, Vicky keeps her head down, praying no one in the room notices the tears pouring down her cheeks. As she turns her head slowly, carefully, first to her left and then to the right, she detects that other women in the group are silently weeping as well. As usual, the official is caught up in his rambling, too merciless to care for the collective grief in the room. With as little movement as possible, Vicky reaches out to touch the hand of the young woman next to her, who responds and undetected touches the woman beside her.

While the puny, egomaniac breaks out in delirious locution, thirteen young women quietly, clasp hands tightly, enduring the anguish of a sentence worse than death.

chapter 24

"In weariness and pain, in hunger and thirst, in fasting often, in cold and nakedness..."

APOSTLE PAUL IN II CORINTHIANS 11: 27 KJV

How is the human spirit expressed during wartime? Since the beginning of the human race, conflicts have demonstrated the best and worst in human behavior. Acts of bravery, sacrifice and benevolence versus shocking accounts of cruelty, savagery and barbarity define characteristics of individuals and their actions when placed under the tremendous pressure of war. Our understanding of World War II has been heavily shaped by scholarly works that explore the human toll, the resulting economic devastation, and the profound and enduring impact of a global holocaust.

The number of victims in every conflict is staggering and those numbers become impersonal when considered in existential terms. Yet each individual who suffer horrific death and the person who manages to survive, is precious, each with their private ambitions, aspirations, and longings common to all human beings.

In Camp Myiata Machi, Sergeant Harry Meijer wants to live! In spite of the excruciating physical pain and psychological trauma, he is determined to survive! Since the disappearance of his New Zealander friend, black clouds of hatred add to the never-ending grief which threatens to annihilate him, anew. Every day alive is torturous, days of waking every morning while it is still dark, facing the bleak hours of extreme, back-breaking work and returning in the dead of night to a meager bowl of broth are circumstances Harry Meijer must not focus on. He wills himself not to obsess about the increasing anecdotes by Japanese guards who eagerly boast about the use of captives as targets for bayonet practice behind the foothills, which explains why every morning at tenko Harry does notice many more of his companions missing. Increasingly, he grows numb as his mind dulls with a fog, making recent thoughts unclear.

The sergeant renews his vow to not give up! …but it is becoming more difficult. Harry must work harder to concentrate on the future, considering that his wife and children may still be alive! Dreams of a different land still gives him hope but is it false hope? Harry has heard that eventually America entered the war too, and what noble reasons would the United States have had to enter the conflict? Harry begins to consider that maybe the Japanese are correct in their assessment of their own superhuman superiority. Perhaps by divine appointment, they are the enlightened ones and the rest of the nations are to serve them. If countries like the United States, Russia and England are so great, why haven't any of those super powers come to the aid of thousands like him, to deliver them from these insane annihilators and emancipate them?

Life is cheap in war. Harry is no longer moved by the sight of dead bodies left in gutters or near the latrines, covered with flies, and with every passing day, prisoner hyak, san, juu, yon does not care. Harry's own body is suffering from tremendous weight loss, with exposed ribs and hips, shrunken arms and legs covered by thinning skin, and as he looks at the emaciated faces of his colleagues with hollowed eyes, protruding cheekbones, extended hair loss, and sallow complexions, Harry is forced to face the truth! They are all dead men, walking!

The wound on his head has not healed properly which caused a couple of minor convulsions, thankfully not witnessed by the guards. Harry reminds himself that his punishment, the injury and its accompanying headaches are a minor interruption, he is grateful to be alive!

In other matters of incarceration, Harry is careful not to become too friendly with anymore prisoners. Daily, new captives are brought in from the Philippines, New Zealand, Australia, Indonesia and surrounding island nations. The pain of losing new internees he befriends, to death and disease has become unbearable and witnessing hundreds waste away every day or dozens murdered by the vicious Japanese guards, breaks his heart!

Harry's musing about leaving the hell-hole alive become more challenging every day and lately he is distraught that the faces of Vicky, little Johny and Walter are fading further and further from his memory, until they appear to be characters he knows only in his dreams.

Lately his immediate circumstances have worsened. Never did Harry consider that the existing situation in the mineshafts could deteriorate and become even more risky. Hazards have increased as water continues to fill the cavern. Many of the prisoners who are too sick to continue with the grueling work are sent to work at the crematorium or put on latrine duty. Every day, new prisoners, younger and stronger are brought into the mining duties to replace weak, ailing captives. Early in their imprisonment, new internees begin with optimism and great courage. Many bring reassurances that they will be rescued. Over time, Harry sadly observes each one rapidly deteriorate into the same, morbid shell he has become.

Sgt. Harry Meijer serving the Royal Dutch Air Force, a prisoner of war, held against his will by the evil Imperial Army of Japan and its maniacal emperor, is slowly sinking into a mire of despair he has for so long managed to overcome and defeat. Just when he believes life in prison couldn't get much worse, hyaku, san, juu, yon is ordered to a new assignment.

Required to transfer from the work inside the mine to the activity outside, where coal destined for the steel mill has to be conveyed from the entrance of the mine to other railway cars, Harry is one of several prisoners chosen to carry large baskets strapped to his back, filled with coal. With the full baskets weighing almost sixty pounds, Harry is amused as he lugs the heavy load up the hill. Surely, it weighs more than he does!

After weeks of the same, physically strenuous routine, Harry believes he will die with a basket of coal on his back.

chapter 25

*"There is no limit to the amount of good you can
do if you don't care who gets the credit."*

RONALD REAGAN/ 40ᵀᴴ PRESIDENT OF THE UNITED STATES

The abhorrent practice of keeping children in captivity was one of many, dismal consequences of WWII! Young children at the cusp of discovering the world around them are naturally curious and full of questions, fortunately equipped with the physical and mental energy to seek answers. Childhood experienced in freedom, offers every youngster the privilege to explore the wonders of their environment. But when liberty is stripped from a child and their natural curiosity impeded by forces they cannot understand, children begin to retreat into a world of finding safety in silence.

Intensely distressed about new impending mandates made upon the camp, Vicky's concerns are greater for young Johny and her toddler, Rene. The majority of youngsters have become quiet, strangely still, not moving unless ordered to, as empty stares fill hollow eyes. Many find comfort in sucking their thumbs, remain in fetal positions, and begin soiling themselves. Mothers are helpless, grieving for their youngsters and Vicky is angry! She is desperate to find ways to help vulnerable families but frustrated as the personal hatred of their captors disrupts her ability to think clearly. Vicky Meijer is frightened by accelerating moments of brain fog coupled with an increase of depression and anxiety.

Life has become even more hazardous for all the internees. It is clear no one is allowed to leave their specified space without permission.

Although she is still required to work in the kitchen and dapur, Vicky is no longer in charge. The new official has replaced her with an Indonesian guard, who is surly, bad tempered and knows nothing about preparing large amounts of food using limited resources. Daily, Vicky feels her annoyance grow because current rules forbid all internees to speak without permission. The young woman risks being severely punished. Several days before Vicky had witnessed the brutalization of an elderly man who spoke out of turn, and the beating two women received when they rushed to his aid.

The worst for Vicky, are the revamped schedules which has made life ever more challenging as the predictable, monotonous, hours are spent sitting motionless confined to her designated, small space. Hours pass excruciatingly slow forcing Vicky to observe at close range the suffering around her. Gaunt, thin mothers and grandmothers of the camp, with the same, empty eyes, staring into space as their starving children, who previously protested loudly about severe hunger pangs, now lie motionless devoid of the strength to let out a whimper.

Vicky is no longer annoyed with the numerous flies, gnats, mosquitoes and other, irritating flying insects constantly landing on her two little boys. She is disgusted with her lack of concern about the rubble, filth and smell of her environment. Even the interminable, looming threat of death from starvation does not frighten Vicky Meijer anymore! The interminable hunger which used to prevent her from sleeping, no longer has the power to keep her awake. Sleep has become a lovely sanctuary and during the welcome hours of slumber, she hopes to take her last breath.

It has become difficult to remember the past. Repeated whispers from demons in her head tell Vicky life in captivity is the only existence she has ever known. For only a mere second or two, a flash of something familiar reminds the young mother it is a lie! Motivated to protect her two children, Johny and Rene's mother realizes she is powerless to shield them from the smell of; pungent body odors, coupled with the acrid stench of rotting garbage nearby, in the midst of filthy, green slime growing in stagnant pools of water which continue to produce untold swarms of mosquitoes. Rat-infested droppings on the slabs of concrete where they sleep, seem to have become something no longer troubling her and is probably the breeding ground of head lice.

Every pre-conceived notion the young mother believed about human dignity, respect, honor and decency, has disappeared. Attributes Vicky learned from Kasmenah about courtesy, humility, or morality, no longer defines them. Selfishness, laziness, self-pity, and poor sportsmanship feel like old friends now and the voices of demons seem to grow louder every hour, scoffing at lofty ideals in this place of death, decay and hopelessness!

The injustice of jailing innocents like Kasmenah has made a mockery of making those values more akin to those who possess a "Pollyanna syndrome." As a young girl, the children's novel about an orphan named Pollyanna was a character Vicky felt much empathy for but not anymore! The silly notion that their lives were worth enough to fight for, was a waste of time and energy. Forever burned into her memory will be the scenes in front of her now! Kasmenah, bone thin, clutching on to her grandsons, Johny and Rene. The permanent wrinkle on her brow expose Kasmenah's burdens of the entire family including her younger daughters Hetty and Dora, who have been sent out on daily duties of mending fences, collecting garbage and since the new official took over, had been relocated to another building on the other side of the camp.

Still there is no news of Bernard and Fentje! The stringent regulations forbade detainees to have contact with family members interred in other prison facilities. It has been years since Kasmenah's sons were taken and rumors that more young people had been transported to camps up in the north, exacerbates Kasmenah's angst about her two missing boys. Unable to ease her mother's suffering, Vicky decides not to tell Kasmenah about the meeting with the Indonesian official weeks before. She believes it was just another one of his imbecilic orations.

Vicky understands the reality of daily ministrations in prison life must be dealt with one minute at a time, regardless of her state of mind. Physical discomforts or mental anguish, debilitating sorrow and excruciating disappointments must be faced head on! The obvious malnutrition her sons suffer from, Vicky is helpless to address as Johny's gaunt torso reveals his thin, pale skin covering tiny bones. Even though she is still nursing Rene, his early development is impacted by her lack of nutrition. Ultimately, it does not matter! This mother of two little boys renews her commitment to do whatever she must to press on, Vicky takes stock of her circumstances, determined to continue. Perhaps the strength she needs to fight will come one second at a time! The lovely, young mother of Johny and Rene Meijer could not know, that soon, Vicky will plead for death to deliver her!

That day begins as usual in Kamp Bandoeng on that early, spring morning. Johny and Rene are calm in Kasmenah's arms, as Vicky sits in the corner nursing another baby whose mother had died in childbirth a few days before. In the beginning, Rene did not appreciate his mother feeding strange babies, and the toddler had made plenty of loud, vehement protests! Now, months later, it is a common sight as the little boy patiently awaits his turn.

Each morning, Vicky leaves the boys in Kasmenah's care for her duties in the dapur to prepare the noon meal. But today, the Indonesian guard who routinely escorts Vicky Meijer to the kitchen, has come for her hours early, directing her to the commissioner's office. Ominous dread overcomes the prisoner as she nervously takes smaller steps, and before entering the administration building, Vicky looks up, taking note of the beautiful sunrise over the horizon. How lovely it would be to be swallowed up by the orange glow!

With heart pounding, Vicky's fear increases as she is led into a different office opposite the commissioner's headquarters. This time, no other woman is present. Upon entering in the usual bowed position, the internee knows to remain standing, and Vicky Meijer finds herself facing an officer of the Indonesian military, one she has not seen before. With ominous dread overtaking her body, Vicky feels her knees buckle. Sheer willpower keeps her upright! The officer remains seated behind his desk concentrating on a file in front of him. Vicky assumes the folder contains information about the entire Meijer-Hall family, quickly takes inventory of the room surrounding her, which she can do without raising her head.

The plush, expensive furnishings in the office are notable, instantly taking her thoughts to the filthy squalor hundreds of innocents are forced to live in. Vicky's best and now familiar friend of bitterness steadily makes its way from her heart into her throat, forcing a cough while the man continues to ignore her presence. Vicky is used to the tactic, easily recognizing the serviceman's uniform which had distinctive markings of someone high up in rank. He could not be bothered with acknowledging the presence of a lowly, soiled prisoner.

The woman accepts it! Life lived in a confined space, surrounded by barbed wire and armed guards is a constant reminder that she is not worth anything at all. The internee does not realize the Indonesian officer is repulsed by the smell of her strong, offensive, body odor.

At the top of his voice, the escorting guard orders Vicky to lift her head, then quickly leaves the room. Without looking up and continuing to read the file in front of him, the officer asks Vicky, "Siapa nama anda?" What is your name? Vicky stands straight, defiantly lifts her head and answers him in her Dutch language, "Ik ben Christine Victorine Meijer-Hall, vrouw van Sgt. Harry Meijer en ik ben moeder van Johny Diederich Meijer en Rene Ludwig Meijer, dochter van Juffvrouw Kasmenah Hall!" 'I am Christine Victorine Meijer-Hall, wife of Sergeant Harry Meijer and I am the mother of Johny Diederich Meijer and Rene Ludwig Meijer, the daughter of Mrs. Kasmenah Hall!' She is hoping that responding in the Dutch language provokes his ire. Early on, the rules of the camp included that Malayan is the principal language used in every communication.

Vicky Meijer is right! The response infuriates the officer, causing him to stand up. Here is a woman with her dignity still intact making the conflict he experiences daily, more difficult. Routinely, facing him every day, are island women who could be his sister, daughter or a neighbor of time past.

Today another lovely creature stands before him, covered in filthy rags, reeking of putrid, bodily odors who does not fear the authority he represents. The irony fascinates him! Doesn't this woman realize he has complete power over her life and that he could snuff it out without question or inquiry? These detainees have to respect his authority in order for him to maintain order over hundreds of incarcerated citizens labeled as domestic enemies. As a disciplined soldier, trained to perform duties devoid from emotion or bias, the officer cannot expose his personal struggle no matter how many times he looks into the faces of women, children and elderly who could be members of his own family! The officer wonders how much longer he can remain committed to treat his fellow countrymen like traitors and in recent times, the official is noticing more resistance from many young women, predominately those with children, like this one, Christine Victorine Meijer-Hall.

Drawing on his most authoritative tone, the Indonesian officer explains that Vicky will be taken to another region in the camp by a guard who will give her explicit instructions. The prisoner Vicky Meijer is warned that any violation of the directive or attempt to escape will result in dire consequences for all members of the Meijer-Hall family. The officer is satisfied that the shudder in the woman's shoulder proves she believes him!

The twenty-five-year-old Eurasian prisoner is escorted by another guard across the camp to a military vehicle which transports her less than half a mile to an area off limits to all internees.

Beyond a large clearing, the scenery changes.

Out of reach from the hundreds of occupants less than nine hundred meters in the distance, Vicky and her armed escort enter a lush, tropical garden, filled with an expanse of beautiful foliage, including her favorite flower, the sweet, delicate, melati, sending fragrant, familiar odors straight to her heart and before she is aware, Vicky is weeping uncontrollably.

Years of speculation about her missing husband, watching helplessly as family members suffer, wondering about dozens of missing family members and friends, anxiously concerned about an unknown future, and the slow, steady annihilation of her dignity as a mother and wife, accumulates in this moment as tears blind Vicky's steps, causing her to stumble. The young, Indonesian soldier grasps the grieving woman preventing her fall, and quickly gives a look of sympathy as their eyes lock for a split second. He has not seen this face before.

Here is the latest catch in the abundant supply of females interred in the camp.

Gently supporting her by the elbow, the guard leads Vicky down a narrow, steep staircase leading them into a wooden structure with a long, wide hallway. At first glance, Vicky is startled to see that throughout the building, floors, walls and windows have been kept immaculately clean. The person she used to be would have appreciated the pristine, undefiled surfaces. Existing in the filth and decay of Kamp Bandoeng has reduced the woman prisoner to loathe the luxury her captors enjoy, including their clean-living conditions!

Following the guard into a beautifully furnished room, Vicky is amused that in the midst of the serious situation, her mind is distracted about money spent by the Indonesian government to keep their officers surrounded in such extravagance, Vicky struggles to hide her smirk. The guard must have noticed because he prods his prisoner with his rifle, reminding Vicky to keep her head bowed.

The guard is aware the reason the young woman is brought to this exclusive location. Like lambs led to the slaughter, the new recruit is in charge of escorting them daily, and every day, he considers requesting a change in duty. From the onset of incarcerating the citizens of Bandoeng, he was assigned in rounding up and separating the comely females immediately. Privately, the soldier has grown more conflicted with his own government as his sympathy increased for the numerous women and girls knowing the brutal, military elite have their way with each lovely victim. It sickened him to have escorted one who was only eleven years of age yet any concern he may have for the innocents would jeopardize his career and quite possibly put his own life at risk.

Leaving the latest casualty in the room, the guard returns to his post in the administration building until he is notified to retrieve the victim from her plight. Many times, officers keep their prey overnight.

The wife of Harry Meijer and mother of Johny and Rene, braces herself once again to fight off the fear which threatens to break down her renewed bravado. The words that Kasmenah lives by are resounding loud and clear as Vicky reminds herself that courage is defined by the ability to overcome the terror she faces at this moment.

Today, Christiaan Hall's fierce, stubborn, eldest daughter understands that within minutes, her life will never be the same! The loss of her freedom years before, compels Vicky to remember she will never accept the forced violation of sacred values. She refuses to be the victim! Vicky Meijer-Hall is proud of her immovable, obstinate choices! However, today is another reminder she has not been free to make her own determination in years!

A man dressed in the Indonesian, military uniform, which Vicky recognizes to be the attire of an officer, enters the room and greets her: "Selamat pagi" 'Good morning.' Vicky returns the welcome in spite of the cotton saliva stuck in her throat. She prays he cannot hear the audible, deafening beats of her heart.

Now, here in the reality of her circumstances, familiar demons tell her to run away and then mock the internee for standing still. Strangely Vicky agrees with them because inexplicably, her feet refuse to move! With chaotic, conflicting thoughts, racing to and fro, Vicky Meijer slowly, deliberately raises her head, defiantly staring at the person speaking. Taller than the average Indonesian man, the soldier possesses a dark complexion and as menacing, black eyes glare back at her, Vicky makes a quick assessment of his wide forehead and distinct, square jaw. He is old enough to be her grandfather. Neither kind nor malevolent but with the familiar detached, assertive tone of authority, the officer instructs Vicky to bathe in the room next door.

The prisoner knows to obey the individual whose power and importance can determine whether she lives or dies!

With head bowed, Vicky is met inside by a young teenage girl, who bows then instructs Vicky to close the door. Inside the crowded wash room, Vicky sees a large, metal tub filled with water and something oily floating on top. On a beautifully upholstered chair, sit two neatly folded towels, and draped on a hook behind the chair hang a new kebaya and sarong. The young girl slowly removes Vicky's clothing, leaving the garments on the floor. The mother of two is taken aback by the stark contrast of the torn, fetid garments she has been wearing and the beautiful outfit waiting for her. Overcome with guilt as she steps into the warm, luxurious bath water, Vicky refuses to savor the moment! The reason the authorities allowed Vicky Meijer the privilege of bathing was far from altruistic! She is no fool to think this is a gift for her sake.

Carefully, she washes her frail, thin body, inhaling the scent of the perfumed water, while the teenager scrubs the filth out of her hair. The young mother's thoughts turn to Johny, Rene, and Kasmenah who deserve clean water too, causing involuntary tears of rage to spill onto her hollow cheeks.

The attending girl departs from the room, leaving Vicky alone with the realization that what is to happen next will forever disrupt her life!

Apparently, Vicky Meijer has languished too long because there is an abrupt knock on the door and the officer, obviously annoyed, makes a demand for the prisoner to get out. Vicky's hands are shaking visibly making it difficult to dry her body and dress quickly. Tightly closing her eyes, then inhaling a deep breath, Vicky tells herself this directive is better than being led in front of a firing squad!

Many horror stories have circulated around the camp about prisoners who refuse to cooperate. Internees told stories of women who were taken away never to be seen again. Other uncooperative prisoners were forced to witness severe retributions of family members, and additional female internees were required to "service" more than one soldier, sometimes multiple in one day.

Mrs. Harry Meijer believes it could be much worse.

When the deed is done, the Indonesian officer, quickly exits the room but not before he reminds Vicky that she is to wear her own clothes back to the compound. Climbing out of the soft, large bed, Vicky furiously jumps up and down hoping to expel his semen, upon returning to the bathroom, she is ecstatic to see the oily water is still in the tub. Slowly Vicky steps in and washes herself, vigorously, until she is raw and bleeding!

Vicky Meijer wants to scream a ferociously loud outburst of protest but she is not sure why! Is she repelled at the thought of putting on her worn-out, dirty garments again? After all, the old man did not kill her, so why is she filled with rage? Surely, Johny and Rene's mother should be grateful to be alive to see another day? Yes, that has to be the main objective! Although the violation of her body is unfortunate, Vicky believes she is lucky to survive the assault. She must concentrate on sheer, unequivocal perseverance for the sake of her little boys. The safety and comfort Christine Victorine Meijer-Hall desperately seeks will not come to her rescue by crying or screaming. Either expression of ridiculous emotion might spiral out of control and cause the young woman to wail and never, never stop!

The wife of Harry Meijer must swallow this bitter pill of fate without complaint!

The same Indonesian guard escorts Vicky back to her family as she keeps her head bowed, not out of obedience but from the weight of shame and humiliation.

chapter

26

"Rejoice always, pray without ceasing."
I Thessalonians 5:16-17 NASB

Weakness invites more aggression during World War II and it is clear that the entire world trembled in the hands of a gang of criminals, a group of depraved, blood-thirsty, vicious hoodlums on the loose, seeking weaker, defenseless victims! All of creation groans while the burdensome tasks of good men fighting to rid the earth of evil, malignant tyrants, becomes more difficult. The United States, England, Russia, Canada and Australia and their European allies are spending more money, increasing their man power, building up their arsenal, bombing major cities, railway lines, bridges, and shipyards to stop the advances of the enemy. Forces on land, air and sea, work tirelessly, sacrificing their lives for the sake of preserving freedom.

In the Dutch East Indies, most of the ground, air and sea conflicts center around the shores of the islands, sparing the internal sections the horrific destruction most European countries suffer in the war. But the interior still needs defending and every ally utilizes the brave, many times, unrecognized, service of hundreds of underground freedom fighters. By the very nature and characteristic of clandestine activity, behind the scenes, these bold heroes lay the groundwork and become the rearguard protection for advancing military operations. The covert activity calls for individuals who are courageous and self-reliant enough to surreptitiously work alone. Sometimes disguised as laymen, these men and women bravely conduct business behind enemy lines to assist in the struggle for political and military freedom. Their services greatly benefit the Allies in the war effort, sometimes at a great price. If caught, many of the individuals suffer torture or death as the enemy would use violent force to expel information from them.

One young man, husband and father of two sons, named Hank Van Haasen, works on the island of Java to obtain and capture illegal radio equipment and weaponry from the enemy. Van Haasen, fearless and strong-willed, like so many of his comrades, hated the Japanese and their control of his beloved country. His years of dedicated effort ended when he is captured by the Japanese in 1943 and sent to the Japanese Seragan Solo prison in Djakarta. There he is interrogated and imprisoned. His wife and children, Art and Iwan, are sent to an internment camp in Surabaya, left to live in a small, enclosed building, holding twenty-nine other innocent, non-combatant women and children. Twelve-year-old Art, his mother and younger brother exist inside a small space in the water closet for the duration of the war.

The cost of war is great and most are fought to preserve an ideology of one country in conflict with the ideals of another. Men are willing to die for a cause they believe is greater than themselves.

Innocent women and children pay the ultimate price. Thousands of non-combatant women and children suffer, including the women and children of the Meijer-Hall family. Vicky's concern grows for Kasmenah whose health seems to deteriorate. Grateful that all of them were spared the onslaught of the malaria outbreak, Vicky understands that much of her mother's failing health is the result of anxiety about her children and grandchildren. She is grateful Kasmenah is unaware of her daughter's latest "assignment" and explains the absences to an increase of work in the kitchen. Vicky is resolute to protect her mother from further heartache.

This is one burden she will carry privately.

Vicky had already begged the guard not to disclose any information with Kasmenah and is surprised that he honors her request. Since the beginning of the Japanese occupation, the young guard has been assigned to accompany harmless, innocent women to the wolves and he is disgusted to be part of it. Whether the soldiers are Japanese or Indonesian officers, in his opinion, every one of them is an amoral, prideful individual, taking advantage of defenseless, helpless women. Most of the officers are married.

The routine for prisoner Christine Victorine Meijer-Hall to "meet" with the Indonesian officer was frequent in the beginning. At times three or four days a week. Vicky has disciplined herself to accept each ordeal with a detached and unafraid reply. It is possible because of the repulsion she experiences every time he touches her! Only once did he slap his victim for not responding properly. Vicky's jumping and washing routine afterwards proved successful in preventing an unwanted pregnancy.

Recently however, much to her relief, Vicky Meijer's schedule has been changed to a meeting only once a week. The young guard revealed to her that the officer had begun using several other women in the camp. Still, the regularity of the assaults make Vicky dub the incidents as her "snake pit assignments."

Vicky is relieved the appointments are less frequent because recently, she is overcome with severe nausea, including overwhelming episodes of vertigo.

On one occasion, Vicky faints in the presence of her mother, hitting her head hard on the pavement. Kasmenah knows the injury is serious because Vicky's eyes have rolled up behind her eye-lids. Believing her daughter is unconscious, knowing help will not come in time, Kasmenah bites Vicky's fingertips hoping it will revive her daughter, desperately calling her name. "Christine, bangun, kau baik-baik saja?" 'Christine, get up, are you alright?' Young Johny is frightened, pushing his mother from side to side to wake her.

But Vicky cannot hear their despairing cries.

Johny's mother is transported to another world who finds herself walking up a steep hill, drawn to a brilliant but not glaring, light. She becomes aware of sounds in the background, including a beautiful resonance similar to the sound of music, however, more refined, pure and exquisite. Arriving at the top, she is greeted by a figure which is the silhouette of a man standing in front of a radiant, celestial gate, encompassed by enormous, resplendent arches reaching high into the heavens. The man speaks: "Ga terug, mijn dochter, het is niet jouw tijd," 'Go back, my daughter; it is not your time.' No, no! Vicky wants to stay! The peace and joy which engulfs her being, going in and through her is beyond description. Vicky does not want to return and she protests, but her declarations are made back in the presence of Kasmenah and two sons.

With great enthusiasm the vision Vicky shares with them is a story she will tell others for the rest of her life!

That evening, bathing and dressing for another snake pit encounter with the officer who is impatiently waiting for her, Vicky keeps her mind fixed on the kind, gentle words of the Man in her dream who calmed her troubled soul.

The comely, Eurasian mother of Johny and Rene Meijer is convinced that one day, she will meet Him again!

chapter 27

"He is a prisoner and he has to follow. His path is prescribed. It is the path of the man whom God will not let go, who will never be rid of God."

GERMAN PASTOR/ MARTYR DIETRICH BONHOEFFER

During WWII, the world is trapped in dire circumstances of ethical proportions. Considering the monstrous evil being committed by the German, Italian and Japanese countries, what could moral, virtuous people do? The victims, whose lives are no longer their own, detained against their will, and suffering at the mercy of corrupt felons, are forced to do unspeakable things. The evil which war exposes, reveals the bankruptcy of man's soul.

While people of conscience debate the ethical concerns about the global conflict, the Allies step up their military campaigns using land armies, underground freedom fighters, tactical and naval support, and Special Forces, everything militarily possible to restore liberate those who were confined, oppressed, abused and unjustly imprisoned. Thousands of prisoners pray fellow comrades arrive to finally rescue them from hell.

Prisoner Sgt. Harry Meijer is among them.

Afflicted with growing, physical difficulty to carry the heavy baskets of coal on his back, Harry wonders how much more he can endure. Each morning, Harry wakes with excruciating pain in his knees, ankles and lower back, and now, newly burning agony in his shoulders and arms have caused Harry to drop his load several times. Miraculously, each time, it was not noticed by the armed guards!

The lack of proper nutrition has left him weak and Harry is disturbed with the routine wandering of his mind, making it harder to concentrate. He is grateful that he is not reduced to eat the rodents, grasshoppers and insects some of his fellow prisoners have been devouring. Still, every day Sergeant Harry Meijer waits for the miracle to be rescued and finally freed from his abyss of torment and suffering.

Of late, Harry is hoping death will take him but the thought lingers only for a moment or two. It feels unnatural for him…alien to his character. Intrinsic of his innermost nature demands that he does not give up!

For weeks, rumors have been circulating about a possible shift in the war but the internees had not seen any significant evidence of it or changes in the routine of prison life which could have reflected some truth to the unproductive gossip. Although their Japanese captors treat the prisoners with increasing physical and mental brutality, existence in Camp Myiata Machi continues with the same, consistent, horrific conditions.

Earlier in the month, the earth shook followed by a deafening, thunderous clap. Harry and his fellow prisoners assumed it was an earthquake. If there was another explanation, their captors did not offer up any statement, in fact, the guards had become more obstinate and irritable than usual.

And then, something did change!

Before dawn one morning, the men in barracks ni, san, hachi are awakened by the uproar and racket of another earthquake. Immediately, several men scramble, falling over one another as they jump towards the small door leading to the outside. Harry follows quickly behind them and instantly he recognizes what is making that volume and intensity of noise!

It is not an earthquake!

Simultaneously, all across the prison compound, camp sirens blare raucously, bringing together prisoners into the open as hundreds of them break out with cries of delight, shouting expressions of emotion, indiscernible because of the roar and tumult above them. Harry rushes outside, looks up and in the dim, early, morning light, and believes he is staring in disbelief at the familiar outline of B-29 bombers dotting the sky. Could it be true? Is it a dream? After all, he and his fellow inmates were in a deep sleep before the chaos began! As Harry takes a closer look above him and slowly brings his gaze across the expanse of the compound, Sgt. Harry Meijer realizes he is not hallucinating!

On the prison yard, Harry becomes one of hundreds of frail, reed thin men jumping up and down in uncontrolled exultation. Dozens of prisoners, who are strong enough, lift themselves onto the roofs of the barracks, shouting, and singing praises to the pilots above. In various languages, Harry hears one familiar word: "Americans!"

In a matter of minutes, Harry's depth of despair is transformed into a vocal emotion of exuberant joy. He is surrounded by fellow inmates waving their arms, jumping up and down, hugging one another, and yelling while running in the direction of the airplanes flying directly above them. The entire camp of Myiata Machi is in chaos and pandemonium but no one is confused! The commotion and upheaval is brought on by a collective realization that help in on the way! As the sun slowly brings the full light of day, the sight of more Allied planes droning overhead, make the most beautiful sound Harry has ever heard.

While in the distance, Harry sees a handful of prisoners immediately storm the headquarters of the Japanese Commander and hastens to join them. Inside, the prisoners of Camp Myiata Machi are not surprised to see the entire building empty. Gone are the guards, officers and civilian staff and in the offices, filing cabinets, desks and furniture have been overturned with papers, documents and empty folders strewn across the floor. Harry and his comrades realize that hundreds of records have been destroyed by their Japanese captors! The paper evidence of their evil deeds has been destroyed but the physical proof of their villainous acts was all around them!

The motivation to dismantle every reminder of his years in captivity returns Harry outside, and he joyfully participates with groups of other prisoners, tearing down Japanese flags and every Japanese symbol, including the numbers off each barrack while dozens of men use the bathroom facilities and shower stalls in the administrative officers' buildings reveling in a shower for the first time in years.

To bring order to the hour's long festivity, one prisoner, who identifies himself as a colonel with the British Army, climbs upon the platform of the staging area and asks for the officers of all nationalities to join him. Reminding the prisoners that they remain members of their country's military, the British officer makes a request for each prisoner to salute the Allied pilots flying over them.

What Harry sees next is a sight he will remember for the rest of his life.

Hundreds of emaciated, bone and skin, gaunt soldiers, clothed in tattered and torn rags, stand proudly in military formation, saluting the officers on the platform and the pilots overhead. In the middle of the crowd, a voice is heard singing the American "Star Spangled Banner'" and all the Americans join in. With tears streaming down their hollow cheeks, some prisoners take turns and sing their nation's national anthem. The solemn moments adding to the collective patriotism of each captive makes Harry even more grateful for the dozens of democratic nations represented.

The officer on the podium requests that every able man assist the prisoners who are sick. Many were too ill to join in the celebration. Sgt. Meijer is one of several selected to begin scouring the commander's quarters for food and bedding to aid the patients. Before he enters the building, Harry looks up at the crowded sky above once more. The entire day, American planes continue flying overhead as Harry joins his fellow inmates grateful for the Americans.

Yes, one day, God willing, Harry and his family will live among them in that great country of the United States!

FREEDOM!! What a word, what a feeling!

Liberated to pursue the dreams and goals for a better life, Harry and his colleagues spend the rest of the day in blessed jubilation! Walking without shackles on their ankles, able to freely move their arms, up and down, to run forward and back again throughout the yard without fear, Harry vows he will never take a simple walk for granted again.

Someone found a ball in the field where the week before several prisoners had been executed for unnamed offenses, and then a soccer game ensued. What a sight for Harry as he takes watches this rag, tag, skinny group, come alive and change into a boisterous, noisy crowd of men who for years, had been muzzled, tormented and enslaved.

The POWs with a medical back round find medical supplies and begin treating the ill and injured. Others begin digging trenches to lay their deceased companions in temporary graves. Quietly, with reverence and with the assistance of two prisoner chaplains, a funeral service is held and every man in Camp Myiata Machi #9, pay their respects to remember all of their fallen mates also keeping in mind those who are missing in action.

The activity of recovery includes every able-bodied man lending a helping hand with clean-up detail or kitchen duty. The officer chosen to be in charge explains that the Japanese had destroyed all the wireless radios making it impossible to obtain any communication with the outside. Understanding that the men are eager to return home, the officer reassures them that eventually an evacuation team would arrive.

Sergeant Harry Meijer doesn't trouble himself about it because he has been waiting four years and three months, counted more than 46,720 hours and felt his heart beat over a period of more than 2,803,200 minutes clinging on to hope he would live to see his family again. The sergeant of the Royal Dutch Air Force can tolerate waiting a few more days. Today he is free…truly, genuinely, authentically free!

Harry Meijer will never allow anyone to control him again!

Fukuoka Camp #9 After Liberation (Sept 1945)

chapter 28

"United in this determination and with unshakeable faith, in the cause of freedom, for which we fight, we will, with God's help, go forward to our greatest victory."

UNITED STATES ARMY GENERAL/34TH PRESIDENT OF THE UNITED STATES DWIGHT D. EISENHOWER

The greatest allied campaigns fought in the European and Asian-Pacific theaters have gone down in history, naming the now famous American generals Douglas MacArthur, Dwight D. Eisenhower, George Patton, Omar Bradley, George Marshall, along with U.K. Field Marshall Monty Montgomery and Prime Minister Sir Winston Churchill. As brilliant strategists, commanders and committed military officers, these gentlemen understood it was the combined efforts of the infantry on the ground, the bombers in the air and the naval forces on the sea which made victory possible.

On Tuesday, May 8, 1945, Germany surrenders. With their cowardly leader Adolph Hitler committing suicide eight days before, the Germany military machine is finished. Italy had capitulated and admitted defeat eighteen months before. The new government of Italy arrests Benito Mussolini and executes him on April 28, 1945.

Even though the allied powers had been successful in defeating Hitler and Mussolini, Japan vows to fight to the bitter end. The battles of Guadalcanal, Iwo Jima, Midway, Saipan, Marinara Islands, the Leyte Gulf, Mindoro, Luzon, Manilla, Burma, and Okinawa are major defeats for the Japanese, crippling the Imperialists economically and militarily. Yet they stubbornly hold on to finish their objectives in keeping the territories they still possess including the Dutch East Indies. With additional plans to invade Australia, convinced they could avoid prosecution for war crimes and preserve the Imperial system, the Japanese leaders mistakenly believe they can achieve partial victories in the Southeast Asian regions of the world. Allied intelligence discover the Japanese strategy to execute those plans in spite of the Japanese disabled, weakened condition, leaving the allied commanders with only one, clear choice, although not all agreed.

Generals Eisenhower and MacArthur discuss storming the beaches of the Japanese islands with more than 700,000 troops but American President Harry Truman is concerned that the partnered carnage and civilian death toll would be in the millions. While he humbly admits that nothing short of drastic measures would stop the stubborn Japanese marauders from blundering their way to world domination.

The Japanese leadership is callous about the sixty Japanese cities which already had been heavily bombed and decimated, equally untroubled by their civilian casualties. Even as the Allies loom overhead, invading Japanese shores, incredibly, Japanese authorities instruct ordinary, civilian citizens to sharpen bamboo sticks and prepare to kill American marines storming the beach!

President Truman, acting in his role as Commander-in-Chief of the United States Armed Forces renders a controversial order which, more than seventy-seven years later is still the subject of analyses, debate and fierce disagreements.

On the morning of Monday, August 6, 1945, an American B-29 drops the world's first atomic bomb - a powerful explosive, nuclear weapon fueled by splitting off the nuclei of specific isotopes of uranium in a chain reaction causing an explosion with the strength equal to that of thousands of tons of TNT - on the heavily-populated Japanese city of Hiroshima. Instantly killing 80,000 people with thousands more dying later from the exposure of radiation, Emperor Hirohito stubbornly refuses to surrender and three days later, on Thursday, August 9, 1945, another Atom bomb is dropped on the island of Kyushu in the city of Nagasaki, killing 40,000 innocent Japanese civilians.

Nagasaki, nestled in the narrow valleys between the mountain ranges of the island, reduces the bomb's effect, limiting the destruction to 2.6 miles. The mountain range also keeps the spread of radiation to a minimum.

According to Japanese historian, Tsuyoshi Hasegawa, history professor and Director of the Center for Cold War Studies at UC Santa Barbara, in his book *Racing the Enemy*; Hasegawa states that the Imperial country and its emperor still refuse to capitulate. Speaking three languages, spending years pouring over primary documents and in the face of fragmentary and contradictory evidence, much because the Japanese had destroyed most of the records, Professor Hasegawa proves that Japan was seeking an alliance with Russia.

With a deep understanding of cultural and linguistic nuance, Hasegawa explains that the atom bombs did not deter the Japanese emperor from backing down. The Japanese leadership in the military and government falsely believe Russia will join them in continuing the war.

They are shocked to receive Russia's response, as Russia declares war on the Japanese Imperialists on August 8.

Seeing no other alternative, the proud nation of Japan surrenders to the Allied nations on Sunday, September 9, 1945 and tragically, more than 10,000 Japanese civilians commit suicide "in shame," including their women and children, as they jump off the cliffs of Japan.

chapter 29

"An appeaser is one who feeds a crocodile, hoping it will eat him last."

PRIME MINISTER SIR WINSTON CHURCHILL

The surrender of the Imperial nation of Japan officially ends the global conflict of World War II. Although there were scattered skirmishes of enemy troops unwilling to admit defeat and continue in their rebellion to fight to their death, most countries agreed to a united Armistice, signing peace treaties, with the exception of Burma, Yugoslavia and India. All countries ceased warfare. Now the enormous task of each nation to repatriate millions of survivors who were ill, homeless, penniless refugees, internees, including prisoners of war, became a global struggle requiring the wisdom, compassion and effort of every available humanitarian organization.

The largest and well-known is the neutral, impartial world-wide organization of the Red Cross.

In 1863, five Swiss citizens set up a committee to look into ideas offered by Henri Dunant in his book dealing with the protection of the sick and wounded during combat. The five gentlemen, Guillame Dufour, a general in the Swiss Army, Gustave Moynier, a young lawyer, Louis Appia and Theodore Maunoir, both medical doctors and Dunant himself, called for an international conference adopting pertinent resolutions and principles, which included for all nations to form voluntary units to help war-time sick and wounded. Taking on the herculean task of alleviating human suffering, the Red Cross has developed around the world and currently continues to serve in both war and peacetime. For World War II, more than 104,000 dedicated doctors and nurses volunteered for military service under the Red Cross banner, thousands more, ordinary citizens volunteer to provide service for reuniting displaced POWs with their families. Sgt. Harry Meijer of the Royal Dutch Air Force is one of those blessed with the help of the American division of the Red Cross.

Founded in Washington D.C., on May 21, 1881 by the civil war-trained nurse; Clara Barton, the American Red Cross becomes the most prolific, productive and philanthropic organization in the world, receiving monetary donations from various, voluntary public contributions which include, wealthy establishments, wealthy individuals, successful businesses and the average layperson.

Help from the Red Cross evacuation teams for the POWs on the Japanese island of Kyushu arrives one month after the Japanese abandoned the prison camps. The Americans drop pallets of food and much needed medical supplies from their B-29's via parachutes to feed the prisoners, who are required to remain until they can be officially processed out. Only the strongest prisoners are given permission to climb up the hillsides of Camp Myiata Machi to gather up the cargo of groceries the freight platforms left behind and Harry Meijer is chosen to be one of dozens deemed "able and fit" enough to accomplish the task.

Typically, upon landing, parachutes partially cover the pallets which had never presented a problem. Until one day, unaware that one of them had struck down an electrical line, Harry grabs a wooden crate as he had done many times since his emancipation but before his mind could process what happens next, he is delivered a thunderbolt jolt in his hands which travels up his bone thin arms, ricochets Harry off his feet, launches him into the air, landing him face down sending his weakened, frail body rolling down the steep hillside. Other prisoners come to his aide and that evening, the doctor on duty explains to Sgt. Meijer that standing on the incline of a precipice had saved his life! Propelling down the steep, descending cliff forced the electricity to release him.

The scar inside his hands would forever remind Harry of God's divine intervention.

Tragically, several prisoners, although they had survived the horrific circumstances of the war and imprisonment, die after uncontrollably consuming large amounts of chocolate candy bars, bread and other sugar-laden foods causing their shrunken stomachs to swell, bloating with toxic gasses. Two had been Harry's friends and he had warned them to be mindful of overindulging yet he understood their fierce desire for food they had been deprived from for so long!

On the morning of Friday, September 21, 1945 Harry joins the first two hundred ex-prisoners of war of Camp Myiata Machi, as they are processed out and transported in utility trucks to the port city of Nagasaki.

While the men had been forewarned about the devastation of the city, nothing could have prepared them for what their eyes observe! The scene before them made Harry's knees buckle. His companions are moved with the same compassion as they survey the rubble left behind after the atomic bomb had leveled the city two months before. What was once a sprawling, port city of 40,000 people is now a wasteland, resembling the vast expanse of an abandoned, friendless desert. Harry is engulfed in despair and falls to the ground, weeping. He thinks of thousands of innocent Japanese citizens who die because the men they entrusted in leadership are hoodlums in high places needing to satisfy their lust for world domination.

Later that same day, the Royal Dutch Air Force sergeant Harry Meijer leaves the Japanese island of Kyushu aboard the American USS Mobile battleship bound for Manilla in the Philippines. Reclining on his bunk bed, grateful for clean sheets and warm blankets, Harry remembers the nineteen-year-old Australian soldier he met on their perilous journey inside the cargo ship bound for Japan. Hopefully the young man survived his incarceration.

The week it takes to make the trip to Manilla, Harry becomes acquainted with the American officials and staff of the USS Mobile. He is on board as one of 500 ex-prisoners of war transported to safety on the magnificent battleship which had seen harrowing war action on the seas of the Atlantic and Indian oceans, sustaining significant damage from Japanese kamikaze pilots (suicide bombers). The USS Mobile has become a ship engaged in missions of mercy.

For the first time since his incarceration, Harry prays that the Americans will be successful to find out the fate of all his family members. With tears of hope, Harry falls into a deep, peaceful sleep.

Arriving in the Philippines the following Friday, the rescued POWs are placed in various camps around Manila, repurposed as makeshift hospitals. Hundreds of dedicated American, French and British Red Cross doctors and nurses provide medical treatment for thousands of prisoners of war suffering from various injuries and diseases, resulting from starvation, beatings and egregious labor regimen.

Sergeant Harry Meijer weighs in at 86 pounds and 9 ounces. A battery of tests and a team of doctors diagnose him with a serious kidney ailment. Sent to the general hospital in Manila, Harry spends twelve weeks healing from more than four years of the inhumane treatment in the Japanese prison camps. Overwhelmed with the blessing of the care and concern of strangers, Harry feels indebted to them for saving his life, and he is highly motivated to heal upon hearing the news that searches for interment victims were becoming more successful every day.

The medical staff is surprised with the speed of Sergeant Harry Meijer's recovery.

Another division of the American Red Cross spends thousands of hours and millions of donated dollars helping prisoners of war in their goal of 'reunification', the daunting task of reconciling lost families. Their job is greatly impeded by the systematic destruction of thousands of files and documents by the Japanese both in prisons on the Japanese islands and Japanese-controlled internment camps around the entire Southeast Asian peninsulas.

Lack of cooperation by the Japanese government hinders the Allies ability to properly assist the Red Cross in reuniting all displaced families. MIAs, missing in action individuals, include not only those who served in active military and war duty, but thousands of non-combatant civilians, women, children and men who were taken by the Japanese, essentially kidnapped, never to be seen again.

Harry prays his family isn't one of them!

On Sunday, December 9, 1945, Harry celebrates his 30th birthday on the British transport ship the Carrcasian, heading for the island of Borneo. In restored health and having gained almost thirty pounds, Harry and several hundred ex-POWs are allowed to leave Manila repatriated with his company and the Royal Dutch Air Force Sixth Reconnaissance Group.

It should have been a day of rejoicing, but Sgt. Meijer is discouraged. The Red Cross had not been successful in locating Vicky, or his children.

Harry inquiries about his siblings and his father, Johann Meijer. He is informed that records are difficult to access because a civil war has broken out in Indonesia between the Nationalist islanders and Dutch colonists.

The Carrcasian arrives less than a week later in east Borneo in the port city of Balikpapan. There, former prisoners of war are told they are not permitted admission on the island of Java because the entire region had become unstable as joint political factions of Japanese and Indonesian rebels fight the Dutch military to maintain control of the archipelagos. Although Japanese Emperor Hirohito had surrendered to western allies months before, many high ranking Japanese officials had begun to support Indonesian nationals to fight for independence from Dutch colonialism.

The bitter struggle for Indonesian freedom is about to get ferocious and thousands of innocent residents of the islands are once again caught in the cross-fire of human ambition, just causes and vindication!

chapter

30

"So they left it for us to live with the legacies of the war. The question is, do we have the courage to overcome them?"

JAPANESE HISTORIAN TSUYOSHI HASEGAWA

The official end of World War II should have been a significant milestone for the Dutch East Indies, but that is not the case for the people of the archipelagos. The islands are trapped in a maze of disorganized and confused state of affairs because the fight for Indonesian independence is about to escalate!

In September of 1945, the victorious Allies were ecstatic to accept Japanese surrender with the Dutch maintaining their plans to restore colonial rule to the islands. But the Japanese occupation had created chaotic conditions both politically and economically, leaving Indonesia torn by contending individuals and forces. As propagandists grossly simplified and distorted the issues, foreign news outlets merely describe it as a dramatic struggle between good and evil with the good Indonesian people fighting against the evil, oppressing colonists.

Months earlier, the Japanese had invested in training younger Indonesian men creating a youthful military group called the Barisan Pelopor (Vanguard Column). Said to have a membership of 80,000 youth, they began guerrilla training months before, both educated urban youths linked to the lower-class of the towns and cities, led by the revolutionary Raden Soekemi Sosrodihardjo otherwise known as Sukarno, and his colleague Mohammed Hatta who also agreed with Sukarno about Japanese collaboration.

Vice-Admiral Maeda Tadashi in charge of the Japanese army-navy liaison office in Jakarta begins to use naval money to finance speaking tours for Sukarno and his Hatta. The Japanese plan to continue the control over the Indonesian military starts to unravel when the surviving middle-aged leaders of Java distance themselves from the radical, unpredictable youth organization. Japanese officials try to unify the movement with the more timid and realistic older leaders but the attempt collapses when the youth leaders insist upon more dramatic nationalistic gestures.

Within their own camp, the revolutionaries are sorely divided and the subsequent national myth that Indonesians stood shoulder-to-shoulder during the Revolution has no historical merit. Plans for an orderly Japanese-sponsored independence comes to a halt because the older leadership are uncertain what to do, yet did not want to provoke a conflict with the Japanese. Vice-Admiral Tadashi steps in and in his house in Jakarta has the declaration of independence drafted on the morning of August 17, 1945. The tumult left in the wake of the war and Japanese occupation, leaves inextricable, highly fragmented, Indonesian leaders, conflicted about their trust in the Japanese and in one another. In the midst of the rising conflict on the islands, thousands of civilians are left in occupied internment camps.

In Kamp Bandoeng, Vicky and her mother Kasmenah sense that a greater change is occurring. The sounds of gunfire in the distance can be heard more often, frightening the children. Food is even scarcer, and a few months before, the Japanese commandant informed all women to cease nursing babies not their own.

There is a greater Japanese presence in the camp and Vicky's usual Indonesian guard has been replaced by a Japanese soldier to escort her to the snake pit site. Brooding and impatient, the Japanese guard shoves her roughly to quicken her pace. Vicky did not think she could ever be frightened again but with the menacing, hostile foreigner, policing her trek to the appointments, cause familiar feelings of dread return and lately, no matter how hard Vicky concentrates in the midst of the assaults, the Man in her dream is slowly fading.

As each session comes to a welcomed end for Vicky Meijer, the Indonesian officer routinely engages in friendly conversation with the Japanese guard, offering to join him with a glass of sherry and a cigar.

Vicky is required to wait, standing against the wall. The young mother's feelings of humiliation have been replaced with a vehement rage because she is not allowed to bathe afterwards anymore, making it impossible to expel the filthy semen inside of her! With head bowed against her will, but grateful for the support of the wall behind her, Vicky trembles, as beads of cold sweat rivulets down her back. The entire episode reminds Vicky of her days spent in the corner of the room hunched over after Christiaan Hall had beaten her.

Engrossed in their conversations, the officer and his Japanese comrade ignore Vicky's presence. The sun has set before the guard ushers Vicky back to the compound.

When the heart dies, it dies slowly! Nothing is left except an empty, deep, dark chasm which envelopes and methodically kills the soul. Victims of abuse recount personal experiences of the body separating from the mind each time the body is violated. Johny and Rene's mother, silent, no longer able to laugh or cry, who has become an abyss of nothingness, a walking shell of flesh and bone, more dead than alive, returns to the cramped, squalid space confining her mother and beloved, two, young sons.

It did not take long for Kasmenah to realize what was being done to her daughter. Their lives have not been their own for years and Kasmenah is powerless to help. Kasmenah's heart is broken. Every day, she finds it more difficult to believe they will survive. For Kasmenah, survival has become a small matter because she is old. She has become aware that her daughter is raped each time the guard escorts her away, causing Kasmenah great pain. The thought of her grandsons never experiencing a normal existence is too much for the grandmother to bear.

However, God gives something special to children! As the years drag on, Johny and Rene continue to give Kasmenah the will to live. In their innocence, the two little boys impart a hope in Kasmenah which the evil of their daily existence cannot destroy. Johny is almost five years old, protective of the two women and his little brother. Each time the guard comes to fetch his mother, Johny finds comfort in his Oma Kasmenah's arms but clenches his jaw and his small hands turn tightly into fists. Three-year-old Rene no longer cries out as his mother is led out of the building yet repeatedly questions his Oma about Vicky's absence. With the wisdom of a grandmother, Kasmenah reassures her grandsons offering words of comfort she cannot believe anymore.

However, several months earlier Kasmenah had received uncorroborated news that Bernard and Fentje were still alive. Kasmenah is trying hard to be grateful for something which had not been confirmed because imprisonment forced survivors to hold on to the smallest strand of hope.

For Vicky, the sexual abuse is transforming into more than just a thing to loathe. Somewhere in her soul Vicky begins to blame her Dutch government, the Japanese, the Indonesians, the military and lately, Vicky finds comfort in laying blame on her husband for not protecting his family who were incarcerated by vile, subhuman creatures! Blaming organizations and institutions feels vague and arbitrary.

Yes, Vicky begins to fixate on a person she can hold responsible and his face is recognizable.

Harry did not protect her and he is not here to rescue his children!

Someone has to be held accountable for their suffering. Vicky Meijer's precious children and thousands like them who have been abandoned by adults who were supposed to protect them, capable adults who have failed the innocents. Vicky finds consolation in the thought that one day those responsible will answer to God for their negligence, apathy, and the deaths of hundreds, defenseless, little ones.

But the guilt weighs heavy on Vicky too. What more could she have done to help the youngsters in the camp? So many children have perished from preventable circumstances. Others have grown aloof and detached, especially if they lost a parent. Kasmenah's daughter struggles with the same, interminable questions which threatens to drive Vicky to the brink of insanity. Perhaps she should have been more demanding with her captors about the children's physical needs regarding food, clothing, blankets and medications. Surely, she should have done more! Youngsters are dependent on adults for care and safety. Vicky feels she has not done enough to help even her own sons. There must be somebody who cares, someone who can help alleviate this ongoing, never-ending pain and anguish? Will the injustice ever be satisfied?

Conversations had been flying around the camp about huge bombs blowing up the country of Japan but Vicky is oblivious to rumors now.

Hope based on innuendo and gossip resulted in overwhelming, debilitating disappointment year after year! Even if the country of Japan is blowing up, the Japanese military is still in charge in Kamp Bandoeng and Vicky Meijer remains locked behind barbed wire fences along with the masses of hundreds of desolate souls!

While Vicky troubles herself about the cares of humanity, the young woman is unaware that her own, private world is about to explode and cause a devastation in her life more than any bomb ever could!

chapter

31

"If the lessons of history teach us anything it is that nobody learns the lessons that history teach us."

Anonymous

The euphoria of Indonesian independence becoming a reality was beginning to sweep across the numerous archipelagos of Indonesia in the summer of 1945. Sukarno is named President of the Republic and Hatta as Vice-President because the political leadership of Indonesia is convinced that only Sukarno and Hatta could effectively manage their collaboration with the Japanese to overthrow the Dutch government.

The Indonesian youths in particular respond to the excitement of a possible revolution. Local Japanese commanders allow the youths to acquire arms and throughout the weeks of the 3rd and 11th of September, 1945, youths in Jakarta take over control of the railway stations, tram systems and radio stations in and around the principality of Yogyakarta, and the cities of Surakarta, Malang and Bandoeng. Mass rallies are held in Surabaya, 430 miles east of Bandoeng. More than 200,000 people fill the Medan Merdeka (Independence Square), on three separate occasions during the month of September, with Japanese forces and tanks standing in position around the perimeter. Sukarno uses his oratorical abilities to convince the crowds to disperse peacefully, confirming the impression that only he could prevent massive violence. The Dutch government however is not about to give up 350 years of colonists' control of the Indonesian archipelagoes!

As Dutch officials return to their previous held posts in the capital of

Jakarta after the Japanese surrender with global allied forces, they become aware of serious challenges to their reinstatements as indications of a revolution begins to emerge on the island of Java. Brawls and skirmishes sprout up in the streets between local Indonesian youths and Dutch citizens. The hatred among ordinary folks explodes organically, suddenly and out of nowhere! Whether in restaurants, cinemas, dance halls, early in the morning as commuters rush to work, in the middle of the afternoon while people go about their daily business, or late in the evening, weapons such as knives, chair legs or beer mugs are whipped out and used by assailants against anyone who is vocal enough to publically disagree.

The Dutch are highly motivated to reclaim and reoccupy Indonesia sending out directives to punish those who have collaborated with the Japanese. Seeking the help of the British and Australian military in East Indonesia, the youth rallies and demonstrations are put down, while Dutch law enforcement arrest many pro-independence officials.

The Japanese are in a difficult position. It is no longer possible for them to ignore their responsibility to the Allies to whom they officially surrendered, so the Japanese suddenly abdicate their loyalties to the youths and on October 3, 1945, massacre hundreds of Indonesian youths in the streets of Pekalongan. Fighting continues in the cities of Bandoeng and Semarang, with the youths retaliating and murdering up to 300 Japanese. When the fighting ends six days later, the death toll is 500 Japanese soldiers and 2,000 Indonesians dead. Meanwhile, the escalating guerrilla warfare increases the Dutch government's concern about the safety and lives of more than 20,000 Indonesian and European internees, mostly women and children, still detained in Japanese-held internment camps on the islands.

The military leadership of the Dutch government send out British and Australian detachments to release the prisoners but locally encounter so much resistance from rebels that sporadic airstrikes are used in attempts to disperse the youth, hindering the Allies' advance to free the non-combatant citizens in the internment camps.

Widely, irregularly fighting continues with no cease-fire in sight. In Surabaya, the heaviest fighting occurs with the help of Japanese Vice-Admiral Shibata Yaichiro who is in favor of Indonesian independence, giving the rebels free access to Japanese arms. Surabaya becomes the site for the heaviest battle for the Revolution.

On October 25, 1945, the British send in 6,000 mostly East Indian troops to help evacuate and free prisoners from every internment camp on the islands but armed Indonesians from another group called the Tentara Keamanan Rakyat (People's Security Army) recruit 100,000 youth to intervene. To prevent the release of the internment camp prisoners, the Rakyat kill the majority of the Indian troops. In early dawn of November 10th, in the face of fanatical resistance, British troops begin a bloody, punitive sweep with airstrikes and naval bombardment. At the end of three weeks, more than 6,000 Indonesian rebels are dead and thousands more flee the devastated city.

The revolutionaries loose much in the way of manpower and weapons in the battle of Surabaya, their sacrifice creates a symbol and becomes the rallying cry on behalf of the Revolution. For the Dutch, it is the turning point for them to face the reality that the fight for independence is made up of more than just a gang of affiliated collaborators without popular support. Sukarno's attempt at leading the revolution becomes tenuous as he calls for the British to arrange ceasefires, which lead many young revolutionaries to distrust him, causing numerous Indonesians to abandon their loyalty of Sukarno. Sukarno's base refuse to support his aristocratic and fascists' ideologies. As a result, several other political parties form in an attempt to unify the conflicts among the various Indonesian groups. With Sukarno's presidential powers limited, the KNIP (Central Indonesian National Committee) is given legislative power to be carried out through a working party called the Badan Pekerja KNIP.

Another faction of the Indonesian uprising comes from the leaders of Nahdlatul Ulama and Masyumi, two Muslim groups declaring "Holy War" in defense of their Indonesian fatherland, laying the obligation of fighting for freedom upon all Muslims. Local radio stations rally support for more fanatical revolutionary enthusiasm throughout major cities.

The older leaders call for political diplomacy, opposing the youth and their intent to continue the struggle with armed weaponry and violence. Other revolutionaries are sharply divided by desiring their own social, cultural and religious ideologies to be the defining identity for the archipelagos of Indonesia.

The competition rages between the elites, the ethnic and communal groups, the older and younger generations, and social classes. As Allied forces increase on the islands of Sumatra and Java, tensions mount and propel those who are whole-heartedly loyal and committed to independence to turn against those who seem apprehensive and doubtful. Mistrust runs rampant and in the name of "the people's sovereignty," young revolutionaries begin to intimidate, kidnap, and murder administrators, village leaders and policemen whose loyalties are suspect. In the confusion, actions made in the name of the revolution are difficult to distinguish from mere justification to rob, loot, extort and settle old scores!

It would take five years of civil war, economic and political chaos, and the deaths of thousands more to perfect the process of national unification.

chapter 32

"I have not failed, I've just found 10,000 ways that won't work!"

AMERICAN INVENTOR THOMAS EDISON

By January of 1946, the Dutch military had made significant advances on the island of Java, taking back control of Jakarta. Fighting continues between the rebels and the Allies, increasing in intensity in isolated areas. The Dutch secure the ports in Jakarta and reclaim control along the Citarum River, the major waterway in Bandoeng. With the assistance of the British and Australian military, who work alongside the International Red Cross, thousands of "politically interred" prisoners are finally, set free.

Sgt. Harry Meijer after waiting more than four weeks in the town of Balikpapan on the island of Borneo, receives news the American International Red Cross has located his wife Christine Victorine Meijer-Hall and their two children. He is informed all three of them survived their interment, are safe and residing in a catholic convent located in the center of Bandoeng.

Harry rejoices at the news!

Every ex-prisoner of war is allowed to enter the mainland of Java to be reunited with family members, with the understanding they undergo an extensive debriefing after reporting to their commanding officers at the Andir Air Force Base. The grateful father and husband is happy to comply as the twelve hour flight aboard a B-25 military aircraft safely returns Harry to his beloved island home.

During hours-long interviews, Harry is told his new child is a boy.

He is the father of two sons! No, three sons! Harry must never forget his eldest child, Walter.

Still finding it hard to believe he is truly free, Harry Meijer reflects upon the years of forced separation, which is finally over! He will take care of his family again, and Harry is determined to be the best husband for Vicky and an outstanding father for his children because life has given him a second chance!

Arriving at the Andir Air Force Base fills Harry with mixed emotions of relief and exhilaration as he stands on familiar ground. Surveying the expanse before him, Harry is reassured to see that miraculously, the war did not cause major damage to the base. The ex-prisoners are greeted by a full entourage of military personnel saluting them as they make their way to the commanding officer's building, where waiting for them is "rijsttafel," the Indonesian banquet-style meal. In a small ceremony following dinner, Harry and several of his colleagues are given promotions.

Sgt. Harry Meijer's rank is upgraded to Sergeant Major.

Afterwards, the commanding officer brief the former prisoners about the ongoing civil war between Indonesian revolutionaries and the Dutch government. He makes clear that the conflict keeps the rules of engagement of war, in place!

It is many more, very long days before Harry is given permission to be reunited with his family. For safety concerns, military personnel are allowed access outside the base with military escort only. Accompanied by a two-man, security detail, Sergeant Major Harry Meijer is driven to the Catholic monastery where his family resides.

Eagerly anticipating he will be greeted by Vicky and the boys, Harry is surprised to be received at the door of the monastery by several nuns. One nun steps forward extending her hand and introduces herself as the Mother Superior in charge of the convent. Gently, the Mother Superior directs him from the foyer into an office closing the door behind them, indicating to the sergeant to sit down. Their conversation is lengthy.

Back in the foyer, the men who accompanied Harry, viewing through a large, office window, see the sergeant suddenly slump over covering his face with his hands. Unable to hear any sound, but noticing his body visibly trembling, it is clear that the sergeant is weeping uncontrollably!

Long minutes pass before Harry is able to compose himself. The

Mother Superior escorts him out of the office leading him into a large auditorium. Set up to accommodate a large number of people, Harry is taken aback by the individuals who fill up the space. The room is filled with dozens of women and children seated around the perimeter and many crowded in the middle of the room. Never has the sergeant witnessed so many women and children together, all of them staring at him as he slowly walks past them. Perhaps they are hoping to be reunited with loved ones too.

Harry's gaze reaches beyond the center of the room, resting his focus upon three figures seated on a faded, well-worn sofa. Instantly, Harry realizes he is looking at his wife and sons for the first time in more than four years! Vicky, painfully thin, is holding a small child on her lap as the older boy desperately clutches onto his mother.

This man walking towards them is a stranger and as he bends down to greet them, Johny sees tears in his eyes and Mommy is crying too! Frightened and confused, the younger child on Vicky's lap begins to wail. Maybe this man is bad like the other bad men in the prison camp. Johny clenches his jaw and balls up his fists to protect her because no one will ever hurt his mother again and he will make sure of that!

However, Mommy stands up to give this intruder a hug and their embrace seems to last a very long time. How is it possible that she could be friendly to someone she has never seen before? Vicky had explained to Johny and Rene that they would meet their father but that didn't make sense. They have never known any man as a father.

Two little boys join hundreds of children like them who are too young to understand that a world war brought their parents terrible loss and in the face of untenable circumstances, is now impacting their reunion with deep wounds of untold heartbreak!

As the sergeant releases Vicky from his embrace, Harry sees that his beloved wife is heavily pregnant.

This was the news Mother Superior had given the sergeant, warning him that reconciliation could be very difficult. Sergeant Major Harry Meijer's wife is expecting another man's baby!

Seeing Vicky heavy with child hits Harry like a thunderbolt! And it is reflected on his face. Harry's initial look of tenderness turns into an expression of displeasure. Vicky feels the stiff and sudden release of his embrace as her husband makes a sudden turn, walks back through the crowd and exits the room.

Not surprised at his rejection, Vicky vacantly stares at her husband as he departs.

In her mind, she had played this scene over and over after the certainty of her pregnancy had been established. Vicky had made several attempts to lose the child by deliberately ingesting poisonous vegetation growing in the camp. Despair gripped her when she failed to miscarry. Fearing the worst, Vicky had prayed for the strength to throw herself down the narrow stairs leading to the officer's snake pit. The temptation presented itself each time Vicky Meijer/Hall was summoned but she lacked the courage to carry out the mission.

Finally, now is the moment of truth as Vicky looks straight into the face of the familiar monster of shame again. Harry's disapproval is minute compared to the disgust she feels for herself so what if her husband didn't understand! No one could fathom what she has lived through, certainly not that man who should have rescued her! Johny and Rene's mother cared less about Harry Meijer's opinion. The hardness in her heart is the reason Vicky Meijer survived!

Exiting out of the crowded auditorium, Harry collapses to his knees behind the closed door. The Mother Superior helps him up to a nearby chair, offering him a glass of water. She has witnessed many husbands react in similar ways. Nothing is new to the nuns in the convent. These women of the ministry have been dealing with dozens of anomalies resulting from the evil brought on by war and the Meijer family is no exception!

Understanding the pain of all four members but primarily concerned with the confusion of the two young boys, the nuns advise Harry to allow his wife and children to remain in the convent until the baby is born. They assure the sergeant that their safety would not be in jeopardy explaining that the entire building and its surrounding property is protected by the International Red Cross and cooperating Dutch military personnel.

However, the Mother Superior makes clear that the choice about placement of the newborn will be the burden for the couple alone.

Overcome with grief, Harry returns to the Andir Air Force Base without his family. Troubling thoughts are competing with feelings of anger, confusion and a strange sympathy. Although the Mother Superior had explained the circumstances of Vicky's pregnancy, Harry questions her reliability to know the true story.

Harry makes up his mind. The discussion Harry Meijer will have with his wife will include conversations not just about the baby but whether or not he will remain in the marriage.

Several options come to Harry's troubled mind, including taking the boys from their mother and raising the children himself. Almost instantly the consideration becomes a revolting one! Deep in his heart, in the private place where no one else can reach, Harry wondered if Vicky really was the victim the nuns claimed her to be!

Two weeks pass before Sergeant Major Harry Meijer returns to the convent. He understood his family's need to adjust to his reappearance. As he struggled with conflicting thoughts about the marriage, Harry definitely had made up his mind about the stranger's child.

On his next visit, the Mother Superior greets him at the door inviting Harry inside to meet with Vicky privately in her office. Although seeing one another again is agonizing for the Meijer couple, without the boys' presence, their conversation flows free from interruption.

Harry proposes to his wife he is willing to continue in the marriage if Vicky gives up the child.

Vicky is not surprised. Does she dare confess to her husband that she had made up her mind to give up the baby months earlier! The circumstances of conception were not of her free will and as far as Vicky is concerned, this is not a child she identifies with. Johny and Rene belong with her, not this stranger in her womb.

The decision is an easy one . . . she would not lose sleep over it!

After the day comes, Vicky Meijer will not sleep peacefully again for more than thirty years.

chapter 33

"Come tell me all these years your tales about the end of war, tell me a thousand times or more and every time I'll be in tears!"

DUTCH AUTHOR/POW SURVIVOR - LEO VROMAN

In January, 1946 the issue of civil war in Indonesia is raised in the United Nations for the first time which place pressures on both sides of the conflict. But the U.N. fails to put sanctions in place and the civil conflicts in the archipelagoes increase, with new groups forming and older, established groups splintering off.

One coalition is formed by yet another radical group named Persatuan Perjuangan (Struggle Union), resembling more like a gang of angry youths. The Communist Party (PKI) which was controlled by former activists and former underground leaders increases in greater numbers in early 1946 as did several more Islamic political parties. The Dutch and the elder revolutionaries try to solve their differences through negotiations, which include partial and limited independence for the Indonesians, specifying certain territories and limited political capital. The various radical youth groups who may have been splintered on ideological fronts come together united in one cause of 100 percent independence! They refuse to consider any suggestions about a partial independence! The conflicts continue to destabilize the whole country of Indonesia.

On a warm Saturday morning, February 2, 1946, two days after her 27th birthday, Mrs. Vicky Meijer with the help of a nun who serves as the midwife, gives birth to a tiny, baby girl. During the long hours of labor, Vicky had made it clear to the midwife that she has no desire to make any contact the child. She had remained detached from the child during the long, nine, agonizing months of pregnancy.

Yet the sound of the baby's cry betrays the commitment the young mother had made to herself. All of Vicky's resolve to stay disconnected with the child disappears and she asks the midwife to bring her daughter back. Trembling with mixed emotions and feeling the strong, familiar pull of maternal instinct she recognized from the births of Johny and Rene, Vicky puts the baby girl to her breast, praying her husband will change his mind. He must understand this child is another victim of circumstance! Harry's wife finds the courage to make a desperate phone call to her husband and begs him to reconsider.

Harry remains adamant! He does not want to raise another man's child! Vicky is left to choose between this innocent baby and her precious, equally innocent, two sons. Harry says she has six weeks to make a decision.

Life in the monastery with her boys and new born daughter is peaceful for Vicky. Cradling the child in her arms, toddler Rene gently touches his sister's tiny fingertips and strokes her head full of jet-black hair. Dark, brown eyes stare back at him and he giggles with delight. Johny, who had passed his fifth birthday two weeks earlier, asks his mother if baby has a name. "Mona," his mom replies, "zelfde als de beroemd Mona Lisa," like the famous Mona Lisa.

Vicky desperately loves her daughter, spending every, free minute with the child. Observing Johny and Rene fussing over their baby sister fills Vicky with hope. Mona is a beautiful baby and her mother prays Harry will change his mind. But six weeks pass quickly when a live-changing decision has to be made. During their third meeting, Vicky pleads with Harry to reconsider his ultimatum, however, her husband remains firm in his decision.

Steeped in turmoil with the thought of abandoning her baby, Vicky believes she could not, under any circumstances, give up on her own flesh! Mona is guiltless and bears no responsibility with the events which brought her into the world. Vicky is furious with the man she married who refuses to acknowledge the painful choice she is forced to make. What kind of monster was he? Surely Harry could understand that the child could die without her. How can he expect his wife to make a choice between Mona and her equally, two innocent sons?

Oh yes, Vicky remembers now! Harry had given up on Walter! This man, devoid of sympathy, lacking any compassion for his wife and her children. Vicky wrestles with hell itself and as the torturous weeks of ambivalence pass, the mother of one baby girl and two, little boys, makes a gut-wrenching decision. But Vicky vows that Harry will pay dearly for putting at risk the life of a child they could rescue!

Mona is placed with the care of the nuns at the monastery who assure Vicky she will be notified if a suitable couple becomes available to adopt the child, adding a warning that the identity of the adoptive family will not be disclosed.

Vicky loses sleep at the thought of strangers caring for her baby. A firestorm of thoughts, relentlessly full of accusations and self- condemnation flood Vicky's daily existence. Abandoning her own flesh makes her as cruel as the man she married! Why couldn't she make her husband understand? Vicky regrets signing those papers which turned Mona into a piece of throwaway merchandise. Where was her determination not to do that very, cowardly thing? Didn't she pride herself on being brave, unafraid, even a woman of courage? Perhaps she should have tried harder to find an opportunity to kill the Indonesian officer! The thought of murder had entered Vicky's thoughts each time he approached her.

Overtaken daily with self-directed remorse, adding to the bitter feelings of anger, the victim forgets she was powerless during her years of imprisonment and forced rape!

On the day of departure from the safety of the convent, inside the military vehicle, surrounded by her husband, Harry Meijer and their two sons, Johny and Rene, searing, hot tears of hatred stream down Vicky Meijer's cheeks as she looks back at the building holding captive another innocent child she could not save.

The tragic story of Vicky's daughter Mona would impact Sergeant Major and Mrs. Harry A.D. Meijer for the rest of their lives!

Former prisoners of war, Master Sergeant Harry AD Meijer and Vicky 1946

chapter 34

"A true soldier fights not because he hates what is in front of him, but because he loves what is is behind him."

ENGLISH PHILOSOPHER/AUTHOR G.K. CHESTERTON

War causes obvious damage to land, structures and all things physical but the manifestations of deep, psychological trauma and the emotional destruction upon its victims take years to expose. In most cases, victims want to forget the horror of abuse, leading to the suppression of severe traumatic events which result in serious disturbances years later.

Life continues for the Meijer family and they are once again residing on the air force base at Andir. Both Harry and Vicky learn their extended family miraculously survived imprisonment and internment, including Harry's brother Rudy, the test pilot who lives through two incidents in which Japanese fighter pilots shoot him down.

Relieved that young Walter and his grandparents endured through their internment too, every Meijer and Hall family member, receive assistance from the International Red Cross and Dutch government in placing them away from the hot spots of the civil war between the Indonesian nationalists, Japanese sympathizers and Dutch military.

Sergeant Major Harry Meijer, his wife and two sons are assigned to live in a converted garage inside the Andir base while they wait for regular housing on base to become available. The Dutch government in the Dutch East Indies, struggles financially caused by the continuing cost of World War II recovery and the added economic burden to fight the Revolutionaries in the ongoing civil conflict throughout the Indonesian archipelagoes.

Vicky doesn't mind living in the garage. It is luxurious and a place of safety compared to life in the internment camp. All her earthly possessions fit in two small suitcases but she is grateful to be alive, thankful that her entire Hall and Meijer families had miraculously survived the Great War. The twenty-eight-year-old mother and two sons only require lots of clean water for bathing, a soft, clean bed to sleep in and a small stove for cooking. Yet, Vicky's attempts to keep on existing within a normal routine of one day at a time, is consistently interrupted by the deep, wounding pain caused by the loss of her baby daughter, Mona.

Harry returns to his usual assignment at the Sixth Reconnaissance Unit with the Royal Dutch Air Force as the military remains engaged in continued war between enemy inhabitants on the island and the Dutch government. The island of Java is split in half with the majority of Dutch military on the south end of the island positioned for combat and the rest of military operations on the north, where Harry is commissioned under orders to "hold fire" unless directed to do otherwise.

For the citizens of the Dutch East Indies, it is a time of more fear and more war with ongoing sounds of random explosions, automatic gunfire, airstrikes, sirens blaring and the challenges of continued, frugal living.

Even in the face of the worst of circumstances, life moves on and one year minus one day after Mona's birth, on Saturday, February 1, 1947, Vicky Meijer gives birth in the Andir Base Hospital to another baby boy who she names Jack Arthur.

With the increase of the family, the RDAF gives Harry and his family accommodations in regular base housing. In the little bungalow, the Meijer clan lives for another two and a half years in a stress-filled environment which includes the inability to leave the base and a 7 p.m. curfew with the Meijer family grateful to receive the living arrangements and the protection of the Dutch military.

Violent oppositions continue to rage over the islands of Java and Sumatra, not only limited between the revolutionaries and the colonists but among the various rebels fighting for their differing ideologies. Bitter animosities result in violent clashes between the aristocratic administrators (uleebalang) and religious Islamic leaders (Ulama) causing the deaths of whole families, which morphs into the slaughter of hundreds more led by communist, leftists' attacks. Three hundred people are killed when fighting breaks out among the Christian Bataks (Toba) and the Islamic Bataks (Karo) because of an "ethnic" conflict.

The rebels on all ideological fronts continue to murder, torture and kidnap anyone they believe is against their cause. Harry and Vicky experience the horror first hand when the young child of a close friend is kidnapped and never seen again. The Meijer couple become fanatical about the safety of their three boys, keeping them in close proximity. Vicky does the shopping on base for food and necessities.

In the midst of caring for three little boys, Vicky's grief about her missing daughter increases. Triggered by the presence of another baby in the family, Johny and Rene begin to ask their mother about Mona and ask questions about her disappearance. Months before Mona's first birthday, Vicky had received news that a childless husband and wife had adopted Mona changing her name to Anna.

Vicky wept for the child but is forced to turn her attention to the new member of the family and the care baby Jack requires. Numerous distractions and constant demands for the family offer Vicky refuge from the strained relationship of the marriage too. Harry is allowed leave from his post up north only a few days monthly, making the couple's time together even more difficult. Outbursts of anger occur frequently between them, with each walking away frustrated as the conflicts between them increase and remain unresolved. Both husband and wife are too distracted to notice that a chasm is growing and one day would burgeon into the immensity of a grand canyon!

Harry's absence is a blessing for his wife as she endures a life of more war, a lost child, three, dependent little boys and a difficult marriage, challenged with the stress of a pain-filled past.

However, the couple demonstrate great resilience to remain committed to their relationship with the understanding that the immediate challenge for them, Sergeant and Mrs. Harry Meijer and family are trapped in the middle of another ideological and political conflict occurring right outside their door.

The Indonesian struggle for Independence proclaims to make life better for the majority of its citizens instead, sends every individual into a maelstrom of ongoing, never-ending misery. As death and destruction continue to rise on the battle fronts, the nation of Indonesia endures the spread of regional crimes including murders, kidnappings, muggings, embezzlements, extortions and corruption in various factions of leadership. Consequences of alarming numbers increase in malnutrition, illness and suicide in local municipalities!

All this civil war does not prevent the Meijer family from growing. The responsibility Vicky loves most is her role in motherhood and on Thursday, August 19th, 1948, Vicky gives birth again and names the child, Maudy Gloria.

Delighted with the addition of a girl in the Meijer family, my father is hopeful my birth will help mitigate the pain and bitter feelings his wife continues to suffer from the loss of her first daughter. But the addition of a baby girl exacerbates the acrimony between my parents, prompting Mom to claim that Mona would have been a wonderful, big sister for all her siblings. Within days, my mother is annoyed that I find comfort sucking my thumb.

In September, Dad receives word that his father, at fifty-seven years of age, perishes from complications related to heart failure. Opa Johann had survived his internment during the war, suffering from hypertension and malnutrition, only to experience extreme distress brought on by the civil conflict in his beloved country. Johann had never changed his position of supporting the Dutch government to remain in power in the Indonesian archipelagoes. He believed that Sukarno's policies would bring about more corruption impacting the citizens of Indonesia. The continued violence and subsequent division among people Johann loved on both sides of the civil debate left him grief stricken. My father deeply mourns the loss of his father. Their relationship had greatly improved when Dad matured beyond his teenage years and became a father himself!

The continued pressures of war is constant on my parents but they find some comfort when the news report that 110 Japanese officers are indicted, with several executed for war crimes committed during World War II. Dad is extremely happy to hear that Yuhichi Sakamoto, commander of the Miyata Machi Camp is among those imprisoned but is equally disturbed about the controversial news that Emperor Hirohito is absolved of all war crimes and considered a hero with some of the leaders of the free world. Unlike Johann, my father chooses to keep his opinions about all things political confined inside the walls of his own home.

With the family growing in number so is Dad's concern about our safety. He is frightened that soon, even the presence of the Dutch military on the islands would not prevail against the rebels, and eventually lose their ability to sustain adequate protection on Andir. Dad moves our entire family onto Opa Johann's expansive estate located in a remote area of Bandoeng. His four siblings and their families join us. Miraculously, the baboe and her family who had been Kasmenah's faithful servant before the war, is reunited with Mom and Oma, chooses to work for the Meijer/Hall families.

The war between the colonists, the rebels and the Indonesian Army carries on with increased, intense fighting. The Indonesian Army rapidly begins to emerge as a political force but is far from being a united one! Lines of allegiance blur as individuals take on opposing ideals about the strategy needed to win independence.

Generally, the distinction is between two main groups within the army. On one hand, soldiers who had no formal military training, understanding only guerrilla warfare desired a complete invasion by storming the capital. Others, who previously fought in WWII on behalf of the Dutch queen, no longer felt a loyalty to her released from that oath believe in taking a more "professional" role and ultimately are put in place serving as officials' staff, later taking on political positions.

Meanwhile, the Dutch proceed with their attempt at a federal solution, organizing a conference where thirty-nine Indonesian representatives of the rajas (Hindu-Buddhists), Christians and several other religious groups support the idea of a federal state with continuing an arbitrary connection with the Dutch. The plan is to incorporate the United States of Indonesia, with the Dutch queen as the symbolic head of a Dutch/Indonesian union of sovereign states. A ceasefire would be agreed upon, and the British and Australian troops would withdraw.

This peace agreement survives only several months, as both sides continue to distrust each other deeply and in both the Netherlands and Indonesia, ratification of the agreement provokes bitter, political controversies over the concessions each would be required to make. Realizing that federalism would not be an easy solution, the Dutch make a serious mistake by unleashing Captain Raymond "Turk" Westerling onto rebel youths, who had conducted further military training on the island of

Java. Westerling is known for using arbitrary terror with the understanding that he will decimate various youth groups which continue to spring up in the south side of the island of Sulawesi. In less than three months 3,000 Indonesians are dead with thousands of young rebels disbanding and scattered.

For the Dutch the cost of keeping a 100,000 active, military force in Java is a serious financial drain on the already war-torn Netherlands economy. They need to regain access to the products of Java and Sumatra, and to accomplish that have to conduct a wide, military campaign sweeping of both islands from their positions in Surabaya, Jakarta and Bandoeng. For now, they are successful in gaining control of all the deep-water ports in Java, securing major positions in Sumatra around plantations, oil and coal installations. On the fringes, outside of major conflict regions, rebel forces take revenge against Chinese aristocrats who were assisting the Dutch effort in their immediate areas, killing hundreds.

Conditions within the revolutionary forces in Java are chaotic in 1948! With more than six million refugees fleeing to the interior of the island, the production and distribution of rice and other life-sustaining products are depleted, causing the price of rice to soar and sending the economy into unprecedented inflation. However, the result benefits the peasantry, wiping out their debt, while legitimate wage-earners watch their incomes fall. With conflicting consequences, hatred and distrust dominate the two classes, causing major, violent and deathly clashes among the citizens. Finding no place to for safety, innocent, non-combatant, homeless refugees are caught in the violent cross-fire of the varied, always changing battles and tragically, hundreds die from unattended wounds and injuries.

In West Java, many militant Islamic guerrillas are led by a Javanese mystic named, S.M. Kartosuwirjo. Expelled from medical school for radical political ideas, Kartosuwirjo became active in Partai Sarekat Islam in the 1920's but was removed from membership in 1939 over policy disagreements. Taking advantage of a cult following of several hundred youths, he becomes head of the local Hezbollah guerrillas. In early summer of 1948, Kartosuwirjo proclaims himself imam (head) of a new state he calls Negara Islam Indonesia, more commonly known as Darul Islam, basing his political views on ideals on Islamic law which he believes should be administered by religious teachers of Islam. Opposing factions are disturbed to witness Darul Islam survive as a regional rebellion controlling much of the countryside of West Java.

By mid-September 1948, open warfare breaks out between PKI and pro-government armed forces. On September 18, PKI supporters take over strategic points, killing pro-government officers. Sukarno denounces the rebels and calls upon moderate Indonesians to rally behind him and Mohammad Hatta in support for his plans for a Soviet-style government. Thousands of Sukarno/Hatta military forces put down the PKI rebellion, killing prominent PKI leaders and more than 8,000 of their followers.

In the Meijer/Hall household, eight-year-old Johny and Rene now seven, take a trip with the husband of our family's baboe outside of Opa Johann's compound. My brothers return home with stories of seeing dead bodies strewn across country roads and along river banks where rebel forces have taken over the countryside. These rogue groups initiating full scale, guerilla warfare result in more localized victories resulting in an increase of civilian casualties but divide over rationalizations regarding the kidnappings and murders of innocent citizens. The Sukarno/Hatta team realize they have to find a way to strengthen and unify their splintered army.

Meanwhile Dutch forces make significant advances, taking back major towns and cities in Sumatra and Java, however, the Dutch military leadership make a terrific blunder upon the U.N. Good Offices Committee located in Yogyakarta, characterizing those in charge of the committee as 'contemptable'. The U.N. demands an immediate cease fire.

On December 31, 1948 on the island of Java, the Dutch honor the cease fire but guerrilla fighting continues in the interior as rebels refuse to stop with demands that only after the Dutch troops completely evacuate, will the rebels cooperate. The incident in Yogyakarta, infuriates the U.N. Security Council and with the support of the United States Congress, cuts off aid to the Dutch insisting they evacuate all troops and transfer power to the Sukarno/Hatta military retaining Sukarno as President and Hatta as Vice President. Negotiations and political haggling would continue for almost an entire year, with several top leaders of the rebel forces imprisoned for various, criminal offenses.

Under much pressure from allied nations, minus any fanfare, on December 27, 1949 the Netherlands formally transfer sovereignty over to Indonesia, and recognize the leadership of the Sukarno/Hatta team.

Earlier that month on Thursday, December 8, 1949, one day before Dad's thirty-fifth birthday, Mom gives birth to another little girl naming her Sonja Yvonne. The pregnancy and birth had been difficult. Mom experienced more than usual fainting spells. Months before, Mom's eighteen-year-old brother Fentje, had succumbed to pneumonia. Kasmenah is overcome with grief from which she never recovers. Burdened with the heartache of the loss of her younger brother, Mom carried the weight of Kasmenah's sorrow, greatly impacting her own health and sixth pregnancy with Sonja. Weighing less than five pounds, Sonja is born with the umbilical cord wrapped around her neck but the swift action of the doctor in charge saves the infant's life and much to Mom's dismay, baby Sonja finds comfort sucking her thumb in the same manner I have.

Like the majority of Indonesia's citizenry, the Meijer/Hall relatives cannot afford to wallow in despair. Every adult member and older children of both families feel fortunate to survive the dreadful years of war and imprisonment, with our parents joining thousands who remain devoted as a united front in loyalty to the Dutch government.

The conflict on the islands of Indonesia continues in spite of the efforts of the United Nations. Regardless of the new sovereignty, many regions remain unstable with the greatest oppositions to the Sukarno/Hatta unitarist movement coming from pro-Dutch, Christian Ambonese loyalists who regard the revolutionists as left-wing Marxists. Fighting continues between splintered groups not willing to capitulate to the tenets of the U.N. agreements and remain determined to institute their form of ideologist government.

Thousands of European/Indonesians grow increasingly anxious believing the state of affairs are worse in the archipelagos than when the Dutch were in control, becoming more suspicious about the pro-Communist Sukarno/Hatta regime, laying blame on them for the uncertainty of the future of the country.

The internal instability of the political and communal upheavals continues in spite of the Netherlands finally recognizing the Dutch East Indies as the Republic of the United States of Indonesia on December 27.

The Revolution formally ends, with sporadic, bloody local conflicts put down by dubious authorities.

In human casualties the toll adds up to more than 30,000 deaths by the time the revolutionaries cease fire. The collateral damage in that number is the majority of lives who were thousands of innocent, non-combatant Indonesian citizens. The death toll of the Indonesian revolutionaries came to be more than 15,000, while the Japanese suffer a loss of more than 1,000 soldiers. A number of 1,200 combined British and Australian soldiers lost their lives not including those missing in action with almost 1,000 Dutch military casualties. Soon, it became evident that beyond victory over the Dutch, the fundamental problems of social, religious, communal, ethnic, cultural, and economic questions still remain.

The Revolution has not resolved them after all.

chapter

35

"I waited patiently for the Lord; He inclined to me and heard my cry."

Psalm 40:1KJV

The new year of 1950 ushered in a war-weary, battle-ridden Indonesian archipelago with millions who were tired, discouraged, unemployed and destitute, desperately depending upon the wisdom of the new Indonesian leadership to pull the country out of a decade of the nation's domestic challenges. Authoritarian traditions, extensive mass poverty, widespread social injustice in pockets of rural districts, far reaching economic upheavals, and pervasive political corruption starting up from local provinces increase under Sukarno and Hatta's regime, reaching high onto the political stage, preventing national unity.

The end of the Revolution does not erase feelings of suspicion and distrust my father has for Indonesia's "new" government. Harry Meijer is aware of Sukarno's ideology leaning towards Communism and believes the corruption of his administration will continue. Experiencing ten years of war and desperately desiring a normal, peaceful existence for his family, Harry Meijer joins many other Dutch/Indonesian families who are considering leaving the country of their birth. It is a difficult decision for him. Born of a bi-racial ethnic group, the majority of citizens, like my dad identify with their Dutch ancestry in the important aspects of core, social values. My father had spent his teen years reading about America and experienced enough life to trust in free markets, less government and free speech! Harry Meijer expressed those ideals to family members and friends believing these were the answers in order to live a full, abundant existence. Educated by the same system which the Dutch applied in their European schools and with Dutch as his primary language in the public and professional square, my father echoes his opinion with thousands of Dutch/Indonesian citizens who choose to lean towards the western values of their Dutch birthright. Harry Meijer is grateful for the government of the Netherlands. He believes Indonesia progressed much better under colonialism, more than people were willing to admit.

As the political leaders, companies and educators from the Netherlands begin to withdraw their presence to make room for the new Indonesian dictatorship, my father feels the ominous approach of troubling events yet to come. Warning many in his circle of influence, including Kasmenah, my father reiterates his concern about the communist ideology of the Sukarno/Hatta regime.

Thus, Harry Meijer joins many Dutch/Indonesian inhabitants as the son of an island mother and love of Indonesia, torn and conflicted with the strong compulsion to leave. Privately, my father questions if he could abandon island life with neighborhoods inhabited by people who are hospitable and generous. Could he leave that behind? Indonesia is his home yet Harry concedes that years of violent conflict and dramatic political shifts have changed the archipelago nation.

On the national level, the government of the Netherlands understood the obligation to their colonies. The Netherlands political leadership alongside the Dutch monarchy feel the responsibility for the lives of thousands Dutch/Indonesian citizens, whose livelihood would be negatively, severely impacted by the Sukarno/Hatta regime.

Beginning in the new year of 1950, Dutch Queen Juliana sends out a decree which allows the Dutch/Indonesian population, prioritizing those who fought for the Netherlands in the two wars, to procure Dutch citizenship and immigrate to the Netherlands. Although the dream of America is still his long-term goal, Dad knew he could not accept the new government in Indonesia. The thought of leaving the land of his birth is heart wrenching but as he explained to Mom, their beloved island country is forever changed. My mother balks at the idea of leaving until Dad addresses the existential problems our family will face if we remain under

Sukarno's rule and my father aptly reminds Mom that even the landscape of the Indonesian archipelago looks different!

War, with its violence, carnage and destruction has devastated thousands of acres of Indonesia's plantations, reduced vast areas of the lush green islands into empty, barren spaces and decimated much of her once beautiful sea shores. Thousands of homeless refugees survive by taking up those same, large areas, using whatever material they can find to form shelters for sanctuary.

Overnight, mass concentrations of squatter-type huts are erected with litter left over from the war. The impoverished, indigent population finds fragmented sheets of lumber, scraps of metal and steel poles covering them with coconut branches and banana tree leaves to use for roofs and flooring, characterizing miles of the islands with hundreds of ramshackle dwellings creating larger expanses of kampongs.

Harry and Vicky Meijer spend long nights discussing their options, and eventually present their ideas to other family members, including Kasmenah. Three of Dad's siblings say they would leave but his brother Jan married to an indigenous girl will remain. Desperate for Jan to reconsider, Dad and his siblings Rudy, Ida and Ellie believe that the Sukarno/Hatta regime will destroy Jan's ability to live a comfortable life. They fail in changing his mind. My mother's siblings and their spouses agree and also choose to leave.

Mom insists that Kasmenah immigrate too, offering our Oma a place to live with us.

…Kasmenah is conflicted.

For Oma Kasmenah, nothing could be done to change the past. The ruinous destruction of her island home is not enough to discourage her and Kasmenah has faith that neighborhoods, villages and surrounding townships will eventually be restored back to the serene life-style of the islands. The elderly woman does not concern herself with irritating politicians.

So, Kasmenah Hall has a different point of view from her children. Life can remain simple and uncomplicated! Kasmenah longs to return to her neighborhood, visit with friends, and sit on the veranda once more to watch the world go by. And she could not leave her precious Fentje behind, whom she missed so desperately!

Our beloved Oma would get her wish and never leaves the tropical land of her birth!

For her eldest daughter Vicky, Kasmenah's decision to remain brings more heartbreak. Triggered by familiar feelings of disappointment, Mom accuses Kasmenah of being irresponsible and selfish, demanding her mother joins us. When that proves to be unsuccessful, Mom tries a different approach making a case about Kasmenah's safety yet Oma is resolute and wants to stay!

Meanwhile, Dad faces new challenges with an important member of his family. After the war, he resumes visits to his eldest son alone as Walter's grandparents have made it clear that Vicky was no longer welcome. Concerned about Walter's future, Dad offers his grandparents Frank and Esme to join us in leaving Indonesia. Frank reassures Dad he will migrate to the Netherlands without his help.

Walter is only one of my father's reason to feel stress. The turbulence in his relationship with Mom has increased as both feel pressures of a growing family and an unsure future. Issues of the past are not dealt with, which continue to hamper their attempts to communicate respectfully with each other.

Four years since Mona's birth and now packing to relocate to a foreign land renews feelings of guilt for Mom who broods daily about her first-born daughter. Agonizing over devastating choices our mother has already made, Vicky Meijer reluctantly accepts that once again, destiny demands the mother of six to release all circumstances beyond her control. Struggling emotionally, Mom buries feelings she believes are selfish!

On the warm, balmy evening of Monday, November 6, 1950 seven members of the Harry Meijer family board the aircraft of the Koninklijke Luchtwaart Maatschappij (KLM) Airline, taking leave of the beautiful, tropical, island nation, arriving three days later in the foreign, harsh, winter-cold land of a country in western Europe called The Netherlands.

Mom has not yet informed Dad that she is two months pregnant.

chapter 36

"You can take the girl out of the country, but you can't take the country out of the girl."

AMERICAN ANTHROPOLOGIST MARGARET MEAD

The Netherlands has been described as a "very big, small country." The popular saying comes from merit and praise the Dutch people give their ancestors for creating more land originally located under the sea. Approximately 17% of the Netherlands' land mass was reclaimed since the early 1300's. Covering an area the size of the state of Maryland in America, approximately 16,300 square miles, the small country sits on the edge of Western Europe wedged between the North Sea, Belgium and Germany. Famous for beautiful, perennial cup-shaped flowers called tulips which cover the countryside during the warmer months, the landscape is dotted with hundreds of windmills, an icon of the Netherlands. Long before they became the star showpiece on thousands of postcards where windmills played a vital role in the Dutch effort to reclaim the low lands. "Nederland" means low country, because Nederland is situated below sea level. Dutch ingenuity and clever engineering-built windmills on dykes throughout the country, used to pump the water and produce mass drainage of the land. The invention of the steam engine which replaces the windmills in the 20th century, makes them obsolete but the government and its people showed great interest in saving a thousand of them to retain the vintage character of Nederland.

From the air, the windmills look like little toys for one of the Meijer boys. Three-year-old Jack squeals with delight at the sight of hundreds of them as our plane descends.

On November 9, 1950, the Meijer family lands in the airport of Amsterdam Luchthaven Schiphol in the city of Amsterdam, on a day which blusters with freezing wind accompanied by miles of snow flurries. Exiting the plane, Dad holds me in his arms, sheltering me from the cold. Mom keeps baby Sonja close to her chest as Johny and Rene tightly clutch on little Jack's hands with all of us huddled as close together as we struggle our way forward. The foreign, icy precipitation makes the long walk on the tarmac difficult for the family of seven. Used to warm trade winds cooling off the tropical humidity in the country they have just departed, my parents discover Nederland's weather to be a brutal shock to the system! Thick condensation from exhaling makes them feel they have arrived on a different planet as storm clouds above us color everything a misty, dull gray.

During the trek, Mom does not hesitate to loudly remonstrate Dad with criticism, exclaiming they have made a mistake! Our island mother insists that she could not exist in a bitter, frigid cold country, taking further notice that there is not a tree in sight! Dad ignores the scolding, pushing ahead towards a group of gray buildings. Privately he admits his wife is not wrong about this dismal, first impression of Nederland.

Perhaps he has made a mistake.

Regretting yet another decision, our mother pleads with Dad to return! She is desperate to go back to the warmth of sunshine, back to Indonesia and Kasmenah! What is she doing here in this strange land? How has her life ended up in this bleak, frigid land with five children in tow? Will she ever see a palm tree again?

My father turns a deaf ear to his wife's rebuke as Mom continues to opine and complain.

Somehow, we make it to the building which shelters us long enough to warm our freezing cold hands. A kind gentleman offers us hot tea while we wait for the bus to arrive. Young Jack declines but makes a comment about the man's big nose!

Several miles into our journey, the bus we board to take us to a little, gray hotel in the small, gray village of Driebergen, slides on thin ice covering the road and slams into a tree. Mom laughs with a sound that comes from deep inside her chest and jokes saying she got her wish for a tree while tears pour down her cheeks. As we wait for another bus, our parents are amazed with the numerous bicycles on the road in spite of the freezing cold weather. Mom takes note about so many people with pale complexions and never has she seen so many beautiful, blue eyes. She exclaims that people are tall! The small island lady stands in awe as she stares at individuals who make up the population of the country called Nederland.

The drastic contrast in weather, landscape, culture, and people open another major chapter and challenge in the lives of Harry and Vicky Meijer but they had done their homework. Dad, who kept his commission with the Royal Dutch Air Force, had insisted that the transition from Indonesia to Nederland be made as smooth as possible for his family! All the arrangements for required immunizations, passports and stacks of paperwork our father had completed in a timely manner while Mom spent weeks knitting woolen scarves, gloves and hats to keep us warm.

For the first time in more than a decade, Harry and Vicky Meijer's vision to live a life free from the threats of death, torture, imprisonment, and poverty, seems possible. No longer did they face imminent death and gone were days of walking with head bowed, and fear of systematic abuses.

The nightmare is over, hopefully they are free to begin a life of peace.

However, the dream of settling down has now been complicated with the move to an alien country, coupled with the responsibility of caring for five children and experiencing the painful departure from family and friends. Life for my parents is no longer defined by the winds of a beautiful island and soft, warm rays of sunshine. Gone is the sweet fragrance of the melati flower and the irreplaceable sounds of the gorgeous, papagai parrots. Pushing past her disappointment of accepting that blissful days of languishing on the veranda surrounded by beautiful ferns, palm trees and endless blue skies are over, Mom also mourns the end of visits to the bustling pasar with Kasmenah and tropical evenings spent outside with friends, enjoying conversation and breathtaking sunsets.

The luminous moon sitting on the flaming horizon has disappeared like the nostalgic days of former times.

Vicky Meijer is also a realist and has not forgotten about the horrific years spent imprisoned behind iron gates!

My parents are in a different land, in a different time. Their environment of gray skies, bleak, cold weather patterns which includes months of rain and snow, determines that the life they once had on their beloved island of Java will never be theirs again. Sergeant Major and Mrs. Harry Meijer make a vow to each other by depending on the same inner strength which enabled them to overcome the trials of a decade of war. My parents renewed courage comes from the understanding that the entire global community suffered in agony!

The country of Nederland like all European nations were impacted by the untold loss of thousands of their citizens during World War II. Destruction of land and buildings took their toll but the spirit of the Dutch people could not be demolished! As a nation, the citizens of the Netherlands were determined to rebuild and by 1950 have made great strides in spite of financial limitations.

Before the Royal Dutch Air Force is able to provide us with permanent housing, the entire Meijer family is placed to live in one room in a nearby hotel. It remains our living quarters for more than one year! Forced to adjust not only to the cold weather of the Netherlands and also challenged with seven people living in one room, my parents work tirelessly to make their five youngsters comfortable. Rene and Johny, active eight and nine-year-old boys begin attending school with Rene scoring high on the placement exams and placed at Thorbecke Lijceum Academy. Johny is sent to De Hooge Burger School with a similar schedule. Jack, Sonja and I are kept busy with Mom at the helm. Our parents do their best to cope with the piercing, brutal winter weather in our newly adopted country.

Not soon enough, spring comes with the welcome of sunshine, lovely tulips and the birth of another little girl for the Meijer family. Saturday, May 12th, 1951, Peggy Ann Louise is born, frail and small, weighing not much more than 5 pounds. Mom is gravely concerned for her baby's health because Peggy is pale and lacks an appetite. The cramped hotel room becomes even more difficult with the addition of the new baby. It would be another five months before the RDAF could secure a home of our own!

By the end of October, 1951 carrying six suitcases, our parents' only possessions, we move into the small "row" house on 35 Hondsdrafstraat in the town of Arnhem in eastern Nederland. Arnhem is the capital city of the province of Gelderland, located less than 20 miles from the German border. All but leveled, many areas in Arnhem still required major restoration to be made to buildings which suffered severe damage during World War II.

Row houses are prevalent in many European countries. A series of red brick residences identical in design, stand in long rows with each home situated side by side joined by common walls.

Sparsely furnished with donated items from the military, our home contains a narrow staircase near the front entrance. Three very small bedrooms and a tiny bathroom containing a toilet, bath tub and sink make up the second floor. Back on the first floor, a cramped water closet containing a toilet and small sink, an inadequate, diminutive kitchen and a meager space used for dining, is attached to an area used as the living room. Outside the front door, a narrow space serves as the front yard which leads to a sidewalk, onto the cobblestone street facing identical row houses across the road.

Although the space inside covers an area less than 900 square feet, for Mom it is a palace! The year spent crammed in a hotel room, eight of us, including four children under the age of five, had become more than a great burden for her. With gratitude, Mom is happy to settle in a home of her own. From early morning rising before the gloomy rays of day peek through homemade lace curtains, until well past midnight, our mother does not cease with the exhausting, endless labor required to care for her growing family. Preparing breakfast, lunch and dinner for eight people is a full-time job. Nursing another, new baby Peggy and caring for a 16-month-old Sonja, 3-year-old Maudy and 4-year-old Jack, Mom works unfaltering with the help of Johny and Rene. On laundry days, she boils water in a large bucket on the small stove in the tiny kitchen for washing clothes which our two older brothers agitate using big wooden dowels. Outdoors, in the little courtyard behind our house, which also contains a small shed to hold coal used for heating the house, Mom hangs laundry on the clothes line, hoping the sun manages to peek through heavy clouds that day. The alternative was to suspend the wash and miles of cloth diapers across the small living room inside. Many winter days, the dangling laundry would greet us as we enter through the front door!

Every weekday morning Dad walks to a nearby depot to catch the bus to work at Deelen Air Force base. As he pushes past snow flurries which stick to his face, he wonders over and over if he made the right decision, however, the father of many children continues to press on to provide for his family. Thoughts of Walter are always on his mind. His son, now thirteen years of age, corresponds with a letter every few weeks. It is in one of Walter's letters that informs Dad, Frank and Esme Ries have agreed to move to the Netherlands too. They will reside in a town called Hilversum.

Life in the cold European country is challenging for my parents. The weather is bleak many months of the year. Potatoes, kale and knockwurst is an insipid cuisine for my parents whose palates previously had only known the wonderful, fragrant, full-flavored condiments of Indonesian spices which make up the succulent dishes of Southeast Asian cuisine. However, not a word of complaint come from Dad or Mom about bland, European dishes because many years of hunger, war and imprisonment remain vivid in their minds.

Purchasing groceries in Nederland is a different experience for Mom. The butcher, vegetable and dry goods shops are located in separate buildings near the Hondsdrafstraat neighborhood. Milk and various other dairy products are delivered via the local milk man but there are some annoying aspects of our new surroundings which my parents have to face head on.

The obvious attention our family draws in public is unsettling for them. In 1950, it is evident that Dutch citizens are uncomfortable by the sudden influx of brown people who possess Dutch surnames and masterfully speak the language. The country, which is still recovering financially and structurally from the destruction of World War II feels a national burden increasing as Nederland welcomes 200,000 Dutch/Indonesians over the following five years and the national resentment is transparent in several news outlets.

Across the country, Dutch communities are struggling with personal feelings of racial prejudice. My parents notice the lack of welcome in the Hondsdrafstraat neighborhood for the intrusive, brown members of the Dutch/Indonesian Meijer family but the unfriendliness of our neighbors does not deter Mom from doing what she knows best! In fact, our mother is slightly amused and challenged by their ignorance as she works to win over the suspicious, white folks by beginning with a campaign of preparing and delivering delicious homemade breads and cakes with all of us in tow. Vicky Meijer introduces herself to everyone covering the entire neighborhood, including families residing on each side of us, across the street, and those who live in row houses behind us. In a matter of weeks, the small community knows our names and before long, friendly neighbors are encouraging us to play with their children. Soon, Dutch housewives exchange the latest gossip with Mrs. Meijer and their husbands invite Mr. Meijer to join them in a game of cards or billiards.

Finally, life for the Meijer clan begins to look and feel like the typical, ordinary family surrounding them in the suburbs of Arnhem. Father sets off to work every day, providing financially for the family while mother stays home, busy with chores, inundated with the care of six children. All should be good in the Meijer household, solid, steady, unshakeable, hopefully a home secure with individuals who are happy and content, no longer impacted by the horrors of the past!

Tragically, settling down in a daily routine becomes the fertile ground against the bliss and harmony our parents have been desperately seeking for more than a decade.

Dad and Mom, (Left to Right) Maudy, Rene, Jack, and Johny, circa 1949

chapter 37

"Family pain is the worst kind of pain!"
AMERICAN PSYCHOLOGIST/FAMILY THERAPIST - DR. JAMES DOBSON

At the end of World War II, global efforts began the work of restoration and rebuilding. The economic, financial, industrial and political aspects demanded great effort on behalf of all nations. The combined, estimated financial loss of all countries involved was 1.5 trillion dollars. In today's calculation that number would add up to be more than $4,000,000,000,000 but reconstruction and repair of buildings, lands, and all inanimate objects was straightforward, even simple compared to the rehabilitation the human race would require. The global impact of more than 70 million fatalities which made up 2.5% of the total world population could be calculated in objective terms but the existential fallout was measureless!

The soul of all of humanity desperately needed the restoration of hope. Those who miraculously survive the years of unspeakable loss in human dignity, self-respect, or self-worth long after the external threat is removed, add millions more to the list of casualties. Not until decades later does the American Psychiatric Association recognize a syndrome called post-traumatic stress disorder [PTSD], leaving millions of survivors without proper resources for the mental health support they desperately need.

In countless numbers of individuals, the healing of deep, unseen wounds of war's dehumanization would take years, while in others, healing never comes! The repercussions and eventual consequences of the evil perpetrated upon its victims, suffering from a high degree of emotional pain, physical distress, and psychological torment threaten to destroy marriages, families and extended associations even decades later! How survivors assimilate successfully back into society, transitioning to the changes in their circumstances, was largely determined by the strength of emotional connection to their closest relationships before the existential violations began.

In the Meijer family, coming to terms with the abuse they suffered would be put to test for Harry, Vicky, Johny and Rene. Each one had experienced the horror of incarceration, sustained injustice individually, distinctively and separately, with each member enduring private, debilitating pain. Yet they suffered together, universally, equal with millions like them, who were robbed of their liberty, stripped of personal dignity then threatened to become victims again as they struggle to overcome the impact of heinous crimes perpetrated against them!

In a short period of time, Harry begins to realize that Vicky and his two eldest sons do not trust him.

Survival for Vicky and her boys in the internment camp was forged by maintaining a symbiotic relationship between mother and her children, keeping them mutually alive. Thousands of families are grappling with similar manifestations. The re-acceptance of an absentee father after imprisonment gives rise to severe conflicts within families causing more emotional and psychological damage on both sides. Surviving children are solely devoted to the woman who had kept them safe, causing great strife with the man reclaiming his role as husband and father, the man who desperately wants to reclaim his position as protector and provider. He is seen as a major disrupter, and characterized as the unwanted interloper!

Although Johny and Rene are very young when Harry re-enters their safe space, the five and six-year-old boys' sense of protection for Vicky is foremost! During incarceration, protecting their mother was the main coping mechanism which helped two little boys persevere. The man who now controls their everyday life is a stranger, interfering in the place they had managed without him! The brothers cannot possibly understand that Dad's ardent desire to be reunited with his family helped him endure the arduous years he suffered as a prisoner. They could not know the horrors our father had to overcome. Equally disturbing was my Dad's inability to grasp the abominable conditions his wife and sons had lived under in the internment camp. Stuck in a zone of disappointment, misplaced hostility and blame, the groundwork is ripe our family's ongoing conflicts and misunderstandings.

Mom is caught in the vicious trap of guilt and shame, then coping by projection and deflection. Like many women survivors, the trauma of imprisonment and its related issues of forced rape, poor nutrition, overcrowding and fear, produce erroneous, emotional cognitions challenging her understanding of the eventual consequences, leading our mother to blame herself first and then others. The error in judgment leaves Mom with a personal appraisal that she is inadequate and weak as she projects her husband to be even more pathetic than she is. The disrespect Mom feels for Dad grows more apparent every day. Without provocation, she does not hold back vocalizing her disdain for him, even at times when he makes a simple request.

Harry desires to be provider and protector of the family again but Vicky asks herself, where was this person when his family needed him most? This same individual who claims to love them is the lout who required her to choose between their little boys or baby Mona. How is Harry different from the Indonesian officer who physically forced himself on her, time after time? What does she do with the conflated hatred and disgust she feels equally for both these men? Additionally, Vicky Meijer struggles to trust this individual who could have chosen to rescue our two helpless siblings, Walter and Mona! Mom feels the growing pressure to admit that this man who fathered her six children continues to disappoint her. Trapped with persistent conflicts whether or not to remain in the marriage, our mother is beginning to show signs of severe anxiety and depression!

Harry Meijer's struggle is of a different kind.

In his mind, Harry's identity as a man was continuously called into question during the years of incarceration. Now my father deals with private frustrations about his role as father and husband in the midst of efforts he makes for a better life for our family. Squarely facing the realization that he was powerless to protect the ones he loved, Harry Meijer is burdened with personal demons of scorching pain, condemning himself with endless, scathing feelings of failure and weakness.

The wide-spread range of negative, emotional trauma in families with a husband, wife and children who have been victims of long-term, villainous abuse typically leads to an increase of self-induced guilt and continual feelings of shame, which keeps each member imprisoned in a revolving door of never-ending despair, as the distrust among them grows. The years fly by with ruinous emotions remaining unchecked, exacerbated by expectations beyond what each broken partner is able to deliver.

Harry and Vicky Meijer join thousands like them who are paralyzed in the trauma of a past they are so desperate to leave behind!

It is Johny and Rene who experience first-hand the consequences of the vocal animosity between our parents. Dad and Mom's continual, unpleasant exchanges eventually rise to the level of loud, vitriolic shouting. Always ready to protect their mother, both brothers do not hesitate to defend Mom during the heated arguments she has with Dad. Johny and Rene see themselves as guardians of Mom's dignity which collides with Dad's accusations of her disrespect for him. Our mother continually struggles between feelings of overwhelming victimization competing with the desire to be the conqueror in every altercation. She fluctuates between silent submission and escalation. Increasing resentment grows between Dad and my brothers as Johny and Rene become the focus of our father's misplaced rage.

In spite of the marital dysfunction broadening to include Johny and Rene, Mom is ecstatic to continue having more children and over the next 34 months, the family is blessed with the birth of three more babies! On Wednesday, June 4, 1952, Harry Gustav is born, healthy, adding to Mom's joy, because unlike Sonja and Peggy he is plump and has a healthy appetite. With the previous children, she was bent to fatten us with food! Little Harry did not need to be coaxed because he is a happy, content baby.

The following year, another daughter is born to Harry and Vicky's burgeoning family and on Saturday, August 29, 1953, Mirna is born. Mom always described Mirna as the poor child who was not given a middle name because her long labor made our mother too exhausted to think of one. The baby is blessed with a sunny disposition however Mirna is brought to the doctor several times within a few months following her birth because of projectile vomiting after each feeding. The physician believes the baby's upset stomach is caused by acid reflux, a symptom he explains, is aggravated by strife and contention in the home.

One and a half years later, the last Meijer son is born on Wednesday,

April 1, 1955. Excited about the baby's good health, Mom names the child Buddy, believing the moniker comes from America in the context of friendship. Dad and Mom agree to give our baby brother the middle name of Johann in honor of our grandfather Johann Meijer and one of Christiaan's brothers, Johann Hall.

Two more times Vicky Meijer becomes pregnant but the obstetrician convinces her she is not strong enough to birth any more children prescribing our mother the use of a device which enables her to terminate the pregnancies at home. The consequence of the unskilled abortions leaves Mom dealing with a severely infected uterus, exacerbating her fragile condition leaves her more vulnerable to existing feelings of despair. Mom's lack of coping skills causes her to look for comfort in the company of her two eldest sons Johny and Rene. Their symbiotic, faithful bond has endured for more than 15 years, with each one confident in finding refuge and strength in their common solidarity and trust! It is a bond they rely on every day.

The crowded, inadequate house on 35 Hondsdrafstraat is teeming with activity from early dawn until late in the evening. Visitors describe our home resembling the circus, full of pandemonium. Mom loves it and is living her dream of many children! Our father isn't so sure. He needs peace and quiet.

The noise and ongoing, rambunctious activity is a welcome distraction for Vicky Meijer. Memories of the internment camp, the never-ending grief over the loss of her baby daughter, the sudden death of her youngest brother Fentje, and the disturbing news that Kasmenah refuses to leave Indonesia, burdens Vicky every day. Demands of eleven people, including seven very young children help mitigate the concerns she carries in her heart.

Not long after fleeing their beloved island nation, Dad learns from his brother Jan that the Sukarno/Hatta administration require citizens of European descent to give up family names as part of the continued eradication of everything connected to Dutch colonialism. Our uncle tells Dad his name of Jan Meijer has been changed to a common Sundanese surname. My father is extremely disappointed with his younger brother that he doesn't repeat Jan's Indonesian name. The new regime in Indonesia eliminates everything European including the Dutch language. Bahasa Indonesian is the accepted, native tongue.

Seemingly overnight, the island nation of Indonesia is transformed.

Maintaining communication with his beloved mother-in-law, Harry makes many attempts by telephone and letters to encourage Kasmenah to come and join us in the Netherlands but Oma remains resolute. She will not leave her beloved Indonesia! Mom struggles with resentment against her mother's desire to stay. However, our mother finds creative ways to cope with her disappointment.

Music continues to be our mother's passion. One item of furniture included by the RDAF, is an old piano which Mom plays, encouraging us to sing and dance. How wonderful it is to jump, hop and skip around the house as the keyboard makes tinny sounds with many keys off tune. As she choreographs our steps, Mom instructs us to join her in three-part harmonies. Vicky Meijer returns to days long since passed when she participated in the youth choir at the Lutheran church in Indonesia. Mom is happy as we join her in learning the krontjong songs of the islands as well as the melodies of Dutch lullabies, including Mom's favorites of "Konijntje Lief," "Zaagen, Zaagen," and "Slaap Kintje, Slaap."

The joy our mother experiences raising nine children is evident in the boundless energy she spends making our home a place filled with music and laughter. Buddy, Mirna, Harry, and Peggy are under four years old, dubbing us to refer to them as "de vier kleintjes," the four little ones. Our mother is busy with constant child care yet manages to take time when we jump into bed with her in the early morning to cuddle, singing her favorite island songs. It is not unusual to see tears rolling down her cheeks as she tightly holds on to us all. The weekdays are full of merriment and noisy activity however, Saturdays and Sundays are remarkably different.

Dad is home on the weekends and his demands for peace and quiet are strictly enforced!

The atmosphere in the home will remain undisturbed with levels of activity brought down to a minimum. The children are required to stay in bed until 7:30 a.m. Mom, Johny and Rene rise early to begin the preparation for mealtimes, begin the laundry and tidy up the house but even three of them must do so as quietly as possible. Dad wants to sleep in or read in bed with the understanding that he is not be interrupted!

However, eleven family members occupying a home measuring less than 900 square feet is a constant challenge for Mom and our brothers to keep free from disturbance.

In the 1950's for the Meijer family living in Arnhem, there is no television available to entertain seven, active youngsters. Along with many other responsibilities on the weekends, Dad demands of Johny and Rene to keep us occupied in two, tiny bedrooms during the early morning hours. But developing serotonin in the Meijer children needs release and eventually six youngsters crowded in a small space, begin jousting, wrestling, tossing pillows, accompanied by the laughter and giggling typical of children who enjoy making lots of noise! The youngest of us, Buddy squeals with delight from his crib as he observes his noisy siblings constantly stimulated with ongoing, rambunctious activity.

It is a particularly challenging time for Johny and Rene to keep seven youngsters amused during the cold months in Nederland stretching from October well into April which require us to remain indoors on most days. Wet, cold, windy days accompanied with hail, sleet or snow keep most northern Europeans inside their homes.

At times, Mom is happy to make an exception. The blanket of pristine snow covering the landscape looks so inviting that she bundles us up in homemade knitted sweaters, hats, scarves, gloves and bravely takes seven of us for a walk around the block. If Johny and Rene are home from school, they come with us. What revelry and laughter we delight in as we throw snowballs, make snowmen and push one another onto the cold, slushy snow! Mom's laughter lights up her face with joy! Vicky Meijer happily expresses to anyone, a desire that her children would never outgrow a need for her.

Johny and Rene disagree!

Seven younger siblings are a handful for our brothers. Dad requires Johny and Rene to help in every aspect of our care. From diaper changes, potty training, mealtime, nap time, and on their days off school, our two brothers assist Mom to care for us from dawn until dusk. Dad is available only a minimal amount of time but on the days he is home, our father is prepared to comb our hair and make us look presentable before we walk out the door in public. It is a priority for Harry Meijer to present his children looking appropriately groomed to the world outside. It is a priority for Harry Meijer to be known in the community as the father of nine, well behaved children.

Lately on his days off, Mom notices that more frequently, Dad steps out with the men in the neighborhood. Billiards had been his passion as a young man and he feels lucky that in his adopted country there were plenty of billiard rooms available, taking the opportunity to play whenever possible. Harry Meijer also indulges in his other passion as a fan of soccer leaving us at home on many Saturdays while he attends the local games with friends. If his wife dares protest, as familiar feelings of insecurity rise to the surface, Mom begins making irrational accusations against her husband, unable to communicate her emotions properly. Again, the unpleasant exchange escalates into another strident, deafening war of words, as seven, frightened Meijer children run upstairs for cover into any bedroom, with some of us scurrying under beds, covering our ears, and desperately looking for safety in Johny or Rene's arms until the shouting match simmers down.

Eventually, Mom calls us to come downstairs. Typically, Dad leaves the house while Mom continues cooking the evening meal and feeds us dinner without our father present. For Mom, the preparation of food automatically makes everything better in our home. As long as we eat the meals she makes, she is content. Her solution to make her children happy is to satisfy their healthy appetites. She had witnessed too many hungry, starving youngsters suffer in the internment camp and Vicky Meijer had made a vow that her own children would never experience the deprivation of food! Late at night, Dad arrives home and Mom is satisfied that he eats the dinner she has set aside for him. Both of them are at peace once more.

The following morning, the day begins as if nothing had happened the evening before.

Sadly, the days of peace do not last long. The repeated pattern of unresolved hostility breaking down communication between my parents, leads to the predicted, relentless verbal attacks, until the Meijer family becomes the main topic of gossip in the Hondsdrafstraat neighborhood. The shared walls in the row houses make it possible for neighbors to eavesdrop on the private lives of one another. Listening devices are not necessary for detecting vociferous quarrels occurring next door.

One day, my father is forced to face that truth when I ran home from my little friend's house to inform him that I overheard an exchange between Ankie's parents. At five years of age, I am old enough to understand their conversation, freely criticizing my parents. Dad wasted no time in leading me back to Mr. and Mrs. Joost's residence demanding an apology from them. Mr. Joost calmly informs my father that the common walls of a row house did not offer any family the luxury of privacy.

The contempt of Mr. Joost's comment should have stopped the constant feuds between my parents and I begged them to stop but the emotional appeals of a five-year-old are not on my parent's list of priorities. I am too young to understand that the increasing, physical pain in my stomach is caused by the humiliation I feel about Dad and Mom's acrimonious relationship.

Unable to harness his personal demons of anger and bitterness and in spite of the risk to our family's reputation, Dad's destructive hostilities continue, especially against Johny and Rene. For minor infractions not of their fault, our older brothers are severely punished because I choke on a button believing it was a piece of candy. Dad held them responsible for not watching their little sister closely enough. Not long after that incident, two-year-old Harry swallows a toy watch. Johny and Rene sustain corporal punishment for that too yet the most severe repercussion they receive from Dad is the day six-year-old Jack discovers a box of matches and sets the kitchen curtains on fire!

Regularly, Dad's method of punishment is to send my two brothers out into the cold. The sympathy of surrounding neighbors who give Johny and Rene sanctuary spare our beloved brothers from serious illness, although they suffer with pneumonia and frequent colds.

At home Mom is in anguish with tormenting grief, either cowering in the bedroom with the rest of us or standing at the top of the stairs screaming obscenities at our father. Those of us old enough to recognize a familiar pattern, witness the ill treatment of our mother and brothers again and again! We join our mother in calling Dad names, which results in a spanking or slaps across the face. Mom does not hesitate to defend us and begins to assault her husband with her fists. Dad responds by hitting her back in return. On those bad, ugly days, we endure the consequences of the grievous wounds tormenting my parents and our older brothers; all the people we love.

Like most children, my siblings and I believe that someday the deep-seated bitterness will end!

However our parents rely on the same coping mechanisms after each disturbance including denial and/or verbal disengagement. Whatever routine they choose, amazingly, both of them remain focused on their responsibilities as Dad faithfully goes to his job every day while Mom routinely, continues, tirelessly with her demands at home.

Johny and Rene attend school, sustaining the hardships at home in silence. My siblings and I watch their example on how to manage the never-ending family pain and heartache.

Jack enters kleuterklass (kindergarten) in 1952, with me enrolled the following year. Johny and Rene accompany us, safeguarding our walk to school because each morning and every afternoon, we pass a section near our neighborhood which is occupied by a large group of gypsies. These families lived in small, metal trailers making it possible for them to live a nomadic life-style while receiving regular, financial support from the Dutch government. Poor, anti-social and lacking regular hygiene, these strangers are frightening for a five and six-year-old. There were occasions when some of the older children instigate their mangy dogs to chase us but Johny and Rene are not intimidated, carrying Jack and me upon their shoulders, keeping us safe!

All is not dismal and gray in Nederland. Along with every youngster in the entire country, the Meijer children eagerly anticipate the yearly celebration of Sinter Klaas and Zwarte Piet. A weeklong celebration in honor of a saint named Nicholas with his helper/servant Piet. The Dutch people culminate the holiday on December 6th with a parade and joyous gatherings with family and friends.

The legend of St. Nick is based on a story of a kind man who lived in 6th century Ireland, financially assisting the poor in his neighborhood with money, food and gifts. After his death, he is dubbed a saint by the Catholic Church and later becomes Father Christmas in the UK nations of England, Australia, Scotland and Ireland, Santa Claus in America and Sinter Klaas in Nederland, Germany and Belgium. It is a special time for all children because he "arrives" upon the roof of each home with his assistant Zwarte Piet and comes down the chimney, laying toys and chocolate candy in the shape of letters of each child's first initial in our individual wooden shoes. Then there are the wonderful times we enjoy ice-skating on the frozen hard ice of the little creek across the fields near our house. Somehow, the Meijer family makes it through the gloomy, cold winter months.

Spring and summer are beautiful seasons in Nederland. Along the countryside and in gardens everywhere, bulb flowers of multi-colored tulips, blue hyacinths and bright yellow daffodils are a feast for the eyes. Multiple varieties of white daisies, large and small dot the landscape, growing wild wherever a clump of soil is exposed to sunlight.

Suddenly, there is movement everywhere. People leave their houses for leisured, long walks along the cobble stone avenues and canals, visit the nearby city and sit outside little cafes, drinking cups of coffee or tea, enjoying the delicious Dutch pastries, relishing in the company of friends and neighbors. Children are once again playing on the sidewalks or in nearby open fields. Even Dad's spirit lifts and he takes the time to accompany Mom on her long walks with us.

The days of sunshine renews my mother's optimism, making her hopeful about a brighter future for her family, and adding to Mom's need for normality, is the simple chore of hanging the laundry, including miles of cloth diapers, outdoors once more.

Unfortunately, the warm weather does not last long and like the brevity of sunshine in the cold land of the Netherlands, short-lived harmony between Sergeant Major and Mrs. Harry Meijer quickly disappears!

Bundled up for Winter in the Netherlands, circa 1951

chapter

38

"While raising children, days are long and the years are short."
American Actor Julianne Moore

The Netherlands, well-known world-wide for the talent of artists like Rembrandt and Van Gogh, its fanciful wooden shoes, quaint canals, majestic cathedrals, and Gouda cheese served on famous, beautiful blue and white Delftware ceramic platters, usually accompanied by a Heineken or Amstel beer, followed with the famous spiced cookie called speculaas, is also reputable for being the most liberal country in Europe. Dealing with a history of conflicts between the Catholics and the Calvinists, the conservative older generation versus the open-minded, liberal young people, the Netherlands are assimilated with political, social and cultural liberalities which make our parents increasingly uncomfortable. Abortion, euthanasia, freewill dispensing of marijuana and prostitution is legal in the Netherlands in the 1950's.

Unhappy with the growing, fundamental aspects of socialism in the country, Dad and Mom begin to discuss the idea of leaving. Both are conflicted about the subject because Dad's brother Rudy and his family have immigrated to the Netherlands along with their sister Ida. Mom's youngest brothers Bernard and Gus with their families have relocated from Indonesia to the Netherlands too. Mom is especially thrilled about Walter who arrived with his grandparents not long after we did. Walter is allowed regular visits with us, happy to be surrounded by his, noisy, rambunctious siblings!

Nevertheless, everything about the cultural environment and economic conditions in the Dutch nation Dad has conflict with, motivating him to begin an intense search for relocation. He has never given up his dream about America but the cost for moving a large family across the ocean is financially prohibitive and Dad's ability to speak English is greatly limited. My father cannot not imagine how he would accomplish a move to America with a wife and nine children.

Destiny has a way of preempting unforeseen circumstances in the journey of life, making the road ahead suddenly clear.

Mom wakes up on the morning of her 34th birthday, on Saturday, January 31, 1953 to hear the news that the entire coast of Nederland, parts of Belgium, the eastern coasts of England and Germany have been hit with the worst storm in more than 500 years. Twelve-foot tidal waves have swept away many seaport towns with more than 2,000 people drowning, including thousands of farm animals. Thousands more people are trapped by floodwater threatening to rise and claim more land, more victims and more livestock. Dad joins hundreds of Dutch military troops summoned to assist with much needed aid. The United States, Canada, and many European countries send help from the Red Cross along with financial aid, military personnel, machinery and food. Every evening, Dad shares with us his gratitude to work side by side with people from all different nations pulling together for one common cause.

Two of them are American soldiers who had finished tours of duty in the Korean conflict. Describing their experiences, the two men are a reminder for Dad that war is a thing of the past for him. Later, the world learns that 55,000 Americans lose their lives including 5 million Koreans. My father invites the men back to our home for dinner with Mom delighted to meet 'real' Americans, who enthusiastically share their love of the United States. The experience re-ignites my father's passion to consider America as his only choice for relocation.

The summer of 1953, shortly before Mirna's birth, Dad received a telegram at work. Arriving home, he hands the piece of paper to Mom, who refuses to read it. Mom tells him she suspects the news is about the death of Kasmenah because she had a dream about it weeks before. The rest of that day, our beloved mother remains in her bedroom, something she had never done before. Jack joins Sonja and me sitting on the floor in front of the closed-door hearing Mom weep and patiently wait for her to come out. Hours later, Mom opens the door allowing us to come inside.

The three of us climb on the bed as she cradles us up against her bulging stomach. Through her tears, Mom asks for Johny and Rene. Oma Kasmenah had been present when we were born and enjoyed us when we were infants but Jack, Sonja and I were too young to remember her. It was different for Johny and Rene. Oma had been a supreme force and an important influence in their lives, making her a major reason they survived those dreadful years in the internment camp.

At thirteen and twelve years of age, our brothers agonize over the loss of their beloved Oma Kasmenah Hall. Mom did not waste any time making long distance phone calls to her sisters to ask about the circumstances surrounding her mother's death. Dora and Hetty explain that Oma refused to sleep in the same house occupied by her two youngest daughters and their husbands because she did not want to be imposing on their lives. Instead, Kasmenah slept in a tiny shed near a ditch. Doctors surmise that the cause of death was due to a bacterial infection brought on by the dirty, stagnant water in the ditch.

Vicky Meijer is furious! She blames her sisters for not being persistent enough with their mother, accusing them of neglect. The tragedy causes a devastating rift among the three sisters.

Oma is buried next to her son, Fentje. Kasmenah was 49 years old.

The untimely death of her mother triggers in Mom an irascible anger, making her more hostile, unreasonable and easily agitated. Dad becomes the object of her rage as she renews more accusations against him including the needless circumstances about Walter and Mona, blaming Dad for abandoning Kasmenah and the life we now live in the "freezing, God-forsaken country" of Nederland. Unable to respond with sympathy or understanding, Dad takes the opportunity for revenge by placing culpability back on Mom!

It takes years for our mother to put to rest the tragic circumstances of Kasmenah's death. It takes decades for Mom to forgive her sisters and Oma Kasmenah's death is one more, painful addition to the list of many grievances our mother has against Harry Meijer.

The winter days are long for our parents in the Netherlands. Somehow the damp, cold climate contributes to their mutual animosity and continuing lack of respect for each other. Confined for weeks indoors, the walls seem to close in on all of us as the dreary, daily routine further add to feelings of hopelessness, culminating all at once one, horrible day.

Waking up one early morning while it is still dark outside, the piercing sound of the howling wind and the incessant, loud splatter of rain on the window cause Sonja and me to climb out of the bed we shared. It was freezing cold in the room, which ordinarily would have sent us back under the warm blankets but the commotion interrupted our sleep making it impossible for us to get anymore rest. Quickly we realize, it is not the noise outside which woke us but rather the ear-piercing volume and intensity of angry words hurling between our parents in their bedroom. Clinging to each other, Sonja and I sneak down stairs hoping to find refuge on the couch in the living room. As we crawl under a homemade Afghan, my younger sister and I wait patiently for the argument to stop. Both of us rely on sucking our thumbs which instantly ease our trembling and calms the fear we experience during our parent's constant altercations.

Suddenly the shouting stops and Sonja and I exchange sighs of relief. Instead, a loud crash made us leap from the couch to see Mom crumpled in a heap at the bottom of the stairs. Johny and Rene have already made their way down followed by Jack, Peggy, Harry and Mirna who were crying hysterically. My older brothers insist on calling the authorities but Mom discourages them, reassuring us that she is not injured! As eight, distraught children surround our mother with hugs, filling the cold, night air with sobs of anguish, I look up to see Dad at the top of the stairs holding his head in despair. Buddy is curled up in his crib wailing in distress!

In the melee of our family's chaos, Buddy is alone. While the rest of us find reassurance in one another's hugs, our littlest, baby brother is forgotten in his bed, desperate for someone to console him! It seems to define Buddy not as the typical, indulged baby of the family, but as the youngest child of Harry and Vicky Meijer left behind. With each disturbance, Dad and Mom suffer the consequence of dealing with their children's physical, adverse effects.

Several trips to the doctor for Sonja's headaches, my chronic stomach aches and Mirna's inability to sleep is diagnosed by a team of physicians as stress related syndromes. The pediatricians blame our parents, making urgent recommendations for family counseling because their issues stem from years of systemic abuse during the war but our parents do not accept the professional assessment, believing counseling will make them victims all over again!

Following every disruptive incident, Mr. and Mrs. Meijer go about their day as if nothing unusual happened the night before. My parents' strict routines of mealtime, bedtime, playtime, and schoolwork are adhered to everyday, which somehow gives us a sense of security. Nine children continue to believe that life is normal with parents who argue, fuss and fight as the Meijer children find safety and trust in one another. We learn not to confide in anyone outside of the family!

The years spent in Arnhem allow Harry and Vicky to make acquaintances in the social circles of the neighborhood but our parents keep them at arm's length. Together Dad and Mom agree on one thing; both are convinced there had to be a better place to raise their children. Growing weary of the consistent frosty cold weather, my father is reminded of the winter seasons in Japan. Mom readily agrees with him about leaving because her longing for palm trees and endless sunshine has grown stronger and Vicky Meijer is growing more vocal in her frustration at the unavailability of Indonesian spices and ingredients. Those items would not make their way to the small, Dutch country until years later as the influx of Dutch/Indonesian immigrants rose.

In January of 1954, Dad receives the special honorary title of knighthood bestowed upon him by Juliana, the queen of Nederland, for service rendered "above and beyond the call of duty" in two wars which acknowledged his bravery, decade of hardship and personal sacrifice. Sergeant Major Harry Meijer accepts the award humbly but in his acceptance speech, defers to those who deserved the recognition more than he did.

Yes, Harry Meijer is Indonesian and Dutch, whose entire life up to this point, proved to be loyal to the Dutch monarchy and her government.

It should have been a milestone for our father, one that might have solidified a choice for him to remain in the Netherlands and serve in the Royal Dutch Air Force until retirement. Instead, the celebrated commemoration spurns my dad to leave the past behind with all its sorrow and disappointment. Our father determines the future would be better and brighter not spent in the Netherlands.

The beautiful medal and framed certificate are not hung in a place of prominence in our home. Sergeant Major Harry Meijer stores both items in a trunk which never see the light of day again.

Sonja, Jack, Peggy, and Maudy (Left to Right) in front of our "row" house Arnhem, Nederland circa 1952

Our last photograph in Arnhem before moving to America, January 1957 Maudy, Harry, Johny, Mom, Buddy, Rene, Jack, Mirna, Sonja, Peggy (Left to Right)

chapter 39

> *"America, America, God shed His grace on thee, and crown thy good with brotherhood from sea to shining sea!"*
>
> AMERICAN COMPOSER/AUTHOR - KATHERINE LEE BATES

The story of America and its immigrants have filled hundreds of historical documents and school text books. Welcoming the disenfranchised and giving millions of the poor and persecuted from foreign lands a place of refuge, is the reputation America was known for world-wide. Reaching its peak of almost 20 million immigrants between the decades of 1880 – 1924, the United States received thousands of French, Russian, Italian, German, Dutch, Irish, Greek, Polish, and Chinese who settle primarily in the Eastern and Midwestern states of America. Many immigrants arrive in the "new" country establishing replica societies resembling the neighborhoods they have left behind. Instead of integrating, the aliens become a problem for the people of America -whose recent ancestors were immigrants- resent their invasion and refusal to mainstream into American culture. Whole communities are divided by different languages and customs. As foreigners pour into the cities, rampant overcrowding and unemployment spreads, unchecked.

The urban crisis motivates Congress to search for ways to restrict immigration into the United States.

In 1924, the open-door policy of receiving foreigners is shut by placing a cap on immigrants based on ethnicity. Each group is limited, and the total number accepted each year is severely restricted to 153,000. The Immigration Act of 1924 also requires that eligibility requirements include those over the age of 16 to demonstrate basic reading comprehension in any language, to pay an increased tax fee immediately upon entering the country and gives immigration officials permission to exercise more discretion about who is allowed in. Over the years, amendments, statutes and eligibility requirements are either added or eliminated by Congress as circumstances globally or in the United States, changed.

By the early 1950's, Congress is moved with compassion to enact a new law named the "Refugee Relief Act: Public Law 203" which would impact the destiny of thousands of immigrants in Eastern and Western Europe. In response to the many refugees left without a country after World War II, the act of PL 203 would increase the number of immigrants allowed into the United States each year and stay in effect until the end of 1956. President Dwight Eisenhower signs the decree on August 7, 1953, stating, "The Refugee Relief Act demonstrates again America's traditional concern for the homeless, persecuted, and less fortunate of other lands...I am delighted to sign this bill and in so doing welcome the 214,000 refugees who will soon come to our shores. They, as I said in my address to the nation, are men and women of the same character who, generations upon generation have come to America to find peace and work to build for themselves new homes in freedom".

In the spring of 1956, Harry Meijer learns about the American immigration law of PL203. Ecstatic, my father begins asking questions about PL203 motivating him to enroll in a class to learn to speak and write English more proficiently. Dad is informed that through the assistance of an American organization called, Church World Service, thirty-seven Christian denominations recruit hundreds of churches around the United States to volunteer sponsorships for needy families in Eastern and Western Europe. Sponsoring a family would mean that the church's congregation and its pastor become responsible to secure employment for the head of the household, provide a pantry full of food and pay for at least three months' rent.

Our parents are ecstatic to discover that the church also provides the financial means to pay for the family's passage but with eleven members in our family, the Meijer's chances of being chosen, greatly diminish. However, my father is not dissuaded and he spends weeks filling in the information in piles of necessary paperwork, hopeful and consumed with a buoyancy he hasn't experienced in years.

Mom seems happier and less burdened too. She is singing again, a lot, taking time to gather us around the piano as we join her with happy melodies imported from America. We are singing English words Mom has to interpret from songs by Walt Disney's, Snow White. The melody "Whistle While You Work," is Mom's favorite because she had a great ability to whistle a tune loudly!

On young Harry's fourth birthday, June 4, 1956, Dad hands in all the information about our family. In less than ten days, our parents are notified to begin a screening process which includes several interviews with the Methodist Church in the city of Utrecht. The formal face-to-face meetings is necessary for church denominations to determine if the applicants hold the same biblical view as the church willing to sponsor them. With Dad and Mom's Protestant upbringing, the sessions are pleasant and our parents are informed that their application is handled with expedience because of my father's service as a former prisoner of war.

Next, medical examinations including a range of immunizations, begin for all of us with the final report concluding that the whole Meijer family is in excellent health! What a boost that is for my mother. It is her mission in life to keep us healthy, well-fed and warm! Mom is convinced that the tablespoon of cod liver oil we are forced to swallow every morning, is the miracle drug which keep her nine children healthy. However, I sustain a serious, adverse reaction to one of the vaccines causing Dad to reconsider the move. My recovery restores his desire emigrate.

The following months are the happiest days the Meijer family has experienced in more than a decade. Dad reads everything he can to add to his limited knowledge about the history, politics and economy of the United States. He discovers in one of the history books that the United States Supreme Court of 1892 declared America a Christian nation. His dreams about living in America among the "echte Amerikaanen" were about to come true. It still seems difficult to believe that everything he had dreamed and hoped for would soon become a reality! My father is delighted to see his wife jubilant and expressing it as she goes about her chores, singing famous American songs, "Allegheny Moon" by Patti Page,

"Que Sera, Sera," made popular by Doris Day and "True Love" sung by the duet of Grace Kelly and Bing Crosby.

On December 5, three days before his 41st birthday, Dad receives a letter from the Church World Service notifying him that our family will be sponsored by the Bella Vista Methodist Church, located in Monterey Park, California. The following week, Dad and Mom receive a letter written by the pastor of the church, Reverend Fred Coots describing life in America and the joy his congregation feels about deliberately choosing Harry and Christine Meijer because of all the applicants, they were the parents with the most children.

My father and mother are overjoyed! On December 31, 1956, the Refugee Act of PL 203 is terminated. The Meijer family is one of the last to make the deadline.

Elated, Dad and Mom are convinced God had handpicked our family!

The following months, letters are exchanged with Reverend Coots requesting individual photographs of each family member to be placed up on the church bulletin board.

Not completely capable of understanding our parents' delight, nevertheless, we join them in their exuberant mood, grateful that the endless bickering has ceased! Johny and Rene try to help us understand. Our brothers experience their own emotion of happiness, sharing positive sentiments. One weekend morning in the crowded bedroom they share with Jack and Harry, our two older brothers reassure us that our parents will no longer be sad or angry once we arrive in the glorious United States. Johny has tears falling down his cheeks because he believes that a friendship between Dad and Mom can finally begin.

Johny says that living in America will change our parents. Rene is not so sure and calls Johny a dreamer.

Finally, a meeting is required in front of a civil judge. The entire family is to attend. Assembling together in the presence of a government official could have been intimidating, but instead becomes a memorable occasion.

Eleven members of the Meijer clan squeeze inside the small space of the judge's chamber, with the younger children sitting on the laps of the older siblings. With the exception of Buddy. Mom, places our baby brother on the floor. The judge makes us comfortable in the informal setting and the interview goes smoothly and thankfully does not take long. As the elderly gentleman stands up to shake hands to congratulate our parents, the judge almost trips because Buddy, not quite two years old, has tied his shoe laces together! Mom makes an apology and explains that Buddy was born on April fool's Day. The justice bursts out in laughter with the Meijer clan joining in!

It is the perfect culmination of a journey with a past soon to be left behind and a future yet to be told.

The following weeks Mom is engrossed from sunup until well past midnight preparing for our departure. Packing for eleven people to immigrate to another foreign country is a formidable task but one which fills her with joyful expectation.

The pretty, Dutch/Indonesian girl who has endured a lifetime of heartbreak with agonizing loss, is now a woman, blessed with nine of her ten children, preparing for immigration to a country most people dream about.

Many of our Dutch neighbors wish us well but saying goodbye is the most difficult on the day Walter comes to see us for the last time. Our handsome, eldest brother had not completely laid to rest the choices adults made, preventing him from joining our family permanently.

As Walter bends down to kiss us goodbye, my cheeks are wet with his tears and I cling to him tightly. We are never given an explanation why our eldest brother could not join us. No explanation would have satisfied me!

Johny and Rene are very sad about leaving eldest brother behind and Mom is sobbing as she holds Walter for a long, long time.

Walter in the Netherlands circa Feb 1957

chapter

40

*"In all your ways, acknowledge the Lord
and He shall direct thy paths."*

Proverbs 3:6 KJV

Several organizations are created after WWII specifically to help hundreds of thousands of refugees who became displaced persons described as people without a country after the war. Two of them, working in tandem with the International Red Cross, are the International Refugee Organization and an organization called The Doors of Hope. With the cooperation of the U.S., Canada, Argentina, Brazil, Venezuela, Chile, and Australia, these non-profit, humanitarian enterprises mobilize the great undertaking of offering homeless survivors of war a place of safety and refuge. One of the many ways this was accomplished was by utilizing ships, previously employed as cargo vessels or aircraft carriers, and transitioning them into passenger lines, to transport hundreds of families from their land of devastation to begin again in another country. One such vessel is the ship called the "Seven Seas."

Launched in January, 1940, the Seven Seas was built in Chester, Pennsylvania to serve as a freighter and cargo ship in service for the United States Navy throughout the war. Four hundred and ninety-two feet in length, sporting one funnel, she is a mid-size ship with a cross beam of sixty-three feet. In 1948, she was rebuilt as a passenger boat and in 1956 is sold to the Europe/Canada Line Company. Sponsored by the Doors of Hope Ministry, the Seven Seas assists in post war Dutch immigration by taking hundreds of European citizens to gain entry into Canada or the United States.

On a cold, typical, winter Nederland morning, Tuesday, January 29, 1957 two days before Mom's 38th birthday, the eleven members of the Meijer family step upon a long, steep ramp guiding us to the entrance of The Seven Seas, anchored in the harbor of the seaport city of Rotterdam. Dad leads the way and his excitement is palatable as he carries three-year-old Mirna in his arms, grinning ear to ear. Closely following him is Mom, cradling 21-month-old Buddy and she is weeping. I am not sure if she is crying out of sadness or joy, I decide it is probably both. Our mother is distressed to leave Walter behind, yet looking forward to our future in America.

What a wonderful picture the Meijer clan makes! Dad is dressed in a brand new gray suit, with white shirt and tie, overlaid by his long, military overcoat. Wearing a blue dress she made especially for the journey, Mom stays warm with a black, woolen coat and a little black hat to match. Both our parents still look gaunt and thin from the years of war but their faces are radiant with joy. Johny, who had celebrated his 16th birthday the week before, has grown tall, wearing a formal white shirt and tie, with a dark vest and slacks that match. Looking more like Johny's twin, Rene is two months away from turning 15 years old, and shares the responsibility with Johny for the rest of us, making sure older children are holding hands with the younger ones. Rene takes his role as our brother seriously and is passionate about keeping us safe.

Both brothers instruct Jack, who would celebrate his 10th birthday in three days to hold hands with five-year-old Peggy who is anxiously looking up to make sure no one has left her behind. Sonja who had celebrated her seventh birthday the month before is leading four-year-old Harry, tightly clutching on to him, because young Harry is full of curiosity and fearless with his own idea about which direction he wants to take! In Dad's arms, Mirna is squealing with delight! Our youngest sister has an opinion about everything going on around her! In Mom's arms, little Buddy is subdued as he wipes Mom's tears off his own cheeks. Holding my hand is Johny and half way past eight years of age, I pepper him with a flurry of questions about our impending journey.

Wrapped in warm jackets, with new scarves around our necks, heads covered with hats and our hands itchy in woolen gloves our mother had spent weeks knitting, eleven of us walk the ramp, some of us realizing our lives will never be the same!

Entering the ship is frightening. Long, dark, narrow corridors cause me to cling to Johny closely, attentively listening to him speak words of encouragement as we wind our way to our stateroom. Side to side swaying of the ship made for unfamiliar movement under my feet as I take slow, unsteady steps. Immediately a strange, foreign smell sends my head into a spin and I vomit my breakfast onto my scarf, coat and shoes. Within minutes, Sonja does the same causing both of us to shed tears of embarrassment.

Over the next two weeks, traveling the choppy, winter seas of the English Channel and North Atlantic Ocean, is a horrific experience as we all suffer from severe headache pain and debilitating nausea. Unfortunately, the small cabin assigned to the Meijer family is located near the engine room. It is the intense foul odor of the fuel and constant, clanging noises made by mechanical equipment which exacerbates our discomfort, making the journey even more difficult!

Only our little sister Peggy is spared any symptoms of seasickness. Adding to the challenge are the sleeping arrangements with two children sharing one bed. Placing our heads on the opposite ends of the bunk, we lie with our feet touching. Buddy is encased in a little crib standing on wheels and with each roll of the turbulent waves, the crib noisily glides from side to side, adding to our difficulty of sleep.

My parents are grateful for the German attendants on the Seven Seas who are especially sympathetic for us as they go beyond the call of duty to make us comfortable, routinely bringing fresh linens, snacks, puzzles, crayons, and coloring books to our cabin. But it's three times a day, at mealtime, that the trip from our cabin to the dining room requires extra caution and patience as we climb up the steep, narrow ladder to the upper deck. Every step taken is a chance for mishap because the ship is easily tossed to and fro in the turbulent sea.

Seven days into our journey, I discover how difficult it is to maneuver around the unsteady vessel. Dad left Jack in charge to stay with me in the room while the rest of the family attend in the dining room for breakfast. Most of the time I was too nauseated to be present for any meal, which left one of my older brothers chosen to remain in the cabin with me. Jack is not happy with the assignment, so he convinces me to get up and accompany him to the dining room. Afraid to follow him but equally too fearful to be left behind, I manage to get dressed and walk behind him as he steps into the dark corridor. Within minutes, Jack realizes we are lost because the tight, small passageways look the same. The puzzled look on Jack's face frightens me more than the strange, ominous hallway looming in front of us.

Suddenly, it occurs to me that we are both going to be punished for disobeying our parents! The previous year, Jack and I got into trouble for picking daisies from the private property of the farmer who lived across the dike near our neighborhood. We were spanked for stealing but Dad didn't make us return the flowers.

This time is worse and I reassure my brother that we are in dire straits! Begging Jack to turn back falls on deaf ears as he is determined to find the ladder which would lead us to the dining room. Unaware that outside, a storm is brewing until the ship begins to pitch from side to the side, swaying profusely. Instantly, the boat heaves up and down in a linear, vertical motion, sending us onto the floor. I throw up what food is left in my stomach from dinner the night before and faint as Jack leaves me to find help. Hours later, I awake in my bunk bed wearing clean pajamas with my parents anxiously hovering over me. Thankfully, Jack and I are not punished.

The following week, the whole family is well enough to attend a party the crew put together to celebrate Mom and Jack's birthdays. Other patrons in the dining room join in the celebration and soon the story of Dad and Mom's journey is circulated among them. I am too young to appreciate what a novelty our large family is in public and the attention we attract. Even the captain of the ship comes to participate in the festivities. Enjoying our company, he holds me on his lap but I am nauseous and expel my lunch onto his beautiful, blue and white jacket, soiling his uniform and spoiling his mood.

With party hats, birthday cake, fresh fruit and the kindness of strangers, that day for the Meijer family is an unforgettable one!

The rest of the journey is uneventful until we reach Nova Scotia, Canada. As we prepare to disembark the ship for a few hours of rest on land, our younger sister, the only one not plagued with the dreaded seasickness, is suddenly not feeling well, and unfortunately, Peggy is the only one not eating the food we enjoy in the Chinese restaurant in Halifax that afternoon.

On the "Seven Seas" 1957
Harry, Mom, our favorite attendant, Jack, Peggy,
Rene, Sonja, Maudy (Left to Right)

chapter 41

"America, America, with streets lined in gold and freedom for everyone who set their feet upon her silver shores."

IMMIGRANT FROM RUSSIA CIRCA 1920

For millions around the world, the United States of America stands as a beacon for freedom, justice, independence and international friendship. Nothing symbolizes those principles more than a grand lady, the Statue of Liberty. Donated to America in 1876 by the people of France, Lady Liberty stands 151 feet tall and is protected from the elements by a thin sheet of copper covering the entire statue. She makes her home on Liberty Island, located next to Ellis Island, the nation's premier federal immigration station for those who arrive by boat. For decades she was the lighthouse for ships which sailed into New York harbor and is the first sighting for immigrants who arrive by sea. Liberty stands upon a pedestal which is 150 feet tall, supporting her enormous weight of 250,000 pounds and sending her more than 305 feet high into the New York harbor sky. With her right foot raised above broken shackles and chains, she depicts moving away from tyranny and oppression. On the inside of the pedestal are engraved the words of the famous sonnet written by a young lady named Emma Lazarus. The most familiar words of the sonnet, written into hundreds of tunes and poems, accurately describe the millions seeking refuge in the safety of American shores:

> "... give me your tired; your poor,
> Your huddled masses yearning to be free.

The wretched refuse of your teeming shore.
Send these, the homeless, tempest-tossed to me.
I lift my lamp beside the golden door."

Late one morning, an announcement is made on the ship of the Seven Seas that within the hour all passengers interested in viewing the Statue of Liberty are required to be present top deck on the starboard side of the vessel. Harry Meijer immediately springs into action, assisting his wife and two sons in washing our faces and combing our hair, ignoring the protests from Sonja and me because we are too nauseous to make the trip upstairs, Dad promises it will be an experience we would never forget and he is right!

We join many fellow travelers on the top deck, some who are talkative, chattering with excitement. Dad makes sure Mom and his children stand close by, instructing us to be quiet, loud enough for the other passengers to hear him. Respectfully, they lower their voices when suddenly, less than half a mile away, the regal lady comes into view.

But I am not looking at her! I am staring at our dad, holding Mirna in his left arm, saluting the statue with his right arm as his tears spill onto my baby sister and Dad's gray suit. Never had I witnessed such emotion from our father. Mom, clutching Buddy, is weeping silently too. Johny and Rene are somber, quiet, while keeping their eyes on the rest of us. As my gaze turns to the tall, imposing figure of the lady, I break the silence by rudely blurting out that she is not very pretty painted in that dull, green color. Thankfully, Dad ignores my comment. Mom, Johny and Rene join in the poignant moment and following their example, the rest of us stand motionless for several, very long minutes.

Not a word is spoken as we make our way back to our cabin for the last time, the mood for my parents is somber. In hushed tones, Mom tells Dad that she is feeling melancholy. In a rare moment, my parents hug each other in our presence. During the next hour while packing, Rene explains to us that the copper covering the statue oxidizes to a green patina when exposed to the outside elements.

Within an hour of passing the Statue of Liberty, eleven members of the Meijer family happily disembark the Seven Seas, exchanging words of appreciation and hugs with the crew members who had served us so graciously. Dad and Mom are giddy as we walk down the ramp but hesitate a moment before they step onto American soil! My eyes are riveted on them.

Our beloved parents, former prisoners of war, who suffered violent persecution, reprehensible abuse, grievous oppression, endured deplorable conditions, survived and persevered through more than ten years of unspeakable horror, enter the land of their dreams with tears pouring down their cheeks!

New immigrants Mr. and Mrs. Harry Meijer, with nine children in tow, believe the United States will be a haven for recuperation, a place of safety and become the country they will call home for the rest of their lives! Nothing could dampen their elation, not even the gray New Jersey shoreline, which is not the most beautiful place in America in the winter. Looking across at the New York harbor, the cold weather, rain, wind and crowded immigration building only ramps up my parent's excitement as we enter the United States on Tuesday, February 12, 1957, the day America celebrates the birthday of the 16th and Dad's favorite president, Abraham Lincoln.

Eventually it is our turn in the long line to be processed to enter the land of promise. Proudly my father names each one of us and the dates of our births as he hands our passports to the officer behind the plastic window. I look up in wonder at my father because he is smiling though his eyes are wet with tears.

How could that customs officer, employed to retrieve and inspect the passports of hundreds of immigrants, possibly understand the gratitude our parents are experiencing this day? Who could appreciate the excitement my parents are feeling unless they had traveled on the same journey of hardship, passed through valleys of agonizing loss and still hold on to faith for a better future?

Harry and Vicky Meijer arrive on another continent, enter another foreign country with a language and culture alien to them, yet they are driven by the same, unseen force which pioneers of the past have described as "the indomitable human spirit."

For us to continue the next part of our journey, we are instructed to make our way from the Federal Immigration Building to the New Jersey Central Railroad Terminal of Hudson County less than a mile away. Exiting the immigration building is the most memorable for Mom who makes us stop as she stands in awe staring at the distant, towering skyscrapers looming over the city of New York. Our mother, the petite, Dutch/Indonesian country girl, who can relate best to cooking and caring for her brood of nine children, is thrilled to enter the United States of America!

Mom is beaming with happiness as we board the "Capitol Limited" train in the New Jersey Terminal bound for the city of Chicago, in a state called Illinois. Vicky Meijer is captivated by the sights of towns we pass by and a small porthole on the train does not reduce her enthusiasm of staring at all the automobiles on city streets. In the Netherlands, numerous bicycles and pedestrians covered the landscape and in Indonesia, prevalent on miles of small, unpaved, country roads were people on foot, walking from one village to another. Never has the native, Indonesian girl ever dreamed that streets could be so wide, as long stretches of highway are busy with motor vehicles. Mom asks a hundred questions of Dad, Johny and Rene about the tall buildings, the massive bridges and the far distance we travel.

The rest of us feel safe on the luxurious, cushioned seats of the fast-moving train and Buddy giggles each time the train blows its horn at all of the railway crossings. Several American passengers make a comment to Dad about seven nicely behaved children and Dad, grinning from ear to ear, graciously responds with a thank you as he translates the exchange for Mom.

My parents are strict enforcers of proper etiquette in public, which includes children extending the hand first for a hand shake and introducing ourselves to adults. On some occasions, seven Meijer children resemble little toy soldiers standing at attention with Johny and Rene keeping their hawk-eyes on us as the grownups make their way down the line.

For Americans, our family makes quite a scene. Eleven of us wearing our less fashionable, homemade clothes, sporting the dreaded haircuts our mother had given us before we left the Netherlands. Mom is a great cook, an accomplished seamstress and a tireless provider for our comfort but her talent as a barber leaves much to be desired! The hairstyle on her nine children, whether the boys or girls, look as if my mom has placed a bowl on top of our heads, chopping the hair on the bottom half to the nape of our necks.

It must have amused some Americans to observe so many members of one, obviously foreign family. Several are kind enough to engage in conversation with Johny and Rene. Both boys knew enough of the English language to carry on a conversation and I watch with pride as my brothers confidently answer questions they ask about our family. My brothers had learned enough French, German and English in Dutch schools to hold conversations in any of the three languages.

I am filled with admiration for my older brothers but suddenly overcome with sadness about Walter even more. I take in all that I can about our trip because I want to share every minute and every emotion with my eldest brother. During the train ride, I ask for a pencil and paper and begin sharing with Walter my observations and feelings about our journey. Several hours later, the very lengthy letter is analogous with words in my diary. Mom cautions me to reduce the number of pages meant for Walter because of postage restrictions.

The heavy feeling in my heart about missing Walter has to be set aside as Dad stands up and announces that we have arrived. Our twelve-hour, 800-mile trip from the New Jersey terminal has come to an end and eleven, weary, immigrant travelers disembark the Capitol Limited train at the Dearborn Railway Station in Chicago, Illinois.

chapter

42

"Show me a politician who gets rich and I will show you a crook."
HARRY S. TRUMAN / 33ᴿᴰ PRESIDENT OF THE UNITED STATES

In the spring of 1946, the American Academy Awards of Best Song went to writers Harry Warren and Johnny Mercer for the lead melody of "The Atchison, Topeka, and the Santa Fe," in the movie production of that year called, "The Harvey Girls." The actual railway line, the Atchison, Topeka, and Santa Fe Railway was one of the largest and most extensive in the United States, linking 2,019 miles from mid-west Chicago, Illinois to the west coast of Los Angeles, California. Charted in 1859, the well-known ATSF Railway Company provided passenger service for Americans for more than a century, taking travelers through dozens of large cities, passing hundreds of small towns, journeying miles of expansive desert, traversing along ample mountain crevices and valleys.

In 1956, the ATSF introduced its premier, streamlined, diesel passenger train termed as "The Big Dome." Allowing passengers unparalleled views of the spectacular scenery through elevated roofs which held large, glass windows, the big dome grew in popularity and over the years, the ATSF built twenty big domes which also gave travelers the comfort of reclining seats, lunch room facilities, and comfortable lounges. ATSF also had in their inventory trains labeled as the "Super Chief," the diesels were essentially double decker trains which held passengers on two levels, either top or bottom.

In the very early morning of February 13, 1957, former POWs, Mr. and Mrs. Harry Meijer and their nine children arrive at the Dearborn

Railway Station in Chicago, Illinois. The temperature in Chicago is below 32 degrees and the kind porter escorting our family to the proper area to catch the next train bound for Los Angeles explains how fortunate we are that there is no sign of snow. Johny and Rene interpret for us what the gentleman is saying as we stare at him a little too long. We had never met someone of black lineage before and the Dutch/Indonesian family is fascinated by his very dark skin and tall, imposing height. Dad and Mom respond to the cordial, gracious man who seems pleased to help us with our luggage, explaining that we will board the "El Capitan Super Chief," and in the porter's opinion, is one of the most beautiful trains ever built. Reaching the platform where we will eventually board, I watch as Dad warmly shakes his hand and gives him American money.

The friendly porter is correct. "El Capitan," named for the Spanish conquistadors, is a massive, streamlined train, displaying a red and yellow engine with a "nose emblem" consisting of an elongated yellow circle and cross. The integral tabs off the cross are outlined and accented with black pinstripes and diagonal white stripes have been added to increase visibility at grade crossings. Twenty-four passenger cars pulled by a magnificent engine are painted in a high gloss, silver finish giving the train a fluid, modern appearance. Now, eleven of us are speechless as we enter a beautiful carriage, furnished with plush seats, wide, open windows and plenty of room in between the rows for seven little kids to play on the floor without disturbing the adults.

It is a comfortable journey through the central and Midwestern states of America. Exclamations of excitement about the beautiful mountain ranges as we pass through in the Rockies, the vast display of desert colors in New Mexico and the enchantment with the hundreds of lights shining brightly in the cities we cut across in the evenings are made by each of us. Friendly porters offer us coloring books, crayons and toy replicas of the El Capitan, while Johny and Rene are given books containing large photographs of the ATSF passenger trains. We cannot read the English words but the pictures keep us occupied as my brothers translate the written parts. The train ride, while exhilarating is also exhausting for my parents who make sure that seven, active youngsters confined in small spaces still behave properly. Regularly, Johny and Rene take turns taking the "vier kleintjes" up to the deck where panoramic views made them squeal with delight!

Culminating four memorable days, early Saturday morning, February 16, 1957, El Capitan safely delivers the Meijer clan to the Los Angeles Union Station in Los Angeles, California. An hour before our arrival, Dad and Mom rely on Johny and Rene to help dress the younger children in clean clothes, washed faces and neatly combed hair. In letters, my parents had been informed by the pastor of Bella Vista Methodist Church that most of the congregation would be on the platform to welcome us. In the few minutes it takes to gather us together, my father is trembling. I hear him ask Johny and Rene to assist in translating. My brothers are amused that Dad humbles himself, wanting their help. It is unusual to see our father so nervous!

Following our parents as we exit the carriage, with Johny and Rene bringing up the rear, I realize that our lives are about to change forever.

Reverend Fred Coots is the first person to greet us as we step off the train. From my point of view, Reverend Coots is a medium sized gentleman with brown hair and kind blue eyes. His pleasant smile greets my father first. Dad is holding Mirna in one arm as the two men exchange warm handshakes. Three-year-old Mirna, filled with wonder, is prattling on incessantly which helps Dad forget his anxiety. Buddy in Mom's arms is wide-eyed but quiet. Within moments we are surrounded by other couples of the church, introducing themselves one by one.

Even though the strangers smile, the foreign language they speak make us uneasy causing Jack, Sonja, Peggy, Harry and me to cling tightly on Johny and Rene's trousers. Part of our confusion is brought on by the Americans who introduce themselves by their first names even though Dad insists on addressing them by formality titles of Mr. and Mrs. What baffles us even more is a gentleman who introduces himself as Bill Pieratt. My siblings and I begin to giggle uncontrollably as Dad asks Bill to repeat his name. My parents wanted to make sure they heard correctly because "bil" translates in Dutch meaning buttock! Raising her eyebrows, Mom gives us a look of warning but the gleam in her eye assures us, she is amused too!

Harry Meijer continues to explain to our new acquaintances that in the Eastern culture, it is acceptable to greet someone by first name only after individuals have become close friends and he makes it abundantly clear that under no circumstance are his children allowed to address a grown up by their first name. If the relationship between adults becomes one of friendship, their children designate the adult as "uncle" or "auntie."

Not until our father is reassured by Reverend Coots that his welcoming committee understands the boundary, does Dad inform us that we will be transported in different vehicles to Bella Vista Methodist Church located in a city called Monterey Park, a twenty-minute drive from Los Angeles.

Overwhelmed, Peggy, Sonja and I begin to panic, begging not to be separated from the rest of our family. Arrangements are made to keep Johny with us in the same car while Rene is in charge of Jack and Harry in another vehicle. Following them is an elderly couple named Dr. and Mrs. Charles Emerson who escort our parents, timid, little brother Buddy and loquacious three-year-old Mirna, whose happy exclamations echo in the domain of the beautiful Los Angeles Union train station, towards tall, wooden doors. What a scene we make for commuters waiting to board the train as they observe eleven foreigners accompanied by American chaperones directing us outdoors to a massive, automobile parking lot.

Exiting the enormous, modern building of the railway station, Mom loudly lets out a shout of joy in her Malayan, native tongue when she gazes upward and stares at dozens of towering palm trees! Our island mother is elated with majestic, green, beautiful trees everywhere! In February the California sunshine is still warm so Mom happily removes our coats as her tears spill freely onto the sidewalk. I am moved by the frequency of Mom's weeping but worry if she will become dehydrated and faint. At eight years of age, I had witnessed Mom's fainting spells numerous times.

Collectively, we are stunned by the immense metropolis in front of us with its sky-high buildings, huge parking lots and cars everywhere but my father's biggest surprise is seeing women drivers! A woman behind the steering wheel of an automobile! Never has our forty-two-year-old Dutch/Indonesian, immigrant father laid his eyes on such a sight and he immediately whispers in Mom's ear that she will not be allowed to drive.

In Dad's opinion, it would not be safe!

My siblings and I have never ridden in a car before. The anxiety Sonja and I face increase our discomfort in the back seat as we sit next to Johny who has Peggy on his lap. Before the car exits the parking lot, Sonja and I are instantly overtaken with motion sickness. Mom's ban on my sister and me for thumb sucking in public is about to be violated! I knew if we didn't, our nausea would result in a major consequence for the American couple sitting in the front seat. I ask Johny for permission but Sonja couldn't wait. My poor, little sister already had her aching head in my lap, sucking her thumb!

For Johny, the drive in the automobile is a joy and he is enthralled with the amount of traffic on American roads, enthusiastically engaging in conversation with the husband in the driver's seat unaware that Sonja and I are desperate to get out! Motion-sickness will continue to plague us for the rest of our lives! Thankfully, it is a short drive to our destination.

The wonderful members of Bella Vista Methodist Church welcome the traveler-weary Meijer family with a big, bountiful breakfast and gifts for all of us. My eight-year-old heart is bursting with joy at the sight of the abundance of food on the several, large tables but my eyes quickly wander towards an oversized bin holding toys, clothes and books. As the festivities for both benefactors and recipients continues, Reverend Coots takes Dad aside and explains that Bella Vista also has six Japanese families in the congregation. Sadly, none of them attend our welcome celebration.

Overjoyed, our parents do their best to communicate their gratitude using hand gestures to fill in the gap for their lack of English words. It is Mirna's delightful squeals clutching a doll given to her by a kind lady named Fern Pieratt, which express the feelings of appreciation from the entire Meijer family.

After the meal, several ladies of the church drive Mom, my sisters and I to a local grocery store called Market Basket. Our mother stands amazed, frozen at the entrance as she stares at numerous aisles of merchandise displayed as far as the eye could see. Slowly, Fern Pieratt guides our mother through every lane of dairy, meat, vegetables, and dry goods. Our mother is lost for words and weeping once again.

What a dream come true is the amazing United States is for the grateful, unspoiled, island mother of many children!

As the celebration at the quaint, little church comes to a close, several members of the board of Bella Vista, including Dr. Charles Emerson, Dr. Jack Dennison, Mr. Gloyd Spearman, Mr. Jim Kreutzer, Reverend Coots and Mr. Bill Pieratt, drive us to a town called Rosemead where the church has made provisions for our family to occupy a small but lovely home, complete with furniture including bedrooms furnished with beds for each of us. No longer did we have to share a bed with a sibling! The abundance our eyes take in was too much to comprehend. My hands wished to touch everything but my parents required seven of us to sit on the living room couch until the church's board members had given Dad, Mom, Johny and Rene a complete tour of the house.

In hall closets, shelves are filled with rows of linens, bath towels, more toys and Mom's squeal of delight is heard as she opens kitchen cabinets which hold pots, pans, and dishes including a pantry filled with canned goods! A white stove which contains four burners and an oven with a tall, white refrigerator standing alongside it brings tears to Mom's eyes. On the small porch in back of the bungalow, Mom cries with joy at the sight of a wringer washing machine and a clothesline in the back yard. In the meantime, Dad is surveying another area of the property.

The lawn in front of the house is large, with an area big enough for nine children to play, however, Dad shares his concern that the yard is not fenced in. While Mom is transported in the joy of having her own home, Dad shares his reluctance of occupying a home located on a street very busy with traffic, including commuter buses and large freight trucks. Years of dangerous living, has made our father hypervigilant about the safety of his family. He asks the owners of the home if they would consider fencing in the front yard.

The first night spent in our little, bungalow is a sleepless night for Mom. I find her at the kitchen table writing a letter to Walter. She lets me crawl on her lap while she composes sweet words of affection to our eldest brother, and allows me to suck my thumb as more of her tears fall onto my pajamas.

Part of the agreement with the requirements for our immigration, the church had arranged for Dad to go for an interview with a company called Fluid Packed Pump Company in nearby Los Nietos, and within two weeks of our arrival, Harry Meijer is employed will remain in the firm for more than thirty-five years. In America, our father will never have another place of employment.

Wasting no time, Dad begins to take driving lessons. In Indonesia and the Netherlands, public transportation was abundantly available and many, small, urban communities made walking to the local grocery store, the post office or the doctor's appointment, commonplace. But America is vast and the suburban life-style requires at least one member of the home to own and drive a car.

Life in America has begun with its advantages and cultural differences for the eleven members of the Harry Meijer family. The language barrier and the western, relaxed attitudes are especially challenging for our parents yet compared to the trials of their past, nothing they cannot overcome.

My parents find peace in the wonder of being in the United States, believing they have arrived in the country they will finally call home!

chapter 43

"I looked up my family tree, and found out I was the sap!"
American Comedian/Actor - Rodney Dangerfield

Post-war America, more than any other nation, experiences an economic boom the world has never witnessed before! With plenty of jobs available, companies all over the United States were hiring a record number of people including an enormous demand for women. While the men were away fighting the war, American women proved to be as capable and competent to perform many similar duties as men, which included blue- and white-collar work. As a result, American families were experiencing greater prosperity and the middle-class begins to increase in record numbers. With both parents working, the average American family now owns two cars, a much larger home than families of the pre-war generation, with more money available for entertainment and vacations.

In 1957, the culture rapidly moves away from post-war rationing, as the price for gas plummets to twenty cents a gallon, grocery store prices with chicken at forty cents a pound, ground hamburger at thirty cents per pound, bread sells for twenty cents a loaf and a box of Shredded Wheat cereal which costs eighteen cents. Those fortunate enough to buy a three-bedroom home in the average, middle-class neighborhood could purchase a new house for $12,000. Others wishing to rent in the same neighborhood could do so for $98.00 a month. To purchase furnishings enough to fill that home would cost no more than $500 and less than $200 is needed to buy the much-desired television set. A brand new, sleek, 1957 four door Chevrolet sedan, sporting a V8 and 140 horsepower engine retails for a mere $1,880.

With his educational background in mechanical engineering, Dad begins his job at the Fluid Packed Pump Company receiving the minimum wage of $1.00 an hour. Meticulous as a disciplined draftsman, my father quickly moved up the ranks to eventually attain the highest position possible. He is delighted to receive the opportunity to pursue a future in a vocation he feels passionate about. Immediately, Dad enrolls in college courses to improve his skill in the English language and takes subjects to further his ability in calculus and advanced mathematics.

Meantime, at home to feed, clothe and care for her family of eleven, Mom budgets carefully with her limited resources to include making our clothes using her treasured treadmill, German made, Pfaff sewing machine, shipped from the Netherlands. And to save money, Mom continues giving us those regular, dreaded haircuts!

Johny is enrolled as a junior in high school and Rene enters his sophomore year. Academically, both our brothers are far more advanced than the American schools require in math, science and foreign languages. My brothers enter their new environment with ease.

Not so for those of us who are younger! In the local elementary school, Jack is placed in the fourth grade as I attend third grade and Sonja enters grade one. All three of us experience bullying by several children on the playground, who make fun of our clothes, criticize our haircut, and make jokes about our funny accents. Every recess, we huddle together in the corner of the playground. Several weeks later, I make a new friend with a sweet girl who is bullied and ostracized for being "too tall."

Meanwhile, Dad and Mom are challenged with Peggy who begins kindergarten, with the experience so deeply traumatic for our shy, little sister, requiring Dad to sit with her for the first hour because Peggy's anxiety disrupts the classroom. Every day for weeks, Dad arrives late for work.

Attending school is frightening for all of us that first year! The foreign language is difficult to learn at first. While our teachers are sympathetic, their responsibilities require them to stay on schedule with little time spent helping us along. I am struck by the odd ritual every morning as the teacher in my classroom reads a verse from the Bible and says a prayer after we stand and pledge allegiance to the flag. My parents are informed that practice is repeated in schools all around the United States of America. Dad and Mom are thrilled! The schools in the Netherlands had no such formality.

Jack, Sonja and I are challenged not only to adjust to a foreign culture but in addition, do not cope well with the pressure of being labeled as different. While many classmates ignore us, the few who enjoy intimidating us are persistent, then Sonja and I refuse to go back. Attending school under stress is beginning to take a toll on our school work. Dad takes the matter to the principal who calls in our teachers to bring the bullies into his office. Although the harassment stops, my siblings and I continue to stay close whenever the opportunity presents itself on the playground, while Dad ramps up his presence in the office to protect Jack, Sonja and me from anyone continuing to harass us. Harry Meijer is clear when communicating to the administrators of the school, he would not tolerate any abuse of his children.

Every elementary, junior high and high school we attend, Dad introduces himself to each principal and teacher involved with his children's education. Our father's reputation follows him and every principal of every school the Meijer children are enrolled in, learn quickly that Mr. Harry Meijer is actively engaged in every aspect of our school experience.

Within months of arriving in the United States, the Dutch/Indonesian Meijer family quickly adapts to the fast-paced lifestyle of the west. Dad passes his driving test and the members of Bella Vista Methodist church donates a small, four-door, 1949 Kaiser Sedan.

To attend church every Sunday proves to be a challenge as eleven of us are cramped inside, with Dad in the driver's seat and two small children tucked in between him and Mom, who holds Buddy on her lap in the front seat. Johny and Rene are sitting in the back, each holding a child on his lap with two siblings seated in between them. Before the mandates of seat belts installed in motor vehicles, our family travels the ten miles from our home in Rosemead to attend church in Monterey Park in the little automobile which at times breaks down or during sharp, winding turns cause a door to fly open! In one incident, I was leaning on the door and as it opened, Johny likely saves my life by grabbing my arm!

Before the end of his first year commuting on American roads, Dad receives two traffic citations for driving too slow!

Far from luxurious, my parents are grateful for the little Kaiser but because of safety concerns, Dad trades it in for a 1953 Ford sedan. Immediately, the entire Meijer family falls in love with the American automobile!

The larger vehicle enables Dad to achieve one of his greatest wishes, as he piles us in the car to visit the magnificent Yosemite National Park in northern California. Yosemite is one of many American national parks Dad had read about as a youth in Indonesia. Unfortunately, the 350-mile journey proves to be a challenge for Sonja and me. We are plagued with motion sickness so Dad makes frequent stops to allow his two daughters out of the vehicle which helps alleviate our nausea and happily, Sonja and I are allowed to suck our thumbs in the car.

On the journey home, Dad takes a detour and we stand speechless, staring at giant Sequoia trees growing in the Redwood Forest located in central California. Over the next few years, our parents take us on long trips to visit all of the popular, natural wonders of California, Arizona and Nevada. They invest in a camera called the Brownie Hawkeye, a box camera made of heavy, black plastic. Looking down into its viewfinder, the photographer could see the object in the lens in front of him. My dad takes dozens of photos to document that his dreams of America have come true. He sends copies to his relatives and friends who live overseas

The southern parts of California charm my parents who put aside a few, extra dollar bills, to make small excursions possible. One year, Mom had saved over five hundred dollars tucked under their mattress. At thirty cents a gallon for gasoline, our family could afford many road trips.

Soon, another purchase Dad makes is a radio for our home. Opening another, new world for the Meijer family, with news and music to help our family learn the correct pronunciation and use of English words and phrases. Those wonderful days are filled with lots of music and lots of singing! Dad's favorite tune to sing around the house is "Rags to Riches" made popular by Tony Bennet. Our father sings many popular American tunes, especially loud in the shower and when he doesn't recall the exact lyrics of the melody, he makes up his words rhyme with a favorite line of "in the stars!"

Mr. and Mrs. Harry Meijer and their nine children begin to settle into a life that seems to give them freedom, permanence, stability and the joy of material comforts in the wonderland of America.

Too soon, however, our parents discover that although this great and mighty nation is amazing, America has her share of imperfections and not so noble citizens!

chapter 44

"Learn from the mistakes of others, because you will not live long enough to make them all yourself."

AMERICAN ACTOR/ COMEDIAN GROUCHO MARX

The immigrant population arriving legally into the United States after World War II was a unique group of people. Millions who had suffered great loss at the hands of their dictator leaders or unstable and corrupt governments, were despaired, disenfranchised, displaced, and without country. The land of America and her reputation as a free and democratic republic was the shining light beckoning to the world that the United States was the country of hope, possibility and most of all, liberty!

Migrants, including Mr. and Mrs. Harry Meijer, wished to remain in America for the rest of their lives. With that goal in mind, my parents question the pastor of Bella Vista for information about attaining United States citizenship. Beginning his research in the local library, Dad learns that anyone interested in U.S. Citizenship has to be a legal resident in America for at least five years, earn a proper income to adequately support the family and live according to the laws of the land. After applications are approved, the person desiring citizenship would be required to take a test concerning basic American Constitutional and Judicial principles.

My father launches into an earnest quest to begin studying, bringing home books from the library but he was distracted by one concern. Our little home located on the busy street in Rosemead becomes too much of a burden for Dad, causing him many sleepless nights. The owners of the

Rosemead house refused Dad's request for a fence in the front yard in spite of my father's willingness to pay more rent. One year later, we help Mom pack up everything in our bungalow and to her delight, move into a lovely home in Temple City, located on a quiet, beautiful, tree-lined street. Mom was especially thrilled because in the large backyard stood a chicken coop! Within days, our mother has Johny, Rene and Jack involved with cleaning and preparing the coop for baby chicks. What a delight it is for our Indonesian mother! Weeks later, we are enjoying fresh eggs and Mom is elated to be caring for the animals. The neighbor children, Tootsie and her little sister Sally, handicapped with polio, join us as we feed the chickens and gather up the eggs every day. Mom shares the bounty with our neighbors and with friends at church.

However, too soon, much to Mom's dismay, Dad is notified by the owner of the property he has sold the house giving the Meijer family a month to move out of a home my mother has grown to love.

Several miles further east of Temple City, in a town called La Puente, Dad rents a house on Pocono Street before consulting his wife. The availability of the home is made by the owner who is a colleague at Dad's workplace. Feeling great pressure to relocate and grateful that the owner allows our family of eleven to move in, my father signs the lease without first visiting the property. His choice angers my mother disrupting the peace we have enjoyed for months. Unexpectedly, petty bickering between my parents begins again with Dad desperately trying to explain his reasons for the hasty decision. Mom dismisses his excuses as she struggles with familiar feelings of subordination.

The spirit of disrespect rears its ugly head between our parents once more!

My father's attempts to mitigate Mom's displeasure by taking all of us to the house on Pocono Street for a tour, fails miserably. Even before we enter a small space designed to be the living room, Mom's voice raises to an embarrassing pitch. I am convinced the surrounding neighbors are covering their ears. Her exasperation increases as she glares at a pocket-sized kitchen, cramped dining area and three, miniscule bedrooms but my mother is most indignant about her husband's dismissal of her opinion. Loud, recriminating words are exchanged between them as we survey the property. Mom objects to everything tiny, including the front and back yards while Dad reassures her we will not remain long but Mom has grown weary of packing up the household for eleven people and relocating again!

Vicky Meijer's frustrations increase knowing we have no choice but to move into the little house on Pocono Street. With tension growing, the hope we have for lasting peace in our home comes to an end.

The added challenge of the crowded, cramped living space causes increasing strife between Mom and Dad to interrupt our lives. Daily, their arguments, sarcastic comments and never-ending disrespect for each other, make life difficult for my siblings and me, impacting our school work and disturbing our sleep. One day, another levee of new hostility is breached during a quarrel my parents have late in the evening. On cue, responding immediately to excoriating, loud exchanges between them, several siblings join me huddled under a bed and the rest of them pressed in the corner of a room, their hands covering ears.

My parents' squabbles and bickering had become commonplace but now Dad is using a strange word more and more frequently, glaring as he says it deliberately, slowly enunciating each syllable. Mom responds in frustration while hitting her fists against her stomach, sometimes flinging her tight-fisted hands against Dad's chest and arms. On days when Johny and Rene are home, our brothers step-in, attempting to de-escalate the altercation. Dad punishes them severely for interfering and after beating them, orders Johny and Rene out of the house…my brothers spend nights on top of the roof. We are new to the neighborhood so there is no refuge available for them from friendly neighbors.

Everyone in the Meijer household continue to suffer! Johny, Rene, and Mom find consolation in one another. Sonja still struggles with severe headaches and my stomach aches increase. The youngest, Buddy and Mirna find comfort in rocking themselves to sleep, as Jack, Peggy and Harry crawl under the covers desperately hoping it is not a night with sleep deprivation, again!

The Meijer family is in chaos for days. Eventually and predictably, unsettled hostilities are swept under a metaphorical rug with our parents continuing their parental duties as if nothing has happened. However, tensions build again about the "new" thing between them, as Dad torments Mom with the same word he repeats over and over! I attempt to extract some information from Johny and Rene but they remain silent about things they know, resolute in holding onto the secret in solidarity with our parents.

Sadly, my siblings and I witness the ongoing ruination of our family! Jack, Sonja and I try our best to come up with an explanation for the meaning of the peculiar word but our young minds cannot begin to know where to search for what it means. Mom remains distraught for days, and at times it is only ten-year-old Jack's gentle approach which calms Mom down as she cries holding him. Six of us, younger than Jack, watch helplessly from afar, sidelined by our personal anguish, paralyzed with the belief that what happens in our parent's relationship is normal in every family.

Dad believes he has a solution! Less than three years as a resident of the United States of America, Mr. Harry Meijer has saved enough money to purchase a television, hoping it will assuage the stress-filled atmosphere in our home. And for a time, it does just that! What joy it is as our family gathers in front of the box which entertains us with black and white images. We relax knowing Mom is thrilled that the television is encased in a beautiful piece of maple furniture. She promptly places a large family photo on top of the console.

Saturday evening is our favorite time as we watch "American Bandstand" hosted by a handsome gentleman named Dick Clark, followed by the musical variety program of "The Lawrence Welk Show." The following night Dad allows us to stay up late for the well-known "Ed Sullivan Show" but on Wednesday evenings, choice of television programming belongs to Dad, with his favorite being a wrestle-mania program hosted by Jimmy Lennon. My siblings and I are introduced to moving black and white drawings on the screen called cartoons. Dad and Mom are delighted by them too and television becomes the help we need to mitigate the stress in our home. Still, Mom continues to voice her dislike of the little dwelling on Pocono Street but the issues of the house and its inadequate yard would prove to be insignificant compared to the devastating blow the Meijer family is about to experience.

chapter 45

"Be at war with your vices, always at peace with your neighbors..."

Inventor/Scientist/Signer of the
Constitution - Benjamin Franklin

Most Americans are not aware of the strong attraction democracy is for those who do not live in a country blessed by it. It is normal to lack appreciation for things one has never been deprived of. A country ruled by the people and governed by its citizens is a dream for millions around the world. America is based on a set of laws: the Constitution, which affords every resident protections and certain, inalienable rights. However, as in all world systems, abuses occur and even in a democratic land, nothing guarantees spitefully motivated individuals from causing harm to others.

Before our first year as legal residents in the United States is over, Dad and Mom are distressed to learn that American children are allowed to leave home legally at the age of eighteen. In lengthy conversations about America, members of Bella Vista Methodist Church wish to help our family understand the many cultural differences between Southeast Asia and nations of the West.

Our parents are appalled at the thought of putting a child out of the home permanently at a young age and reassure us they would never force us out. Helping to educate my parents about all things legal in America, Reverend Fred Coots fulfills his obligation with regular visits to enlighten the immigrant Meijer family with information he believed vital to help our parents understand their individual rights as residents of the United States.

He sheds light upon the ability of one individual or group to financially litigate against another, warning us that in increasing incidents around the United States, civil litigation has gone out of control. In his opinion, Pastor Coots feels the abuses have always been perpetrated by those without merit or cause.

In the spring of 1959, barely two years after our arrival, Dad and Mom learn first-hand what a civil lawsuit would involve, finding themselves embroiled in the midst of an American nightmare.

Saturday mornings always began the same in the Meijer household. Dad doesn't go to his job on the weekends, sleeping in, which meant that we had to be quiet and remain in our beds until 7:30 a.m. After breakfast and when our chores are completed, my siblings and I are allowed to watch cartoons on our brand-new television or we have the option of playing outside. Our favorite outdoor activity is to take our soccer ball, invite the neighborhood kids to join us and play on the street.

While my mother continued to be vocal about her disappointment regarding the tiny home we occupied, she is grateful for the friendly neighbors on the block. Juanita Walker, Maria Gutierrez and her younger brother Jimmy, who live to the east side of our house and Laurel Woodworth, whose family resides behind the common alleyway, every Saturday morning after cartoons and breakfast and join us in the street for a game of soccer. Laurel's older brother Woody is a good friend of Johny and Rene and at times, they are available to "referee" our plays.

Living across the street, directly in front of our home, the Smith family reside with John and Elaine who are the parents of a pretty, blonde, seventeen-year-old daughter named Mary-Ellen, a twelve-year-old son, Johnny and a one-year-old toddler named Benjamin. Mom had already made the rounds to introduce our family, bringing delicious baked goods to every housewife she meets. As is her routine, our mother would invite them over for tea, or lunch and of course, the latest gossip. The only person who never accepts Mom's invitation is Elaine Smith. Mrs. Walker and Mrs. Gutierrez explain that Mrs. Smith did not befriend either of them as well. The women agree that Elaine Smith is a bitter lady perhaps because she works long hours in a factory job.

Both Anita Walker and Mary Gutierrez are Hispanic and discovered soon after moving in the neighborhood that the Smith family keep to themselves. Also, some speculated that little Benjamin is Mary-Ellen's child. The rumor mill also freely contributes information that Mary-Ellen is a morally "loose" individual. The tall, pretty teenager dresses scantily and regularly uses language we later learn, are swear words. Peering out the living room window, Mom observes a variety of young men picking Mary-Ellen up any time of the day in noisy, ostentatious, muscle cars. It is clear Mary-Ellen Smith does not attend school.

For Mom, the "Mary-Ellen" saga evokes a greater curiosity, increasing mother's criticism about the parenting style in America. In her Eastern cultural opinion, American mothers who work outside of the home are selfish! She reaches out to Pastor Coots and his wife, Patti, requesting advice from them to properly approach Mr. and Mrs. Smith. Fred Coots kindly advises Mom to stay away from the Smith family and tells Mom to mind her own business.

Unfortunately, those words make Vicky Meijer even more determined to win over the unfriendly Smith family.

One day against the pastor's counsel, Mom walks across the street carrying a plate of homemade cookies, with Buddy, Mirna and Harry in tow, Mom suggests to Elaine Smith that she would volunteer to teach Mary-Ellen to knit, sew and cook. Perhaps it was Mom's thick accent which causes Mrs. Smith not to accept the kind offer of neighborly help and slams the door shut leaving the Dutch/Indonesian lady and her three children standing on the porch. Mom returns home with her confidence slightly bruised but not discouraged and rallies us to invite Johnny Smith to join us when we play ball.

One typical, Saturday morning, Jack, Sonja, and I are playing in the street with the soccer ball, joined by our neighborhood friends including Johnny Smith. This time, however, Johny, Rene and Woody are unavailable to referee, so we make up new rules for a new game. Minutes into the game, Mary-Ellen Smith walks up to Jack and questions our brother about Woody's whereabouts. Apparently, Woody had expressed an interest in Mary-Ellen and she was interested in return! All of us, including eleven-year-old Jack, are intimidated by the tall, imposing teenager who regularly displays an air of impertinence, however at Mom's insistence, we treat Mary-Ellen kindly. Our mother believed there was something broken inside mean people, instructing us to always be kind. Politely, we invite

Mary-Ellen to join in the game. I am surprised that the seventeen-year-old accepts. Soon, eleven of us are enjoying the competition of two teams going after one ball.

Regrettably, it is not long before Mary-Ellen begins to violate our new rules. Protesting loud and clear, I tell her she cannot continue to play. Mary-Ellen responds by slapping me in the face, rapidly increasing the assault by using her fists, beating me to the ground, and viciously, repeatedly, kicking me in my stomach, head and back. The teenager is six inches taller than me, making it impossible for me to defend myself! I curl in a fetal position attempting to shield my face from the painful attack. In the back ground, clamor of shrieks and shouts of my siblings and friends bring out several parents, including my father, who grabs Mary-Ellen from behind and pulls her off from me. He yells at Mary-Ellen to get off our lawn, carries me into the house and lays me on the living room couch. My bleeding nose completely soils his shirt and I vomit my breakfast onto a beautiful rug given to Mom the week before. Mrs. Walker and Mrs. Gutierrez each claim to have called the police and before Mom could finish cleaning the mess I had made, law enforcement officers are knocking on our door.

At ten years of age, I had never been confronted by the police and seeing the two men in uniform frighten me. I am convinced I will be hauled away to jail. Sobbing uncontrollably, I am unable to answer their questions. The officers reassure Dad they had enough witness statements to assemble most of the facts, asking my father if he wished to press charges. Dad asks for an explanation of what it would involve, and afterwards, politely refuses. The officers encourage my parents to seek medical attention for me, cross the street and disappear into the Smith's residence.

That evening, Dr. Charles Emerson, our physician friend from Bella Vista Methodist Church makes a visit to our home to examine my injuries. Filling in a report, the kind doctor takes photographs of my bruised stomach, back, and my face which sports a swollen nose and eyes which have turned black and blue. He instructs Mom to keep me home from school until my headaches and vomiting stop. Doctor Emerson says I have suffered a mild concussion, advising them they should pursue the matter in a civil action. My parents decline.

Ten days later, Dad receives an official letter via a mail courier.

Containing his anger in the subsequent days following the incident, the letter sends Dad into a rage as he reads words from an attorney stating that "the Smith family is pursuing a $10,000 judgement against Mr. and Mrs. Harry Meijer for violating their daughter's civil rights." Pastor Coots recommends an attorney for whom Bella Vista Church will pay a portion of the lawyer's fees. Mom is convinced we will be shipped back to the Netherlands, while I feel responsible for starting the painful ordeal. Johny and Rene spend weeks reassuring us neither scenario will occur but Mom and I are plagued with fear and trembling.

The months leading up to the court appearance are stress-filled for Dad, Mom and I. As the defendant, my father is given a choice to a trial by judge or jury, choosing a trial by judge. We spend many sessions with the attorney Pastor Coots recommended, who informs us that the Smith family gave the police a completely opposite statement. In their version, I am the instigator of the physical assaults and it is Mary-Ellen who was severely injured, naming Dad and me as the perpetrators. In the ensuing weeks, my parents spend their evenings together improving on the English vocabulary. My siblings and I are pleased to see them studying in harmony, united in one cause!

The attorney prepares me for my testimony. He is a large, imposing man, towering above my parents with a deep, hoarse voice probably caused by his chain-smoking habit. Initially, my testimony included that I witnessed Dad pulling Mary-Ellen away and then kicking her in the leg which caused her to trip. The attorney admonishes me to leave "that part" out, warning me that losing the case could result in the entire family being shipped back to the Netherlands. The pressure to rehearse a story which is partially true causes my stomach aches to increase.

The lawyer is not wrong! As mere legal residents without permanent status, any criminal and or civil violations of the law can subsequently repeal our parents' submissions for citizenship and send us back to our country of origin!

On the first day of the trial while in the hall way waiting to be called in, the pain in my stomach is relentless! In addition, I urinate helplessly before I could reach the public restroom. Mom tries her best to clean me up in the bathroom and is sympathetic, understanding my anxiety. Outside of the courtroom once again, I feel faint so Dad decides to send me home.

There were enough witnesses for the defense and he believed there would be no need for my side of the story.

Dad is wrong. The following week, the judge requests for my presence and testimony in court.

Entering the large, austere courtroom, I am overwhelmed with the enormity of the space and aware of the dozens of people seated on rows of large, wooden pews. A strong odor of furniture polish and leather is overpowering, causing a familiar wave of nausea to make me stumble, however thankfully, Dad has hold of my hand which prevents me from falling. The terror I feel, coupled with weeks of stress brings me close to tears but in his pep talk with me earlier that morning, the attorney reminded me that at ten years of age, I was a capable, young lady and that my father's freedom lay squarely on my shoulders. He made it clear that it was my responsibility to win over the judge.

I do not like this person Dad chose to represent him. The lawyer is not a patient man, easily agitated, and uses aggressive hand gestures which made me fearful of him even more. Privately, I tell Mom that his bad breath is offensive too.

I find solace in an outfit Mom had purchased at the department store for me to wear for the court appearance. A lovely dress made of pale brown material with puffy, short sleeves and a bodice surrounded with white lace. On my feet are white lace socks to match and black, patent leather shoes. It is the first dress I own which is not my mother's homemade creation. Sonja hopes I outgrow the pretty dress soon!

Now gripping my father's hand tightly, I am grateful for my shiny new shoes which take my eyes away from the giant, podium looming in front of me. Earlier, the lawyer had advised me to keep my focus straight ahead, with my head up but he never considered what an intimidating, ominous looking character the judge appears to be for a nervous, ten-year-old.

Prying himself loose from my tight, sweaty grip, my father sits down in a nearby pew, leaving me standing alone, with all eyes of the people on me. The man wearing the black robe behind the huge platform is an elderly gentleman with a head full of gray hair, however, I am drawn to his smile, which reach to bright, blue eyes. With just a hand gesture, the judge beckons me to sit in the witness bench located on his left. In spite of the kind smile on his face, I stand frozen, unable to move and barely breathing. Suddenly, my dad is holding me in his arms as he lifts me up to the large, witness box which is so deep, my eyes barely peer over the edge. My heart is pounding wildly, and I frantically reach out clenching onto Dad's jacket. Gently, my father wrenches himself loose from my restraint a second time, as he whispers encouraging words in my ear. Tears pouring down my cheeks spill onto the lapel on his coat and I am convinced that I will faint and die!

Then things get excruciatingly worse! The horrible attorney forgot to inform me about the part which requires a witness to put their hand on the Bible and "swear to tell the truth, the whole truth, and nothing but the truth so help me God." Trembling with fear that if I tell the whole truth and nothing but the truth, our family would be sent away out of America and if I didn't, a holy God would know I was lying keeping part of the truth out!

Grateful to be seated during the questioning, waves of nausea engulf me but before I realize it, the questions are suddenly over and I am ordered to sit next to Mom, whose eyes are brimming with tears. Pastor Coots and half the congregation of Bella Vista are seated around our family. I had not noticed any of them while on the witness stand.

The plaintiff's only witness is Mary-Ellen Smith. Mary-Ellen looks very pretty in a bright, yellow dress and matching high heels. Her testimony is dramatic and seems credible which makes me wonder if I should have been more animated too. At once, the pretty teen is crying loudly, boldly pointing her finger at Dad and me, calling us monsters. Mary-Ellen Smith makes a convincing witness for her side!

Following her testimony, the judge excuses the entire courtroom and orders a recess because it is lunchtime. Many of our supporters join us as we make our way to a cafe across the street from the municipal building. While lunch is being served, a courier enters the café and hands my father a slip of paper.

Dad is too nervous to eat because we are instructed to return to the courthouse as the judge is prepared to render his verdict.

chapter 46

"Those who say they never let small things bother them have never slept in a room with a mosquito."

CHINESE PROVERB

The U. S. laws regarding immigration and rules for an immigrant to maintain his status as a legal resident are many. One of the strictest stipulations gives the United States Attorney General the right to deport (expel from the country) any foreign national convicted of a crime, civil or criminal.

My personal dislike of the attorney my parents hired did not make him any less correct about the serious circumstances my father is facing as a foreign resident in America. Although the lawsuit brought against Dad is a civil action (which punishes the defendant financially and brings financial gain to the plaintiff), the attorney is correct that officials could revisit the incident on Pocono Street and bring criminal charges against him.

Then in a flash, the frighteningly long, stress-filled months come to an end!

The imposing figure behind the bench begins to speak after everyone in the courtroom has been seated. The judge uses big words like "credibility," "hostile intent" and "financial repercussion." My ability to understand the English language had increased over the past two years and I realize the judge is severely reprimanding Mary-Ellen and her parents. He is addressing them as bullies and describing them as individuals who were morally bankrupt, while extolling the virtues of our father as a former POW characterizing my parents as courageous, immigrants who are welcomed into the United States to make it a better country. In conclusion, the judge orders a writ issuing a permanent injunction which prohibits any member of the Smith family from having contact with the Meijer family. His judgment also renders the Smith claim invalid, making them responsible to pay all legal fees!

With a loud slam of the gavel, the judge orders everyone out of the courtroom except the Meijer family. Hugs are passed around on our side, accompanied by long sighs of relief. The Smith family exit with their heads down as I overhear Mom tell Dad that she has pity for them.

The judge requests my presence in his chambers and includes my parents. Inside his private room, I am thrilled to see dozens of shelves filled with law books and at once I feel inspired to become a judge. The kind, elderly gentleman removes his black robe and suddenly looks like he could be anyone's grandfather. Reclining back on his office chair he asks my father many questions about his life as a prisoner of war and Mom's internment camp experience.

Both my parents pause before they respond. Dad begins by sharing things I had heard before, including offering up more details of events, when suddenly Mom bursts in, interrupting my dad with a flurry of emotional responses. Struggling in broken English but with great enthusiasm, my mother is anxious to answer the judge's questions. An hour later we exit the judge's chambers with his warm well wishes.

The drive home is a happy journey for all of us, however, my parents are no longer "starry-eyed" about Americans and one year later, the nightmare of another, civil lawsuit is about to repeat itself again in the Meijer family.

chapter

47

"Adversity tears from us all we do not wish to be exposed and reveals who we really are."

Pastor/Evangelist/Author ~ Santana Acuna

The 1960's witnessed in America, the longest, uninterrupted period of economic expansion in its history. By 1961, the five largest industrial corporations accounted for over 12% of all "assets" in manufacturing. America is pushing forward past World War II and the Korean conflict of the early 1950's. John Fitzgerald Kennedy made true on his 1960 campaign promise to "get America moving again" by stimulating the economy through tax cuts for businesses and giving them a 7% investment tax credit. The 35th President of the United States also convinces Congress to raise the minimum wage 25% to $1.25!

Mr. Harry Meijer, a husband and father, employee of the Fluid Packed Pump Company and recent immigrant becomes one of the beneficiaries to receive the 25-cent hourly raise. My parents feel so blessed they begin to discuss the possibility of sharing their blessing with others. One evening after arriving home from work, Dad gathered us in our tiny living room to inform us that Mom's cousin from the Netherlands would visit and possibly move with his family into our home. We are told that several of us would give up our beds to make it possible. Even Dad and Mom move out of their bedroom to accommodate Oom Oswald Hall, his wife Tante Luce and their two young sons.

Paying it forward was my parents' motto. Oom Oswald plans to find a job within a year and then apply for permanent residence in America. But the year passes, and to Dad's frustration Oom Oswald's expectations in a job are unrealistic. The Oswald Hall family returns to the Netherlands much to relief of the Meijer family. We had all grown weary accommodating four extra people living in our tiny home on Pocono Street.

Within months of the Hall family's departure, Mr. Harry Meijer accompanied by his wife and nine children move two miles and a lifetime away from the Pocono Street neighborhood. I am sad wondering if I will ever see my friends again. I lived for those Saturday afternoons we played with them, as we look forward for the Good Humor Ice Cream truck to come around! The increase in salary allowed Dad to purchase a pre-owned, 1959 blue, Pontiac station wagon, large enough to accommodate his tribe of nine children. My father is extremely proud to own an American-made automobile. He lovingly washes it every Saturday morning, spending hours polishing it, making sure the vehicle is spotless for our Sunday attendance at church. In Dad's worldview, the Pontiac represents a step up into American society and elevates our status from humble immigrants to valued citizens of the community. However, one day, my dad is forced to reconsider his evaluation of the status symbol!

On a Saturday morning in May of 1960, exiting the I-10 San Bernardino Freeway near the campus of California Polytechnic College, Dad waits at a stop sign before proceeding cautiously 100 yards to another sign requiring him to stop again. With Rene in the passenger seat next to Dad and Johny in the back seat directly behind the driver's seat, it is obvious to them that the way is clear. Before the Pontiac has travelled more than twenty feet beyond the second stop, it is hit broadside on the driver's side, sending Dad, Johny and Rene into a tailspin. By the time the three of them realize what happened, the Pontiac comes to a complete stop on the other side of the road. The beautiful, blue station wagon is demolished on its left side but miraculously, none of the three occupants are seriously injured. Dad feels a sharp pain in his left hip, yet manages to exit the vehicle on Rene's passenger side with Johny luckily only bruised on his left shoulder.

Across the street, my father and my brothers see a crumpled, 1955 Ford Fairlane, the vehicle which had struck them. Quickly running towards the car which had violently crashed into a tree, Johny and Rene gingerly assist the driver out of the destroyed automobile. A young man about 17 years of age, asks the two brothers if they can find his passenger. Further down the road in a sandy ditch, my brothers discover another teenager, who had been thrown from the Ford, groaning in pain. Fortunately, neither of them sustains any serious injuries. The police officer who arrives on the scene takes a report but Dad is not satisfied leaving the information up to the interpretation of the deputy, returns to the scene of the accident later that day, and meticulously drafts his own calculations in relation to the accident including distance, speed, all things he knew in physics and math. My father takes photographs of every angle, curve, skid mark, the positions the vehicles ended up in, including distances between the tree and where the passenger landed after he was thrown out of the Fairlane.

Dad's ordeal with the Smith family has made him skeptical about the way Americans deal with facts and believed he needed to be prepared for another challenge.

Sadly, his suspicion is right. The father of the young driver is a professor at the nearby college of California Polytechnic, who retains an attorney. Dad receives a summons to appear in court to answer a civil lawsuit against him demanding financial compensation for the mental suffering of the professor's son and the destruction of his vehicle.

The news infuriates Mom. Her anger at "litigious-happy Americans" has no limit in excoriating remarks she makes describing people who our mother once believed, were beyond reproach.

The trial by judge lasts less than three days. Rene and Johny's testimonies corroborated the evidence offered up by Dad's attorney. In conclusion, the judge sides with my father, severely reprimanding the police officer for assuming the driver of the Ford had told the truth. Our side of the courtroom is filled with our family and many of the Bella Vista congregation. This time, Mom feels no sympathy for the professor and his "lying son." Dad's computations about the accident convinced the judge that the teen driver went through the stop sign, driving at a much higher rate of speed then was originally reported. His friend admitted on the witness stand that he and his friend were arguing about a joy ride experience when the crash occurred.

The trial ends with the judge asking Dad a question which make my mother's ears perk. He asks if Dad wished to counter-sue, explaining that it was my father's right to seek financial damages from the professor. Dad is emphatic as he says "No."

On our way home and for months afterwards, Mom does not hesitate to tell her husband what a foolish decision he made. The financial pressure she suffers from every month, making ends meet falls on deaf ears. Dad stands his ground, trying to make Mom understand that the end did not justify the means.

For my father, the subject is closed!

But my mother would have appreciated extra, financial help and we all agreed. Mom's growing brood of nine children are requiring an expansion in our wardrobe and shoe demands, notwithstanding, our increasing appetites! The necessity to put more food on the table and clothes on our backs is becoming a greater burden for Mom. Days she spends at the sewing machine making handmade garments are not enough as we outgrow the outfits faster than Mom can produce them, even as we hand them down to younger siblings! By the end of 1960, Jack and I are on the verge of becoming teenagers with Mom feeling the pressure of five smaller children intensifying too.

Thankfully, Rene and Johny work part-time jobs after school contributing to the Meijer household and the tenacious, always resourceful woman of the Indonesian islands always finds ways to stretch a dollar. Arriving home from school, we would find our mother in the kitchen preparing food, in the garden tending to her home-grown vegetables, or seated at the sewing machine making a variety of homemade attire for us. Saving money is always at the top of Mom's list, so it is not unusual to find that she has climbed up a tree to trim its branches or is standing on a ladder holding a paint brush because she has decided to change the color of a room. Mother's philosophy about economics and the budget includes whatever she could do herself, to make life less burdensome. More and more, she relies on our help to assist in that endeavor! Without Dad's knowledge, our mother is thrilled to add more coins and dollar bills to a pile she keeps under the mattress of their bed.

One spring day Mom informs Jack, Sonja and me that we were to join her on an errand. The year before, Mom had defied Dad's rule about obtaining a driver's license and unbeknownst to him, had begun taking driver's education classes. Surprising us, Dad lovingly admitted that he was proud of her and purchased a pink, 1958 Rambler for his wife to drive.

Enjoying a level of freedom she had never experienced before, the excursions make Mrs. Vicky Meijer aware that American grocery stores regularly throw out food in large trash bins located discreetly behind the supermarkets. Mom is shameless in approaching any store manager requesting permission to salvage groceries from the bins. Eventually, every manager in our neighborhood stores become acquainted with the little, brown lady, speaking English with a heavy, foreign accent and politely endure her lecture about wasting good food in the abundant land of America. Our mother deems much of the throwaways are still edible!

Unable to scale the large, deep containers where the food is tossed, Mom insists that Jack, Sonja and I scavenge the enormous sized receptacles for loaves of bread and any other food to rescue. She is clear that regardless of a few moldy slices, Mom considered the bread good enough for us to consume. Dozens of large bags of vegetables and fruit we retrieve are brought home for us to separate spoiled items from unblemished produce. But my siblings and I hate the scavenging and we express our concern about the safety of food discarded into dirty trash receptacles. Our Indonesian mother's standard response is that we are ignorant and too young to understand what it means to be genuinely hungry!

Vicky Meijer, a former prisoner of war, reminds us over and over again about the decade she experienced during two wars and as tears pour down her cheeks, she recalls her powerlessness to rescue innocent children who perished needlessly from starvation and disease.

Mom's sentiments about the dreadful years of horror reach deep into our hearts but Jack, Sonja and I refuse to eat the scavenged food!

Mom in choir

chapter

48

*"I love to give away homemade gifts...
which one of my kids do you want?"*

QUOTE ON A BUMPER STICKER

Every family has its cast of characters and the Meijer family is a house full of them. The beginning of 1960, less than three years as residents of the United States, Johny, Rene, Jack, Sonja, Peggy, Harry, Mirna, Buddy, and I are growing up, each blessed with intrinsic, individual temperaments and separate personalities. Our two eldest brothers, Johny and Rene are well into their teens. Johny is reserved, measured, also kind and patient. Like Jack, he is able to calm our mother when she is sad or angry, while Rene honestly displays feelings of intense emotion. Intellectually bright, Rene excels in school, and without much effort, consistently receives top grades in every subject at school. Dad believes Rene has an intelligent quotient on par with Dad's sister, Tante Ida.

Jack, Sonja and I follow closely in age. Jack's quiet and sweet temperament, helps lighten the anxiety Sonja and I experience in our home. The vier kleintjes; the four little ones, Peggy, Harry, Mirna and Buddy, are still very young and need help in understanding the challenges within the Meijer family. Peggy is shy, easily frightened by situations she cannot control, as Harry tries his best to ease her insecurity with his sense of humor. Just eight years old, Harry easily commits to memory words of songs, repeating with ease details of current events or conversations he overhears. Our family physician, Dr. Charles Emerson is convinced little Harry is blessed with a photographic memory. The happiest child in our house is Mirna! Nothing dims the smile on her friendly face. Mirna's sunny disposition easily helps her form many friendships. The youngest of us Buddy, at times is left behind as he struggles to find his place in the loud, chaotic, large family of Mr. and Mrs. Harry Meijer.

For my parents, providing to meet our physical demands is uncomplicated compared to the psychological and emotional needs their nine children require. Dad and Mom are not equipped, or even concerned with our mental health. Their pragmatic approach to life has always to been to consider survival first and foremost.

Our parents have no time or patience with theoretical, idealistic considerations!

Motivated by providing a roof over our heads, clean clothes and food on the table are priorities which keep my father and mother fully occupied. The physical and dental health demands of their brood take up more than hours in a day. Neither one tolerated minor distractions which could interfere with their daily objective to raise nine children to responsible adulthood. Our parents are strict enforcers of rules they lay down to maintain family cooperation with the least amount of disruption. My siblings and I are expected to figure out disagreements or disputes without their intervention, including finding ways to work collaboratively with one another to clean the house, wash the dishes, assist in yard duty or help fold laundry.

Dad and Mom's experiences in prison lead my parents to be dogged about team work and the cooperation required to make daily life less stressful. Neither of them had the time or patience to deal with petty complaints or hurt feelings and they meted out corporal punishment to us, not rising to the brutality of what Johny and Rene received but punishment none-the-less!

Yet, as families tend to be, Dad and Mom are also our greatest allies when a threat comes from outside the family. Our parents believe us first before they consider an outsider's explanation. Conflicts among their children however is not tolerated and are treated with a slap on the back with an admonishing to work it out! They had no patience for tattling.

The beginning of the 1960's have added up to considerable changes since my parents' release from imprisonment. Spending more than two decades moving from one residence to another as world events determine the path my parents were forced to make, including crossing three continents, Mr. and Mrs. Meijer find themselves eager to purchase a home of their own. Dad and Mom push against the pressure by their Dutch/Indonesian friends to relocate to communities where many Eurasian families reside close to one another. In his studies about the United States, Dad learned that for more than a century, America witnessed her immigrant population re-creating areas of commonality with neighborhoods they had left behind in the old country. Harry Meijer is clear with his mates that he desires for his children to integrate with Americans. With the financial help of the Pierrat family, and Johny and Rene who had unselfishly saved money from their part-time jobs, Dad purchases a home in the city of La Puente, California for $12,500.

Within one week of moving in, the proud owner of the home on 535 North California Avenue hangs a large American flag on the front porch!

Larger than any of the houses my dad had previously rented, the four-bedroom, two bath home covers little more than 1,000 square feet and again Mom is very dissatisfied with another small, inadequate kitchen. But Dad did not qualify for a bigger loan and he reassures her that the large front and back yards will accommodate their growing, active nine children. She reluctantly relents but wastes no time to seek the help of Johny, Rene and Jack to build a large chicken coop on our newly obtained property. It does not take long for Mom to revel in the emancipation and empowerment of home ownership as she begins planting a vegetable garden and with coins and single dollar bills kept under her mattress, Mom purchases small fruit trees, including multiple banana trees and several palms. Within a year, the warm Mediterranean climate makes the home on California Avenue look as though it could have been a residence in Indonesia!

Putting aside her concerns about the small kitchen, Mom's days are spent outdoors happily tending her garden, caring for the baby chicks and a puppy named Daisy who joins our family. The expectations she has for me and my sisters is a long list, including becoming adept with sewing skills and being skilled in the kitchen. While Dad's principal aim for us is to do well in school, Mom's priority centers on the proficiency she believes we need about all things concerning life in the home. It is compulsory for my brothers to be accomplished in using a hammer and saw and she also demanded they learn how to cook complicated dishes of Indonesian cuisine. Mom's joy knew no bounds when she discovers the beloved Indonesian herbs and spices are readily available at local Asian stores!

It seems the bickering between my parents comes to an end as their appreciation about life in America mitigates the acrimony between them. Enjoying the respite from the painful environment, my siblings and I are relieved the pernicious war of words has stopped. What has captured our parent's attention is their excitement to become United States citizens and their attendance of classes to prepare for the Constitution exam. Eventually, Dad, Mom and Rene pass the test, which required memorizing of the Preamble to the Constitution, names of famous U.S. Presidents, relevant civic and historical facts, including knowing all of the major Constitutional Amendments.

On Friday, July 6, 1962 Dad, Mom, and Rene are proudly sworn in as U.S. citizens, pledging to renounce all loyalties of foreign governments and countries and proudly promising sole allegiance to the United States of America! That weekend, Mom and I cook all day as friends, neighbors, co-workers from Dad's work and congregants from Bella Vista Church come to celebrate the glorious event. My father is beaming as he offers up a short speech to dozens of his supporters with a message of gratitude to God, his family and the community of American friends. My siblings and I believe Mr. and Mrs. Harry Meijer have turned finally the corner on the horrific years of the past!

Like most things, they do not remain the same forever.

Too soon, Johny and Rene move away. With America getting involved in a controversial war in the Southeast Asian country of Vietnam, Johny receives a notice from the government and is drafted into the U.S. army. Instead, with Dad's advice, my brother chooses to enlist in the United States Air Force. Johny is sworn in on December 21, 1962 as a United States citizen and member of the U.S. Air Force. After basic training, Johny is deployed to Vietnam. Within months of Johny's departure for service in the military, Rene is married.

These major changes in Mom's life impacts her fragile emotional and mental state. She struggles adjusting with Johny and Rene's absence. Almost daily, we hear her weeping in the back yard as she works. Vicky's two eldest sons, who had been the security and comfort our mother relied on during the most tumultuous years of her life, have left home

My siblings and I are depressed too. Suddenly the atmosphere in our home grows quiet because we are downcast, sadly missing our big brothers. I struggle with familiar feelings of loss which remind me of the day we said goodbye to Walter. But the Meijer family still has nine people living under the same roof and any sentiments have to be put away as our pragmatic parents make it patently clear that Jack, Sonja and I are expected to fill in the gap regarding household chores.

Whatever idealistic conceptions Dad might have had about America as a prisoner of war in Japan, quickly dissolved within the first several years as U.S. immigrants. My father's personal struggle with both lawsuits made him realistic that in a democratic land, aggressive, greedy individuals still find ways to propel a person's life into chaos. The negative aspects of American culture begin to bother him.

In the United States, the 1960's are marked by major political, economic and social changes. Our parents are distressed to witness the political and social upheaval of America displayed in newspapers and televised on the evening news. Assiduously engaged in watching every nightly, news program, my parents stay informed as they regularly view "The Twentieth Century" hosted by journalist Walter Cronkite, "The Huntley/Brinkley Report" co- anchored with Chet Huntley and David Brinkley and every current report programs which highlight major developments in domestic and foreign issues, especially an increasing tension of the cold war between Communist countries and the United States.

Portrayed as a major, dangerous threat by the United States, the Soviet Union begins to increase its idealistic, socialistic propaganda globally with its leader, Nikita Khrushchev. Khrushchev who borders on lunacy while addressing the U.N. General Assembly in September, 1960, threatens to "bury all Western ideals and its people." He is quoted saying that "eventually America herself will be attracted to socialism and it will be too late when its citizens realize America has become a communist nation too!" During one speech, the portly, sixty-six-year-old man removes his shoe and slams it onto the podium in front of him.

In my twelve-year-old perspective, I believe Khrushchev could carry out the threat. But my stress is reduced when my father shows us newspaper cartoons making fun of the 5-foot, 3-inch Khrushchev as caricatures of his round, bulbous stomach and puffy red cheeks are exaggerated in drawings of major news magazines and newspaper articles. But the odd, eccentric leader of Russia makes his point as Communism continues to intimidate other free countries with its political ideology already practiced across China, North Korea, North Vietnam and Cuba.

Menacing, hostile harangues from Khrushchev including stories from news sources covering his references to using the atom bomb cause wealthy American families to build underground bunkers on their private properties. The fear spreads like wildfire nationwide in the United States as many in the middle-class justify going into debt to finance expensive construction of underground shelters in their backyards. In schools across the country, the fire drill is accompanied by standard procedures mandated for "Atom Bomb" drills, training us to run for cover under desks or hide in closets.

My father is amused at the naiveté of the average American who doesn't understand what kind of destruction an atom bomb can cause, he had witnessed the devastation of an atom bomb. Running for cover under a desk or hiding in a closet would not spare us!

On Tuesday evening, January 17, 1961 our father requires the entire family sit in front of television to watch President Dwight D. Eisenhower's farewell address. The message which lasts less than ten minutes includes a warning for Americans citizens to remain diligent in respecting and adhering to the mandates of the United States Constitution and to prevent the free land of liberty from succumbing to the military, industrial complex. Eisenhower reiterates his warning about giving unelected technological and scientific corporations the power to make public policy.

Remaining engaged with all things political and cultural, Dad agrees with President Eisenhower. His own life had been greatly impacted and almost destroyed by governments making bad choices for its citizenry. But an incident involving our fourteen-year-old brother Jack disrupts Dad and Mom's focus on American domestic and foreign policies.

Jack's friend John, a neighbor boy two years older than our brother invites him for a drive to school. John was proud of his newly acquired driver's license. Unbeknownst to Jack, John changes direction of the vehicle, taking a route to nearby Mt. Baldy. The two boys enjoy their day playing hooky from class but on the drive home down the steep, mountain pass, the inexperienced, sixteen-year-old driver loses control of his father's vehicle as it spins out of control hitting a large embankment. Jack is knocked unconscious, waking up hours later in the nearby hospital. John, who fled the scene of the accident, has his license revoked but is grateful Jack's injuries are not life threatening. Days pass before Dad visits the place where the accident occurred, informing Jack that the barrier prevented the car from plunging two hundred feet down a cliff! As Jack recovers, my parents reclaim their interest in American and world news.

Beside growing global tensions, my parents see disturbing stories revealing increased, race- related friction across America. As accusations of police brutality within black communities gains national attention, it gives rise to a number of organized black civil rights groups such as the Southern Christian Leadership Conference headed by the young preacher, Martin Luther King. Groups such as the NAACP (National Advancement for Colored People) join King in organizing marches and rallies in the southern states where black neighborhoods are prevalent and the use of excessive force by police is systemic. Much to our horror in our newly adopted country of the United States, we are glued to the television watching telecasts of fierce and deadly demonstrations spreading across the south. Nightly, various news programs broadcast violent clashes which reveal the frustration of black demonstrators and the police forces using any means to repress it.

The brutality my parents experienced during the war years make them more vigilant about our safety. This is a time when only wealthy families can afford complex, electrical alarm systems installed in their homes. Every evening before bedtime, Dad begins to prop up a chair against the door knobs of our front and back entrances. He places round, wooden dowels inside the casings of every window, hoping it is enough to deter an intruder. Mom asks him to consider purchasing a firearm for protection. Our father declines saying he did not want a gun with young children in the home.

Increasing pressures of the Supreme Court ruling that prayer and Bible readings are no longer allowed in public schools worries Dad but it is later that year, on Friday, November 22, 1963, when the world learns of the murder of President John Fitzgerald Kennedy, that our father begins to voice with alarm that America may not be a safe country to reside in after all. Both Dad and Mom had registered with the Republican Party shortly after they received their United States citizenship but like most Americans, our parents supported John F. Kennedy, especially appreciating the patriotism President Kennedy had for his country.

Much of President Kennedy's work is left undone, most importantly, his unwillingness to send more U.S. troops to an ongoing war in South Vietnam. Although, America had sent some armed forces to Vietnam in 1954 following the withdrawal of the French, President Kennedy was hesitant to get America involved on a larger scale. The country was just beginning to heal after the loss of 37,000 American servicemen in the Korean War making many Americans uneasy about another conflict in Southeast Asia. The controversy about Vietnam ramps up in debates across national news agencies, with horrific live feeds of Buddhist monks publicly lighting themselves on fire, committing suicide in protest of the Vietnam War!

President Kennedy understood that full national support was needed before the United States would embroil itself in another war in a country so far away, making it clear that the debate would continue in Congress. Following his assassination, opposing factions inside Washington D.C. increase pressure upon the American public to side with controversial, cold war policies instituted in 1955 by the Eisenhower Administration to stop Communism worldwide.

The death of President John Fitzgerald Kennedy destabilizes America even more. It doesn't take long for curious citizens to begin questioning the official findings of the Warren Commission which holds Lee Harvey Oswald solely responsible for President Kennedy's murder.

As the turmoil in the United States is not just isolated on political and social platforms, our parents become agitated at major, radical, cultural changes, which continue to make headline news.

Dad and Mom's story in the La Puente Valley Journal, Sept 1961

chapter 49

"A country is only as strong as its citizens, its citizens are only as strong as their families, and their families are only as strong as their faith in God."

40ᵀᴴ United States President Ronald Reagan

In his book, *The Greatest Generation*, written by television news anchorman Tom Brokaw, the author describes a generation which sacrificed everything selfish for "the sake of doing what was right." The same American generation of the 1930's which lived through horrific years of the stock market crash and the Great Depression became the adults of the 1940's who fought in the Second World War and continued living lives of selflessness believing the next generation would receive the opportunities of American values for "life, liberty and the pursuit of happiness."

But it is not unusual for the sacrifice of one generation to fuel entitled selfishness in the next. "Baby boomers," a term used to describe those who were born post-war between 1946 and 1964, are about to revolutionize the American culture on their own terms.

On the fringes of society, beatniks of the 1950's are a counter-culture group which advocates the use of illegal, hallucinogenic drugs and counter-culture attitudes. Anti-government, anti-marriage, anti-religion and anti-establishment, their mantra suggests that all things mandated by conventional society would result in emptiness and frustration. By the early 1960's, beatniks give rise to a younger generation, some who identify as hippies. Describing themselves disillusioned with government, religion and traditional family values, tens of thousands, almost entirely white, middle-class teenagers follow the advice of self-made guru and ex-Harvard professor, Dr. Timothy Leary, who proposes that people need to, "turn on, tune in and drop out." Nightly news programs are filled with stories about hundreds of homeless young people living on the streets in the city of San Francisco, overdosing on Lysergic acid Diethylamide [LSD], the potent hallucinogen produced in labs in the Haight-Ashbury District of San Francisco. In addition, reports of a "sexual revolution" begin to appear in newspapers and magazines coupled with the Food and Drug Administration approval of the safety and viability of a contraceptive pill to prevent pregnancy. "The Pill" opens the door for accepted sexual permissiveness, impacting the culture in ways mainstream America had never witnessed.

Less than two decades before, the increase of the female population working outside the home during WWII was applauded because of women's contributions primarily on production lines but the end of the war caused society to shift back to heralding moms to remain as homemakers. Suddenly, organized women's groups spring up in the United States to bring public awareness up front and center about the benefits of more females in the work force. Feminist movements spread across the country, pushing boundaries of traditional mores against conventional expectations of women in American society. Popular weekly shows like "Father Knows Best" and "Leave it to Beaver" begin to wane in popularity. The accepted father figure as the bastion of wisdom and sole provider of the family is called into question. In the years that follow, the role of fatherhood is mocked in advertising media on television with increasing family programs highlighting flawed male characters like Archie Bunker in the popular show "All in the Family."

In 1960's America, rebellion against authority, disrespect, irresponsibility, and selfishness are glorified in movie theaters, magazines and rock music. Mr. and Mrs. Harry Meijer and their peers are appalled! It seems as if the very fabric of American culture is deteriorating! Gathered in front of nightly television, we are assaulted with media coverage of growing dissension and increasing violence between young college students and law enforcement in city streets. Protesting groups gather by the hundreds against the U.S. Government and its military actions around the world. Furious about the news stories showing young people burning the American flag, Dad does not hesitate to vocalize his disdain for all rebels, insisting each one of his children support the Constitution of America and the country's rule of law. Harry Meijer makes it clear that any subordination would not be tolerated in our home. Mom enthusiastically agrees!

With his seven children seated around the dinner table, Dad makes the case for the United States and its institutions, holding fast that America is still the greatest nation on earth. Stories of his imprisonment in Japan, the subsequent civil war in Indonesia, feed Dad's skepticism of liberal socialism in the Netherlands and his reiterations about the bulwark of the U.S. Constitution, enabling America to survive any crisis, are his favorite subjects.

I am beginning to understand that my father's delight about liberty in America is derived from a past of great suffering and loss. Entering high school, subjects in political science and civics become my favored classes.

As each Meijer child turns eighteen years of age, Dad escorts us to the local voting precinct to register with the Republican Party. Our father had done his homework about the two major political parties in our adopted country, convinced the values of conservatism, including small government, were the best ideals for any country. Harry Meijer's life experiences under colonialism, communism and socialistic rule have left him staunch and supportive about a democratic nation ruled as a republic. My brother Rene disagrees and joins the Democratic Party, believing the party of President John F. Kennedy is the better choice in tolerance and compassion.

The ongoing civil and political unrest around America brings up troubling memories and I closely observe my parents' reactions as they grow more concerned about the American political, cultural and spiritual struggles. They battle familiar feelings of despair which rise in conflict with their determination to believe strongly for their adopted country. Many of their Dutch/Indonesian friends who have immigrated to the United States, including Dirk and Miel Wildenboer, share negative, frustrated feelings about the disappointment America has turned out to be. Dad's loud, vocal defense of America can be heard by all of us who have been sent outside to play and I hear Mom proudly joining him in reminding their friends that the United States is still "the greatest nation in the world and to be grateful for her!" I do not join my siblings in their activity in the yard instead I stand at the corner of the house hiding behind an open, dining room window where my parents are having detailed, complicated discussions with long-time friends about the freedom America offers. Dad's passion is fueled by his enrollment at Mt. San Antonio Junior College where he signs up for political science, civics and more advanced math courses.

Fortunately for me, Mom requires more help in the kitchen as every weekend is spent in our home feeding dozens of immigrant friends and acquaintances who come to hear Dad expound his opinion of America. Assisting Mom in the kitchen, I do not have to sneak behind the wall anymore to eavesdrop on the conversations and I am thrilled to be privy to it all, serving food my mother and I prepare to people my parents have deep affection for.

Taking advantage of Mom's need for my assistance in the kitchen during long hours of food prep, I gingerly raise questions about her past, asking her to recall an anecdote she might view differently from my father's perspective. My attempts to be subtle were not always successful as discussions of the past leave Mom vulnerable to sudden outbursts. On occasion, without warning, in the midst of a lively conversation between us, my mother begins making angry remarks, and leaves me alone in the kitchen to finish cooking. Unable to take notes as I "interview" my mother, I do my best to commit to memory her narrations, until years of seeking information about my mother's past impacts my own emotions, deeply.

Daily, I begin to struggle with increasing feelings of animosity towards my father. Confessing my negativity about it to Jack, my brother reminds me that our parent's past had nothing to do with us. Jack kindly reminds me that in the midst of reliving past horrors, our parents faithfully devote everyday towards caring and providing for the family! The objectivity from my brother helps Sonja and me to better understand Mom's emotional instability. But it is the unveiling of the long-held family secret which brings to light a major reason for our parent's relentless feuding and ongoing conflicts.

Circumstances surrounding dismal details of Mona's adoption and the definition of the word Dad used to torment our mother required a long, torturous explanation my siblings and I were forced to hear. For years, our parents and two older brothers left the rest of us bewildered about a word that caused Mom repeated, immeasurable grief! Only after Jack, Sonja and

I entered our late teens did Mom trust us enough to share the complete story of what had occurred so long ago...

Trembling and emotional, Mom approached the subject cautiously, making sure it is safe, closely scrutinizing our reactions for any hint of judgment or criticism.

Although the tragic story about our lost sister disturbs me, the truth also brought us great relief! With tears streaming down Mom's cheeks, the heartbreak about giving Mona away tears at my heart too. Jack, Sonja and I immediately have great sympathy for the burden Johny and Rene had carried for so long! Innocent victims in this saga, our brothers were very young, certainly not equipped to carry the weight of adult secrets.

Mom continues in describing horrific events surrounding the birth and eventual loss of Mona, as words prove to be inadequate, our beloved mother demonstrates the agony she experienced by using one hand to symbolically slice her other hand, explaining how her heart was cut in two that day! Throughout the narration, Mom lays blame with Dad, freely admitting that her strident relationship with him grew out of bitterness of forcing her to make an impossible decision. Our mother speaks slowly and deliberately, enunciating every word as her eyes pierce Jack, Sonja and me, making sure we are paying close attention.

It is the Dutch word "Arabier" our father had begun using against Mom! Inaccurately using the term did not matter, as far as Dad was concerned, it produced the right response from his wife. Harry Meijer preferred referencing Mona's father using the Arabic word rather than the larger and more accurate description of "Muslim." While it was difficult to hear the particulars of such a personal nature, it helped Jack, Sonja and I shed some light on the matter and finally understand the bitter acrimony.

But after years of witnessing the hostility between Dad and Mom, the three of us no longer feared the breakup of our parent's marriage. In fact, we reached a point of cynicism, encouraging them to divorce! In spontaneous meetings with other siblings, seven of us strategize together how we could bring about an amiable separation for them. Collectively, the children of Mr. and Mrs. Harry Meijer are exhausted with the ongoing drama. Even the young vier kleintjes begin to voice their disdain for Dad and Mom's lack of respect. We all pay the price in our mental, emotional and physical health.

Our schoolwork suffers as our parents suddenly erupt with more bickering, many times late in the evenings or early morning hours. Mom copes by entering the kitchen and begins preparing food, using ingredients which fills the air with strong, pungent odors of the Indonesian dishes but it is the sound of our mother's weeping which prevents us from falling back to sleep!

Predictably, the following morning, everyone in the Meijer household behaves with business as usual! But my siblings and I walk on egg shells as another eruption follows soon after, making us mindful not to bring friends home too often, sparing us the embarrassment of consequential gossip which would inevitably follow when Mr. and Mrs. Meijer have another loud, unreasonable dispute! On many occasions, we cope by desperately searching for answers to help our parents find some resolution in their troubled relationship. Several times, Jack, Sonja and I would bring home books from the downtown La Puente Library addressing family relationships. Both Dad and Mom handled those suggestions with scorn. For me, the advantage of having many siblings made the rebuffs less personal, because we secretly agreed that our dysfunctional parents needed our help. The Meijer kids are determined to fix them! However, the discord of our parents produces a bond among the nine of us which last lifetimes.

Several talk show programs had come onto American television in the 1960's, and I suggest we watch the "Phil Donohue Show" together as a family project. Phil Donohue was a popular television host offering constructive, layman's advice on relationship issues. Dad's response was predictable. He couldn't believe people aired their dirty laundry on national television. Sternly admonishing me to mind my own business, Dad forbade all of his children to approach him or Mom about the subject of their marriage, unequivocal that it was none of our business! He reminded us to stay focused on school work and the studying required to maintain good grades.

In spite of the negative aspects of my parents' relationship, their loyalty to America never wavers! It is one of the few subjects where they find common ground. Routinely, both Dad and Mom brag about their newly obtained citizenship to everyone they meet. Whether their audience is a checker in the grocery store, or a filling station attendant at the gas pumps, my parents proudly share their mutual appreciation for the country!

United in their love for America, the bond between Mr. and Mrs. Harry Meijer, grows stronger.

Nevertheless more and more, I am surprised to hear my parents admit that their love of America does not offer the long-awaited peace each of them has been seeking. Until one day, Harry and Vicky hear about a man who refers to a "peace which passes all understanding."

William Franklin "Billy" Graham Jr., an American Christian evangelist who rose to celebrity status in 1949 by conducting outdoor rallies, held mainly in large stadiums throughout the United States and around the world, is a Southern Baptist minister preaching the "gospel of Jesus Christ." Reaching audiences numbering in the thousands, Dr. Graham expounds in laymen's terms the veracity and truth of God's Word, the Bible. His message about a loving God, who sent his only Son to die on a cross for every person's sin, resonates with Dad and Mom.

Attending one of the events in Balboa Stadium, located in San Diego, California, my parents bring Sonja and Peggy along and at the end of the message, respond to the invitation of Dr. Graham's request for anyone interested to be "born again." Joined by their friends, Dirk and Miel Wildenboer, and Mom's youngest brother Bernard and his wife Corrie, my parents and little sisters walk to the front of the stadium with hundreds of other people choosing to follow Billy Graham's lead to accept the forgiveness of God through His Son, Jesus Christ. Each of them is given a Bible of their own. Arriving home later in the evening, Dad and Mom wake us to announce that they have committed to a relationship with Jesus Christ. The passion in their tone piques my interest but not for long!

Excitedly, they share the story of Christ's death and resurrection but I rudely interrupt them and question the authenticity of something which sounds like a fairy tale, raising my concern that this story had never been told in Bella Vista Church. After all, were we not members at our Methodist church and wouldn't our pastor have shared an account as dramatic and important as that? My parents dismiss my questions as skeptical, teenage angst! Privately, they are troubled that the gospel is not preached from the church's lectern.

Approaching our pastor with the same question, Dad is not satisfied with the answer and considers leaving the church. In June, 1964, it looks as if our time at Bella Vista Methodist Church may have run its course.

But my parents' devotion to the congregation who graciously sponsored them seven years before, continue attending Bella Vista Church, hoping to hear the gospel message from the pulpit.

The blessings of life come with its trials too as our parents learn that Jack, who like our brother Johny, has also joined the U.S. Air Force and is headed for the escalating war in Vietnam. Dad never concerned himself with the disputes surrounding the conflict because he believes that every war is controversial. My father remains vocal in his strong held belief that every man should serve his country in the military and is extremely proud that two of his five sons serve, yet equally disappointed that Rene, Harry and Buddy choose not to enlist.

In July of 1965, President Johnson sends 100,000 American troops into South Vietnam. When Harry Meijer hears about hundreds of young men exiting the country to live in Canada to avoid the mandatory governmental draft, he is disgusted yet grateful his two sons, Johny and Jack return from Vietnam alive, although Jack goes back to Vietnam for a second tour. Among the three high school graduation classes of 1965, 1966, 1967, Jack, Sonja and I lose dozens of classmates killed or injured in the war.

While the headlines are disturbing and negative, both Dad and Mom verbalize their love and appreciation for America country to everyone they meet. Some individuals are moved with their history which now includes their personal testimonies of salvation in Christ Jesus. My father is thrilled to include the latest addition of his story believing God has given him a mission to share his memoirs for anyone who asks. He is requested by some of our teachers to visit the classrooms and share the interesting accounts of his life. In my journalism, geography and history classes at La Puente High School, I sit among my classmates and listen intently as my father relives, at times with tears in his eyes, his life story, making me feel as though I hear it for the first time. Mr. Harry Meijer would continue sharing his story in many classrooms and repeat the account in my own children's classrooms years later. In the midst of living life in a country which less than a decade ago had been foreign in language, custom and culture, my father harkens back into the past to revel in the blessings of the country he now resides in enjoying the liberty of the United States. Harry and Vicky Meijer are resolute in their faith of America's ability to overcome all her challenges!

My father's greatest joy was his weekend job as the referee of local soccer teams in and around the Los Angeles basin! A lifelong fan of European football, Dad dedicated years to his passion as a referee. Harry Meijer received yearly awards recognizing him as the most consistent in judgment, common sense and keeping calm on the field. My sisters and I take delight in attending the games just to observe our father's wise handling of unruly, challenging soccer players and their fans. It makes us proud to see Dad deal with unsportsmanlike behavior and at times in the face of threats by hostile players, we appreciate our father's shrewd approach and remaining in control.

Life for our parents continues on its chosen path and over the next few years, as each one of their children leave home, Dad and Mom are no longer given the luxury of distraction by the needs nine children demand.

The empty nest forces them to finally deal with the pain and disappointments of their regretful, bitter past.

chapter 50

"Before I got married, I had six theories about bringing up children, now I have six children and no theories."

BRITISH EARL OF ROCHESTER/ POET JOHN WILMOT

We did not give up! My siblings and I continued to hope that the relationship between our parents would improve and on a spring day in 1980, we believed the day had finally arrived.

It was a beautiful, cloudless day on Sunday, May 11th of that year. The reliable, California sun had made spring flowers bloom and the temperature outside was typically warm. Nine of us were at our parent's home joined by our spouses and children celebrating Mother's Day. Although we had all married and been away from home for years, we visited Dad and Mom regularly and each one of us made extra efforts to spend every special occasion and every holiday with them. With residences far away from our parents' home in La Puente, Johny, Sonja, Buddy and their families drove long distances to be present for the Meijer celebrations. Living far away never prevented any of my siblings from attending important family functions. At those times Mom would cook enough food to feed an army and her sadness about the empty nest would diminish for a day.

On this Mother's Day, after the meal is finished, Dad sent the grandchildren to play in the backyard, requesting the rest of us follow them in the living room. I sit at the end of the couch with my husband who has our six-month-old son on his lap and survey the room, surrounded by my eight siblings and their spouses. I reflect upon the passage of time and now here we are, with children of our own. However, the passage of time could not diminish decades of poignant memories which resonate inside the walls of our parent's modest home.

My thoughts are interrupted as I hear my mother make an announcement that we would meet our sister, Mona. The varying reactions around the small, crowded room add up to a mixture of astonishment and joy.

Dad explains that Mom's sister, Hetty, who lived in the Netherlands, noticed an ad in the newspaper placed by a woman requesting information about Mr. and Mrs. Harry Meijer. Tante Hetty called Mom and asked for permission to give the woman our parent's phone number. Within an hour, Mom was talking to the daughter she had not seen in thirty-four years. Mom was in tears as she elaborated on the conversation between her and her long, lost, eldest daughter. The conversation was awkward but they were both anxious to meet.

That Mother's Day is a day of rejoicing for all of us but for our mother, it was a day of liberation and the beginning of relief for her from decades of guilt and shame! That night, Dad said Mom slept the entire night without interruption!

Early in September, four and a half months after receiving the news, we meet Mona. Dad had sent our sister a plane ticket encouraging her to make the visit for at least two weeks but before her arrival, Mona told her story to our parents in a very long phone conversation.

Mona had been a resident in the Netherlands since her adoptive parents relocated from Indonesia soon after the war for independence ended. After finishing school at the age of sixteen, Mona met and married a young man of Dutch nationality and the two became the parents of three boys and one daughter. In January of 1980, Mona had asked her adoptive father for a copy of her birth certificate and for the first time, our sister sees the names of the two people she believed were her natural parents. Our father was unaware that Mom had put Dad's name on the birth certificate because Mom did not want the name of the Indonesian soldier to be known.

While the initial meeting of our long, lost sister was filled with a mixture of emotions, our mother and Mona, dealing with years of troubled sentiments towards each other, had to work hard to piece together a relationship, which included Mona's choice to face the bitterness she carried her entire life, mistaken in the belief that she was abandoned by two uncaring parents. Conversely, Mona is sad to learn that our dad was not her biological father.

Over the years, my parents made several trips to the Netherlands to become acquainted with Mona's family, as Mona made trips to visit us in America regularly.

Tragically, the story about Walter does not have a happy ending. My heart still breaks at the thought of him.

Soon after arriving in the United States in February, 1957, I began corresponding with Walter and two of my cousins, Ronnie and Jennifer Meijer, Uncle Rudy's children. All of them lived in Nederland and I enjoyed writing letters telling them of our life in America. Our correspondence lasted for many years.

One day I no longer received answers to my letters from Walter, although he continued to remain in touch with my parents. Walter had settled down with a woman named Olga and was too busy to write me personally but through letters and telephone calls with Dad and Mom, I learned that he was happily married. Soon, Walter informed Dad that Olga was pregnant and several months later gave birth to a baby girl. Three years later, another little girl is born. Our parents are delighted to have many more additions to the family and make several trips to the Netherlands over the following years to visit with Walter and Mona's families.

On one of their trips to the Netherlands, a miscommunication between Dad and Walter caused my eldest brother to become extremely, unexplainably hostile.

Dad had made a promise to see him on a particular day. At the last minute, for reasons not even Mom was sure clear on, Dad changed his mind and did not call Walter until the next morning. Dad's version of the event was that Walter got the date wrong. Apparently, Walter had been anticipating Dad's visit all day but when Dad called to apologize about the mix-up, Walter hung up on him. It was clear that all the years of disappointment culminated in that one infraction and regardless of the many attempts Dad made to reach out to his son, Walter refused to speak to him. Mom was beside herself with grief and she wrote Walter many, many letters which were returned to her, unopened. Mom blamed Dad and her anger towards him about the situation smoldered in her heart for months.

In January, 1981, our parents received a phone call from Dad's sister Ida, who informed them that Walter had succumbed to a heart attack. He was forty-two years old.

Tante Ida explained that the year before, Walter arrived home from work to find a note on the table written by his wife saying she was leaving her husband, taking their daughters with her. Neighbors informed Walter they suspected Olga of having an affair with a man who visited often after Walter left the house for work. The tragic situation plunged Walter into a pit of desperate anguish. It was our parent's opinion that the failure in his marriage caused Walter to refuse help from family members and close friends.

It is clear to everyone that our beloved, eldest brother died of a broken heart! Mom grieved for months. Personally, I judged Dad harshly for not handling the situation properly with Walter and I told him so! My father was not offended and calmly reminded me that Walter was his son before he was my brother. The comment made me angry and in between sobs, Dad took me into his arms and let me cry. I pray that one day I will see our eldest brother again!

Walter's death was not the only heartache our parents experienced.

At all cost, our parents determined to remain in their marriage and expected the same from us. Sadly, seven of us divorced and remarried, putting our parents through hell! Dad and Mom suffer the pain of watching beloved grandchildren endure the agony of parental breakups. Believing they had sacrificed their own happiness for the sake of their children, they considered us cowardly and spineless! Our parents did not hesitate to express their strong opposition for our broken marriages! Several ex-spouses characterized the Meijer siblings as self-righteous. Those of us who remain in our second marriages for decades are not spared the continued barrage of disapproval from our mother. She didn't care about the emotions or needs of adults who lacked the courage to remain committed in marriage. Johny and Buddy saved my parents the shame of divorce by remaining with their spouses the first time around!

But Mom had plenty to say for the rest of us about our marital failures.

After all, the outspoken, little lady from Indonesia had no problem approaching complete strangers accusing them of neglect if she felt they had not dressed their child warm enough. Those of us in Mom's presence would attempt to help her understand that in polite, American society it was not proper to approach strangers in that manner. Churlish in her response, Mom did not care! For her it was about the innocent child, not the "foolish, thoughtless parent." At times, the stranger would not respond, while others, highly offended, use expletives as they walked away. However, in her defense, there were times Mom's assessment would be correct! Personally, I have witnessed parents bundled up on a cold, windy day accompanied by children dressed without a jacket or sweater!

The way our mother coped with disappointment would be to remind her divorced children that we were selfish and arrogant, repeating over again how angry she is with the lack of our commitment. At times, I would explore with her the possibility that Mom could not overcome her contempt because somehow our failures reflected back on her. Of course, my mother's response did not surprise me as she contemplates the thought for a split-second then slaps me on the back without hesitation and unabashedly declares that I was wrong!

Our mother's favorite claim was that she had a hundred, compelling reasons to divorce our dad but nine, supreme reasons not to!

The stress Mom felt about our shattered families was a burden she carried deeply as the weight of her broken heart refused to heal. At any moment her resentment could be triggered by a thought, a dream or a picture of a neglected child, provoking her to make phone calls to us, many times late into the evening when her torturous thoughts about our suffering children would keep her up at night! Whoever was on her mind would receive the call including her angry rebuke. Much of the way Vicky Meijer handled her own heartache was to repeat an offense to the offender, causing another breach to break, as our family is plunged into another bitter conflict.

With the nest empty, Dad became the consistent recipient of Mom's repeated, verbal assaults until one day, in late November 1987, my father had enough! Although their physical altercations ceased twenty years before, I was about to find out that more than words flew that day.

The morning after Thanksgiving began with my usual routine of making breakfast and sending our three children to school. My husband and I were immersed in a discussion about the escrow for the sale of our house and the purchase of another. When the phone rang, I assumed it would be the real estate agent handling both transactions. I was wrong.

The caller identified himself as a detective from La Puente informing me that Dad had spent the night in the nearby City of Industry Jail. Shocked, I hear him explain that Mom had been hospitalized the night before prompting the arrest of my father for striking her. With his bail set, we were required to come up with $5,000 to release him. My brother–in–law Ray and my husband, Phil, contributed the money, sending me to the facility to pay the fine and pick up my father.

Gravely concerned that my parent's bitterness towards each other had escalated to this level of violence, I wasn't prepared to see my dad in such a pathetic and pitiful condition. A wave of emotion sweeps over me as I see the seventy-two-year-old man behind bars, still in his pajamas, standing on bare feet, as he stares down at the floor. Without a word, hands cuffed behind his back and ankles shackled in chains, Dad shuffles a few steps towards me. I feel an outrage rising inside me but keep quiet as the guard took off the restraints. I am angry because in November, the cell is cold and there is no blanket in sight. The detective assigned to Dad's case made no effort to hide his hostility against his prisoner as he gestures for my father to exit. The prison guard allows the metal door to slam shut, probably meant to intimidate us.

As I finish filling in the paperwork, the detective makes a comment about "unhinged old men." The rancor in my response makes it clear that I believed he had been at his job too long!

During the short drive back to our parent's house it is awkwardly quiet in the car. In my adult years, the relationship I had with my parents had become one of mutual respect. Our conversations were always lively, especially if the subject matter centered on politics or religion. We were on the same page politically and I had given my life to Christ more than ten years before. Many times, my husband and I would accompany Dad and Mom in their convalescent ministry to the elderly, enriching my relationship with them even more.

Today, in the car with my father is different. It is clear Dad does not want to talk about the incident, as tears stream down our cheeks, communicating the mutual sorrow in our hearts. Arriving home, Dad wants to shower, shave and go to bed but not before he makes a phone call to Mom. Since I was scheduled to meet the social worker at the hospital, I invite him to join me to visit Mom in person. With downcast eyes, he explained he was too ashamed and as I exit the house, I overhear my father on the phone begging Mom to forgive him.

The social worker was already at my mother's bedside when I arrive, engaged in a lively discussion with Mom about pressing charges. Seeing me, Mom reaches out her arms to me and in Dutch, asks me to take the woman away but I am taken aback by the injury to my mother's face! Black and blue, Mom's eyes are barely visible in her swollen, distended face. The story she told the authorities was that Dad pushed her during an argument as she lunged forward to hit him. Mom fell, hitting her face against the corner of the bathroom door casing causing the severe contusion. Repeating the incident to the social worker, Mom insisted she did not wish to press charges. Furious and demanding that I try to change Mom's mind, the social worker urges me to have Dad charged with assault and battery. Mom holds fast to her refusal as I escort the incensed social worker out of the hospital room.

The following day, our brother Harry, secures the services of an attorney Dad would need to plead out his case.

chapter 51

"Trials teach us what we are; they dig up the soil, and let us see what we are made of."

BRITISH PASTOR CHARLES SPURGEON

The story of our parents does not end with Dad's arrest in 1987. Although the event was traumatic and equally humiliating for them, court-ordered counseling sessions did much to mitigate their endless hostilities! Forced to reconsider the past and deal with the pain, Dad and Mom found ways to forgive each other and begin anew. One major decision which changed the trajectory to help them overcome the past was to leave Bella Vista Methodist and attend a different church.

Many of Dad and Mom's Dutch/Indonesian friends had encouraged them to seek fellowship where the preacher delivers his sermons in Dutch. My parents agree and delight in the pastor's sermons about a personal relationship with Christ. They become actively involved in the church's evangelistic outreaches, join the choir and Dad begins to teach a Bible class. Immersing himself in the study of God's word, my father enrolls himself at Biola Bible College where he discovers a love of the scriptures, committing many verses to memory, rejoicing in unearthing the biblical treasures of history, prophecy, eschatology, revelation, and apologetics.

With the guidance of biblical discipleship by individuals mature in their Christian-walk, our parents begin to grow in their love for Christ, mostly demonstrated in ways they begin to treat each other with respect. They become more vocal about forgiveness and the work of the Holy Spirit.

Dad's eyes would be brimming with tears as he acknowledged his faults. It made Mom happy to see him humbled!

Soon their days were filled with visiting the sick in hospitals, singing at convalescent homes and delivering food to the homeless and hungry. Johny and Rene and their wives would join them on occasion. In 1990, Mirna, Peggy and I came together as a trio naming ourselves "Joyful Sound," taking our ministry in song to convalescent hospitals, weddings, funerals, and numerous church functions. On many occasions, Joyful Sound would team up with our parents to minister in music together.

In those final, quiet years of their lives, our parents made time to visit and fellowship with their numerous friends, who like Dad and Mom were growing older. They made many long trips to the Grand Canyon in Arizona, Yellowstone in Montana and visited the Calaveras Big trees state park in Northern California. In 1972, I had married and lived in Quantico, Virginia with my husband and two children. It was my parent's opportunity to spend two weeks with us and every day visit the United States capitol in Washington D.C. Dad's show of emotion was greatest as he stood in front of the statue of President Abraham Lincoln.

With their advancing years and evolving perspectives, the core values my parents held deeply never changed! While Dad's emphasis for his children had always been college attendance and good grades, Mom's priorities were for her children to be individuals of good character. When we demonstrated kindness, generosity and hospitality, our mother would approve heartily. My siblings and I continue to live up to that expectation with the help of our spouses. Each one of us open our homes and lives to others who are welcomed in to be part of the family.

My father's greatest satisfaction was distributed among Johny and Rene graduating from Cal State Fullerton, with Rene continuing on to law school, Jack receiving his degree from Redlands University, Sonja, graduating from California Polytechnic and Mirna, becoming a school teacher with a degree from Cal State San Bernardino. With her exotic beauty, Sonja became the celebrity in our family as one of the original island girls in the weekly program called "Fantasy Island." We enjoyed seeing her in the background takes on "Love Boat," "Starkey and Hutch" and other popular programs of the 1970's. Mirna's good looks won her stage presence in beauty contests and pageants.

Our Dutch/Indonesian parents did well adjusting to the cultural, social and political changes their journey required. We had a father who expressed his opinions publicly about all things cultural, socially and politically. Early in 1990, Dad began to voice concern about the shifts he was beginning to notice on the popular news stations. Several cable networks had popped up in America and he was disturbed that the majority of them offered editorialized opinions in place of reporting factual news stories. For the man who had experienced first-hand the political upheaval and major transformation of his birth nation, our father cautioned us that a biased media was one of the first threats to freedom. My dad believed that every citizen of a free nation should be able to make up their own minds about all things cultural, social and political and reflect those opinions at the voting booth. Harry Meijer was clear about the respect every sovereign nation deserved in having its own borders! Entering the United States legally was paramount for him.

Both Dad and Mom learned to speak perfect English, despite Mom's Dutch accent when speaking English, it did not deter her to express exactly how she felt on any topic. Those opinions were not always valued by her western sons and daughters-in-law, challenging our mother to work out difficult relationships with some of them. In Mom's worldview, her opinions and advice, even unsolicited, should have been considered with more value. At times her in-laws didn't always agree, causing Mom great disappointment. But Christine Victorine Meijer–Hall never faltered under any pressure or critique! She would simply dismiss the critic off with the wave of her hand.

And our mother was adamant that one day Americans would embrace iced coffee, retail cinnamon rolls, and finish off a seared steak with melted butter!

After Dad's passing, we were concerned about Mom's well-being and safety. She insisted on remaining in her home, reassuring us that she could take care of herself. Mom did well with each one of us regularly checking up on her every week.

Mona made several trips from the Netherlands to continue visiting with Mom, staying for three or four weeks at a time. On two trips, her husband Anton and her children accompanied her. Mom relished those visits, which gave mother and daughter opportunities to bond.

The following eight years after Dad's passing, Mom fared well living alone. She enjoyed hours of playing Scrabble with anyone who was willing to challenge her. Nine times out of ten, Mom won! However, increasing hearing and sight loss and burgeoning arthritis caused her quality of life to diminish and she resented her body's inability to move the way it used to. Also, Johny and Rene grew concerned about her house. Many cosmetic changes needed to be made and they worried about the structural damage which had occurred over the years, requiring major repair work.

Meeting with Mom on a February morning of 2004, our brothers made a proposal that Mom reside with one of her children until the construction on the house was completed. As it would turn out, Mom spent time in all our homes. On March 12, after the furniture and Mom's belongings had been removed, the demolishing of the walls, floors and ceilings began with the bulk of the work left for Johny, Rene and Jack who were very knowledgeable about everything structural, electrical and plumbing. Johny, with his degree in electronics, had made a good living, providing for his wife and five children. Rene as a structural engineer with a degree in civil engineering had been successful working for the State of California for almost forty years. Both Johny and Rene had retired the year before. Jack, with his expertise and career as a building inspector, joins our two older brothers and between the three of them contribute their talent and experience in many years of construction work. On the weekends we are joined by Harry who understood the regulations required by the state of California because of his work in forty years as a certified entomologist and Buddy, who had spent his entire professional life as a heating and frost insulator, including installing and repairing commercial air conditioners and heaters.

Every day, including every Sunday after church, for more than twenty months, we work tirelessly and with great joy, receiving help from our spouses, children and grandchildren. The project bringing us together once more. The years we spent raising our own families, managing marriages and careers, limited our opportunities for gathering on a regular basis. The daily contacts for those many months become precious. What an adventure it is for us as we work with the hard, difficult labor demanded most from Johny, Rene, Jack and Harry. Many days, Johny, Rene and Jack spent most of their time underneath the house to shore up the foundation, replace old plumbing and reroute the electrical lines. The heavy lifting of structural beams, new windows, new French doors and new bathroom construction required the strength and muscle of all our brothers. Buddy helps with insulation, concentrating on the heating and air conditioning concerns. Meanwhile, the girls spent weeks digging up and replacing Mom's fruit trees and flowering bushes which had overgrown completely out of control as Mom had become too old to maintain her lush, Indonesian garden. How we enjoyed the days the boys needed us to paint! Walls, ceilings, doors, window sills, baseboards, everything received a fresh new coat of paint!

The end of each day gave us the opportunities to reminisce and reflect on times past. The good and the bad were brought into perspective, with each one of us appreciating the final outcome of God's overwhelming goodness and grace on all our lives making it a safe place to admit our own faults and failures.

The motivation for refurbishing Mom's house was to give her a safe dwelling in which she would enjoy her final years. Instead, a fall which broke her hip, would deem her incapable of remaining home alone and much to Mom's disappointment, we were forced to sell her beautiful house.

As the Lord would provide, the humble, little house that was purchased for $12, 500 was sold in September of 2005 for $450,000! Mom wept unashamedly as we took down the American flag which had been proudly displayed in front of her home for more than 45 years. The money made from the sale of her home provided the opportunity for Mom to reside in a lovely retirement residence, offering her the 24 hour care she needed for the rest of her life. She was 86 years old.

When we enrolled her into the Lexington Retirement Home in Ventura, Mom made it clear to the staff and residents her first name was Christine. She would remain at the Lexington for almost five years.

The last four months of Mom's life were extremely painful. Suffering from bladder cancer caused tremendous pressure on her heart. One early Sunday morning, August 1, 2010, the nurses of the convalescent home where Mom had been transferred several weeks before, discover our mother sitting upright in her bed, with the Bible on her lap, wearing glasses and holding a backscratcher in her right hand. She had passed away less than an hour before. Months earlier when doctors alerted us that Mom's heart was rapidly giving out, our beloved mother protested angrily, claiming she would never, ever "abandon" her children, grandchildren and great grandchildren. And for weeks, she asked for her granddaughter Sarah, Jack's daughter, whom she had not seen in years. Mom trusted that her pacemaker would continue working forever, believing she would live to see Sarah one more time!

The one unforgivable sin in Mom's heart was the abandonment and abuse of children. The day before her passing, it was the subject she spoke about most. Her heart broke whenever she heard of children suffering from divorce, the mistreatment from others, or neglect. Mom carried the wounds of troubled children deeply and her last words reminded us to always be devoted to our children and grandchildren.

On that summer, Sunday morning, God called our beloved mother home and I believe that for the second time, Mom stood face to face with the One, who did not turn her away, opened the pearl gates and welcomed Christine Victorine Meijer-Hall to enter her final place of rest and long sought, glorious peace, home at last!

Our sister Mona with Dad and Mom

Joyful Sound – Mirna, Peggy, Maudy

EPILOGUE

"And God shall wipe away all tears from their eyes; and there shall be no more death, neither sorrow, nor crying, neither shall there be any more pain: for the former things are passed away, and He that sat upon the throne said, Behold, I make all things new..."
Revelation 21: 4 & 5 KJV

The earthly journey of my parents has ended but their story continues with us. We are the products of their lives, their love and their sacrifice. How well we represent them and honor them will be judged by the One who judges us all. Who are we? We are their eleven children: Walter, Johny, Rene, Mona, Jack, Maudy, Sonja, Peggy, Harry, Mirna, and Buddy. The Lord continued to bless our parents with 32 grandchildren and numerous great-grandchildren. All are living, something Mom never took for granted as she praised God every day for the health of her family. However, since Mom's passing, several family members have faced challenging, life-threatening issues.

On August 1, 2012, Mirna was diagnosed with stage four "non-smoking" lung cancer. At the time of this writing, she is victoriously, bravely fighting the disease, optimistic that she will overcome and triumph over it! Amazingly, Mirna seizes each day with the same, happy spirit she possessed as a child. Teaching math is her passion, but she is always prepared to give her students a lesson on life. With unbridled enthusiasm and a zeal for living, Mirna is surrounded with loving support from three beautiful daughters, grandchildren and partner of twenty-three years, Richard Mark.

Our brother Harry has been battling a rare blood cancer but more than three years later is still fighting on receiving daily encouragement from his wife Goldie, children and grandchildren. Showing up for work every day and sharing his wonderful sense of humor, Harry's love of God is evident to everyone he meets.

Tragically, my Australian husband of 42 years, Phillip Testro, succumbed to Hodgkin's Lymphoma in March of 2018. His love and encouragement I miss every day! On Thanksgiving Day in November, 2023, our sister Mona lost her battle with type 1 diabetes. She was surrounded by her family on that final day.

Sadly, Rene suffered kidney failure and began dialysis more than three years ago. With the loving support of his wife Debbie, Rene survived until his passing on February 20, 2024. (On his 60th birthday, Rene legally changed his name to Ray, a name he had preferred since his professional days). The youngest of us, Buddy suffered a stroke, thankfully not taking his life but challenging him physically. Under the watchful care of his wife, Inge and his children, Buddy continues to progress and once again has resumed helping people with their air conditioning and heating needs at a fraction of the price! And earlier two years ago, my beloved granddaughter Lauren Elizabeth had been diagnosed with an Infiltrating Ductal Carcinoma. Strong and resolute to battle this terrible disease, Lauren trusts her Lord and Savior to help her overcome this aggressive cancer as she still cares for the needs of her husband and two young children during months of aggressive chemotherapy including a successful recovery from major surgery.

All of the above are reasons for the Meijer family to remain grateful and consistent in prayer!

As I re-read my manuscript for the sake of editing, I began to see that my own words shed new light on the life my parents lived. While I took liberty putting to paper many personal and private circumstances that they would not have appreciated for public consumption, I trust that their story will be an inspiration for many.

Impacted by their profound feelings of love, hate, despair and hope, my words are written to convey all things true about two people who loved much, hated grievously, despaired profoundly, hoped extravagantly and in the end, believed gloriously!

I thank God for my parents! With the choices they made to overcome the challenges life presented them, I do not believe I would have been as successful to master the horror or subdue the mental anguish of the brutality they endured. It is impossible for me to fully appreciate what they chose to overcome! Though my childhood memories are filled with numerous anecdotes and experiencing firsthand the PTSD (post-traumatic stress disorder) they suffered, my siblings and I were in awe of their tenacity to conquer doubt and bravely make choices others would have considered impossible! I am proud to say that our parents Harry and Christine Meijer never used their own victimhood as leverage against us! Whenever they were given an opportunity to share their story, they did not squander that moment by appearing as martyrs. With dignity and humility, Dad and Mom gave God the glory!

Millions of people did not receive a second chance. It was that fact alone which enabled my parents to live in gratitude. Neither Dad nor Mom forgot those unfortunate, innocent victims who lost their lives.

I am indebted to my parents because they believed enough in the goodness of God to entrust this world with many offspring. My parents spent years investing time, money and emotion to raise a house filled with rowdy, rambunctious boys, who loved playing pranks on one another and melodramatic, excitable, moody daughters. Dad and Mom had their hands full, managing nine children under one roof. The noise and level of constant activity would have made the average person dizzy but it was a house filled with hope, faith and compassion. Battling our personal flaws, it is an ongoing journey to demonstrate genuine tolerance, and grace!

My parents left us their legacy. My prayer is that my siblings and I live to continue that heritage of God's amazing love and forgiveness!

Harry and Christine Meijer preferred that I not write their story, believing it was not worthy to be told but they were kind and slightly amused when I insisted that one day it would be put into print.

Neither of them would live to see it.

The last time I saw Dad alive was on the day we celebrated his 80th and Valoree's 4th birthday at Mirna's home. The weather was unusually warm for a December afternoon in Southern California. The beautiful neighborhood is lined by tall, lush pine trees which kept the sun from beating down on us. On the quiet neighborhood street, my youngest son, John and his friend Hyun-Soo demonstrated several ROTC rifle maneuvers in full uniform for Dad as part of his birthday gift. With most of the family present, including several of Dad and Mom's friends, the two young men entertained us with their rifle skills and marching technique.

The display thrilled our father, who enjoyed all military pageantry.

Afterwards, Mirna called everyone into the house because the food was ready to be served. Our family loves to eat and no one needs to be called in twice!

But Dad remained behind standing motionless on the driveway.

Cautiously, I approached him, realizing he was preoccupied and deep in thought. As I drew near, it was clear Dad's eyes were filled with tears. Speaking in Dutch, the language my father was most comfortable using when the conversation was a private one, I asked him if he was alright. "Nee meisje, ik wil naar huis gaan" was his reply. 'No sweetheart, I wish to go home.' "Maar Papa, wij zijn net begonnen met U verjaardag's feest, U ken niet nu naar huis gaan" was my response. 'But Daddy, we have just begun your birthday celebration, you cannot go home now.' As tears fell onto his cheeks, he pointed upwards staring into the beautiful, blue sky, "Ja meisje, die huis wil ik zien, het huis waar onze lieve Heer Jesus leeft, ik ben moe!" 'Yes sweetheart, that house I wish to see, the home where our beloved Jesus resides, I am weary.' It distressed me to hear my father say those words and later I expressed my sorrow about it to my husband. I was not ready to let my father go!

Dad stayed long enough to cut the cake with Valoree and decided to leave soon after. It disturbed me that he did not eat and he looked fatigued. As I walked my parents to their American-made Lincoln town car, Daddy whispered in my ear, "Meisje, zeg aan jouw kinderen en jouw klein kinderen, dat onze lieve Jesus wacht voor ons allemaal!"

'Sweetheart, remind your children and your grandchildren that our beloved Jesus is waiting for us all!'

IN CONCLUSION

"But grow in grace, and in the knowledge of our Lord and Savior Jesus Christ. To him be glory both now and forever. Amen."

2 Peter 3: 18 KJV

This project would not have been possible without the support I received from many people. It was a journey within a journey for me and I received the constant rally cry from the sidelines given by beloved family members and numerous friends to continue.

    First of all, my thanks to our brother Harry for the title of this book! Harry understood my life-long, heart's desire to tell this story about our parents' journey. There were times that Mom in her frustration would call him the "devil child." To this day, I assure Harry, she was kidding!

    My gratitude goes to my late husband, Phillip, who patiently urged me on from the beginning of my first manuscript written in 2013, even when he had to turn down the television volume as he watched all of his Formula 1 and NASCAR races and Australian Rules football games on mute so I could concentrate while I wrote. A whole lot of thanks are offered to our son-in-law Christopher Caruso for the gift of this wonderful Dell computer which replaced my old typewriter and made writing much easier. In addition my daughter, Julia, helped keep things in perspective for me with encouragement "not to get too sentimental." Later, my friend Charles Thorpe gave me his custom-built computer to update my final version. Thank you, Charles!

    My youngest son John is commended for the patience he demonstrated during the countless hours, days and weeks I needed his valuable assistance with design, formatting and editing. My eldest child, Phillip James inspired me with the love a son has for his mother. Much appreciation is also extended towards Cliff Gossage who spent 35 years as an engineer with the Southern and Union Pacific railroads. His insight regarding the trains and their routes enabled me to recall my family's journey more clearly. Cliff's wife Sue and a great number of my brothers and sisters in Christ inspired me with their enthusiasm and encouragement!

I appreciate the time spent with Art and Ida Van Haasen as I interviewed them and they prepared Indonesian dishes which was reminiscent of a meal Mom used to prepare. Inge's mom, Jane Veldhuijzen gave me valuable insight into her personal journey as a child in the internment camp and I am grateful for those, still alive, willing to share their story.

My indebtedness is not limited to those who are still living. My thoughts and gratitude are with all of Dad and Mom's beloved friends, all who have passed on now but recounted their experiences with me over the last forty years. Edwin and Francisca Wyatt, Dirk and Miel Wildenboer, Truiw Pies, Edward and Sunny Ilken, Hannie and Greet Simon, Willem and Coco Broederlet, Jan Wieland, Jimmy and Patti Khale, Willie and Rieky Van Muijen, Moritz and Anne Stebbler, and many more, former POW's, who unabashedly shared their experiences and (raw) feelings about life in captivity. In the early beginnings of my journey to interview them, my parents' friends believed I was too young to appreciate all they had endured, making them cautious in answering my nosy questions. However, throughout the years as they witnessed my emotional growth and maturity, I earned their trust.

In recalling their individual testimonies, it became obvious that much of the men's intense anger was not merely directed towards their captors. The common thread throughout statements from them revealed a painful degree of personal anguish and shame about their own victimization. Growing up in a culture which required men to be courageous and resolute, they struggled to come to terms with the erroneous belief that the world perceived them to be weak and gullible. The men's collective bitterness, excessive frustration and occasional vitriol, using crude language at times, was only part of the evidence confirming their feelings of helplessness decades later. Steeped in the stigma that addressing those very personal experiences would bring about more humiliation, these former prisoners of war put on faces of bravado, denying their deep, emotional wounds. Professionals in the field of counseling and psychiatry acknowledge that many victims mistakenly believe they could have prevented or should have done more to avoid becoming victimized and abused.

And so it was for the women as well. While their pain was not expressed using offensive language, the roots of shame and humiliation associated with the sexual abuse, descended deep into their psyche. These lovely women carried visible, emotional scars yet incredibly, with their grace and dignity intact.

With many of these families, my siblings and I had the privilege of growing up with their children. As the first generation of these former prisoners, each of us shared common stories about each of our parents mainly concerning their approach and methods with child-rearing, the ways they dealt with marital issues, their intrinsic values regarding work and the principles of money management. Our parents' prison experiences made them respond eerily similar in all of these circumstances.

It's important for me to note that my mother's only surviving younger brother Bernard refused my request for an interview because the recollection of painful memories was too much for him to bear. I understand! At 95 years of age, my uncle Bernard is doing well and blessed that he has six lovely daughters to care for him!

At this time, let me say that this story is not intended to disparage the people of Japan or those of Japanese heritage. For more than six decades, the nation of Japan has been a strong and necessary ally for the United States in East Asia. America depends on Japan in major exports of automobiles, machinery, electronics, computers, copper, iron and steel. Politically, Japan aligns itself close to countries of democracy and with the United States.

War brings out the best or the worst in all people. Many examples could be mentioned on both fronts including the tragic story of thousands of missing youngsters who were sent out of England during World War II. Believing they were motivated with benevolent intentions, the British government evacuates more than 150,000 children to the former Rhodesia, New Zealand, Australia and Canada to spare them death and injury as England lay under siege by the Germans. After the war, thousands of these children were never reunited with their families again! In her book, "The

Lost Children of the Empire," English social worker Margaret Humphreys exposes Britain's irresponsibility of keeping sloppy records which were covered up as the government blatantly lied to parents telling them that their children had perished and conversely, told the children their parents had died in the war, making them orphans.

The horrors of war have been used to justify the evil humans inflict upon other humans…regardless of race, country or nationality! Man's sin nature is fully on display during times of crisis.

There is a great deal of substance and value found in the past. The way historical events earmark and possibly help to enrich our lives cannot be overlooked. History, not rewritten but recounted accurately, can be the common, binding force which connects us to the truth of who we are and what our ancestry have done.

In the last decade of his life, Dad made great strides in re-establishing a respectful, loving relationship with his wife and children, acknowledging his dependence on the Lord Jesus Christ! The realization that God directed his steps to the nation of America, offered my father his greatest, earthly acquisition of FREEDOM: freedom of religion, freedom of speech and the right to pursue happiness.

Webster's Dictionary defines family as a group of people related by blood or marriage, however, the explanation from the Bible says: "For this reason I bow my knees to the Father of our Lord Jesus Christ, from whom the whole family in heaven and earth is named, that He would grant you, according to His riches in glory, to be strengthened with might by His spirit in the inner man; that Christ may dwell in your hearts through faith: that you being rooted and grounded in love, may be able to comprehend with all saints what is the width, and length and depth, and height; and to know the love of Christ which passes all knowledge, that you might be filled with all the fullness of God." Ephesians 3: 14 – 19 NKJV.

The love of Christ defines my family with the love we have one for another, not done perfectly yet rooted-in and grounded by the One who is perfect!

My parents have passed on but the soul of who they were endures in the rest of us. Their story resonates not because they were without flaw or super human. No, they were ordinary people who survived extraordinary times. Harry A. D. Meijer and his wife of fifty-five years, Christine Victorine

Hall, recognized that the super-natural connection with their children, grandchildren and subsequent, dozens more descendants would always be woven in and through the love of the Lord Jesus Christ…. yes, God's perfect love, which transcends time, space and most of all, human fallibility!

To my reader, thank you for investing the time to read about Harry and Christine Meijer and our family's journey. May the love of Christ resonate deep in your heart, blessing your life with everlasting grace and peace!

Rancho Cucamonga, California
April 1, 2024

Mom, Dad and Adult children, circa 1980

*Some of the children, grandchildren and great-grandchildren
of Harry and Christine Meijer, circa 2013*

Milton Keynes UK
Ingram Content Group UK Ltd.
UKHW042200280824
447530UK00011B/110/J